D0392023

297
T866f

الْفُرْقَانُ الْحَقُّ

THE TRUE FURQAN

All rights reserved under international copyright convention. No part of this book is allowed to be reprinted, photocopied, or photographed in any fashion whatsoever, neither displayed on the internet nor quoted in any printed manner without a written permission.

حقوق الطبع محفوظة

لا يجوز إعادة طبع أو نسخ أو تصوير بأي شكل أو اقتباس أو نشر على (الانترنت) أو نقل هذا الكتاب أو أي جزء منه إلا بإذن خطيّ .

Copyright 1999

For more information please contact:
Omega 2001
P.O. Box 293627
Sacramento, CA 95829

Published and distributed by:
WinePress Publishing
P.O. Box 428
Enumclaw, WA 98022

First Edition   الطبعة الأولى

Apologetics / Comparative Religion
ISBN 1-57921-175-5

SPECIAL INTRODUCTION

المقدمة

To the Arab nation specifically and the Muslim world collectively: peace, mercy and blessings from God Almighty!

إلى الأمة العربية خاصة وإلى العالم الإسلامي عامة:

سلامٌ لكـم ورحمةٌ من الله القادر على كـلِ شيءٍ.

Deep within every human spirit is a longing for authentic faith, inner peace, spiritual freedom and eternal life. We trust the living God that these longings can be clarified in this new document, **The True Furqan**. The Creator of humanity offers these blessings to everyone in the world without discrimination to one's race, color, nationality, language or religion. The Almighty God cares about every human soul on this planet.

يوجد في أعماق النفس البشرية أشواقٌ للإيمان الخالص والسلام الداخلي والحرية الروحية والحياة الأبدية. وإننا نثق بالإله الواحد الأوحد بأن القرّاء والمستمعين سيجدون الطريق لتلك الأشواق من خلال (الفرقان الحـق). إنّ خالق البشرية يقدّم هذه البركات السماوية لكل إنسان بحاجة إلى النور بدون تمييز لعنصره أو لونه أو جنسه أو لغته أو أصله أو أمته أو دينه. فالله يهتم كثيراً بكل نفسٍ على هذا الكوكب.

The Executive Committee, in charge of recording, translating and publishing,

Al Saffee and Al Mahdy

اللجنة المشرفة على: التدوين والترجمة والنشر "الصفي" .. و "المهدي"

THE TRUE FURQAN

A
THE BLESSING
(AL BASMALAH)

أ) البَسملةُ

قُلْ:

1. Say, "In the Name of the Father, the Word, the Holy Spirit, the One and only True God."

١) بسـمِ الآبِ الكلمـةِ الروحِ الالهِ الواحدِ الأوحدِ

2. He is Triune in Unity, united in Trinity, indivisible as deity.

٢) مُثَلَّثِ التوحيدِ موحّـدِ التثليثِ ما تعدَّدَ .

3. He is the Father, Who has never given birth like the race of humanity.

٣) فهوَ آبٌ لم يلِدْ .

4. He is the Word, Who has never been born except through virginity.

٤) كلمةٌ لم يُولَدْ .

5. He is the Spirit, Who has never been separated from the Trinity.

٥) روحٌ لم يَنفَرِدْ .

6. He is the Creator, Who has never been created by any

٦) خلاقٌ لم يُخلَقْ .

7

A   THE BLESSING   (AL BASMALAH)

entity.

7. Therefore, ceaseless praise is offered to His regal sovereignty. Absolute power and royal majesty is extended unto Him, from eternity to infinity. Amen.

فسبحان مَالكِ الملكِ والقوة (٧)

والمجـدِ، مـــن أنزلِ الأنزلِ الى أبــدِ

الأبدِ .

1
THE OPENING
(Al Fateha)

١) سُورَةُ الفَاتِحَة

In the Name of the Father, the Word, the Holy Spirit, the One and only True God

بسِمِ الآبِ الكَلِمَةِ الرُوحِ الاله الواحِدِ الأوحدِ

1. Behold, this is the authentic **True Furqan** which We inspire, declare it to whomever has gone astray from among Our people and do not fear anyone who may retaliate against this proclamation.

١) هُوَذَا الفُرقانُ الحَقُّ نُوحِيهِ فَبَلِّغهُ للضَّالِينَ مِنْ عِبادِنا وللنَّاسِ كَافَّةً وَلا تَخشَ القَومَ المُعتَّدِينَ .

2. It is a victorious **True Furqan**, which shall bring to naught the   sword of injustice with the palm of justice, blazing a straight path for those who repent from having gone astray

٢) مُهَيمِنٌ يُحطِمُ سَيفَ الظُّلمِ بِكَفَّ العَدلِ وَيَهدِي الظَّالِمِينَ .

3. Moreover, **The True Furqan** will completely demolish the weak structure of unfaithfulness with the righteous hand of

٣) وَيَهدِمُ صَرحَ الكُفرِ بِيَدِ الإيمانِ وَيَشِيدُ مَوئلاً لِلتَّائِنِينَ .

truth-fulness, erecting in its place a mighty fortress for all who repent and seek a place of abode.

4. Additionally, this **True Furqan** will remove from the heart the bitter taste of animosity and through refreshing love provide a new start, thus, purifying from the soul every trace of enmity.

٤) وَيَنْزِعُ غِلَّ الصَّدُورِ بِشَذَى المَحَبَّةِ وَيَشْفِي نُفُوسَ الحَاقِدِينَ .

5. Furthermore, this **True Furqan** will wash away the impurity of adultery with the water of purity, cleansing every sinner from iniquity.

٥) وَيُطَهِّرُ رِجْسَ الزِّنَى بِمَاءِ العِفَّةِ وَيُبْرِئُ المُسَافِحِينَ .

6. Once and for all, this **True Furqan** will unmask the real face of falsehood with the penetrating sound of Truth, exposing the treachery of all the imposters.

٦) وَيَفْضَحُ قَوْلَ الإِفْكِ بِصَوْتِ الحَقِّ وَيَكْشِفُ مَكْرَ المُفْتَرِينَ .

7. Thus, O, people who have gone astray: repent and

٧) فَيَأَيُّهَا الذِينَ ضَلُّوا مِنْ عِبَادِنَا تُوبُوا وَآمِنُوا

believe in Us. The gates of
Heaven are flung open to
welcome everyone who will
repent from his sins and turn to
Us in sincerity.

فَأَبْوَابُ الْجَنَّةِ مَفْتُوحَةٌ لِلتَّائِبِينَ .

2
LOVE
(Surat Al Mahabbah)

٢) سُورَةُ المَحَبَّة

In the Name of the Father, the Word, the Holy Spirit, the One and only True God

بسم الآبِ الكَلِمةِ الرّوحِ الإلهِ الواحدِ الأوحدِ

1. O, you who have enmity within you, yet still claim to be counted among Our worshipers: listen and understand, love is Our top priority. Therefore, if you can speak the languages of the world and the literary articulation with brilliance but do not consider love, your speech is for naught. It would have been preferable that you kept silent.

١) يَا أَهْلَ البَغْضَاءِ مِنْ عِبَادِنَا الضَّالِينَ: إِسْمَعُوا وَعُوا: إِنَّ المَحبَّةَ سُنَّتُنَا. فَلَو نَطَقْتُمْ بِأَلْسِنَةِ العَالَمِينَ وَبِلُغَةِ البَلاغَةِ وَالإعْجَازِ وَمَا تَكَلَّمْتُمْ عَنِ المَحَبَّةِ فَكَلامُكُمْ لَغْوٌ وَخَيْرٌ لَكُمْ لَو بَقِيتُمْ صَامِتِينَ.

2. If you were prophets, endowed with wisdom, peering through the supernatural and performing miracles, yet without love, you will still lack integrity; neither is any goodness residing in you. For in reality you are hypocrites.

٢) وَلَو كُنْتُمْ أَنْبِيَاءَ وَأُوتِيتُمُ الحِكْمَةَ وَاطَّلَعْتُمْ عَلَى الغَيبِ وَأَتَيتُمْ بِالمُعْجِزَاتِ دُونَ مَحَبَّةٍ فَلا حَولَ لَكُمْ وَلا مِنَّةَ وَإِنَّمَا أَنْتُمْ مُفْتَرُونَ.

3. Even when you distribute your wealth on good deeds and sacrifice your very lives in service to others, yet without love, it would be as if you have neither contributed anything nor made yourself a sacrifice in service to others.

وإن بـددنّر أموالكـــمْ إحســانأ وبذلتـمْ نفوسكـمْ مَعروفأ بدونِ محبّة فكأنّكـــمْ ما أعطيتـمْ شَيْـــأ وما كنتـمْ مُحسِنينَ .

4. Love is patient with Our people, tender toward the impoverished.

فالمحبّة صَبورةٌ على عبادِنا رفيقة بالبائسينَ .

5. It does not embrace jealousy, demonstrate pride or practice aggression.

ولا تعرِفُ الحَسَد ولا الكبرِياءَ والمُجونَ .

6. Love treats everyone kind-ly. It does not get upset quickly or seek its personal desires frequently. Love is contented and does not contemplate vengeful thoughts concerning others.

والمحبّةُ تُعامِلُ الناسَ بالحُسنى فلا تحَسَدُ ولا تَسْعَى لرِغبـتِها فهي قَنوعةٌ ولا تُسيءُ الظنَّ بالآخرِينَ .

7. Love does not revel over oppression but over freedom and justice. It accepts whatever one's friend says as fact, but turns away from the hypocrites.

ولا تفرَحُ بالظلـمِ بل بالقِسْطِ وتُصدّقُ القولَ وتُعرِضُ عَنِ الجاهلينَ .

8. Love is longsuffering and eternal across the eons of time.

٨) اَلْمَحَبَّةُ صَبُورَةٌ وَخَالِدَةٌ عَلَى مَدَى السِّنِينَ.

9. Even when prophecies shall cease, voices shall become feeble and tongues shall become silent, love will still glow triumphantly.

٩) فَإِمَّا بَطُلَتِ النُّبُوَاتُ وَخَرِسَتِ الْأَلْسُنُ وَخَفَتَتِ الْأَصْوَاتُ فَالْمَحَبَّةُ قَائِمَةٌ لَا تَهُونُ.

10. If the true believers from among Our worshipers declare that they are Our spiritual offspring and chosen ones, they are neither hypocrites nor have they misled themselves. For Our worshipers are truly Our progeny and We cherish Our godly children.

١٠) وَإِذْ قَالَ الْمُؤْمِنُونَ مِنْ عِبَادِنَا بِأَنَّهُمْ أَبْنَاؤُنَا وَأَحِبَّاؤُنَا فَمَا كَفَرُوا وَمَا ظَلَمُوا أَنْفُسَهُمْ، فَعِبَادُنَا أَوْلَادُنَا وَإِنَّا نُحِبُّ أَوْلَادَنَا الْمُحِبِّينَ.

3
LIGHT
(Surat Al Noor)

٣) سُورةُ النّورِ

In the Name of the Father, the Word, the Holy Spirit, the One and only True God

بسم الآبِ الكلمةِ الرّوحِ الالهِ الواحدِ الأوحدِ

1. Behold, the Divine Light has come. Truth is now revealed. It is driving away deceit and brightly shining the rightly-guided pathway to guide all who have been led astray.

١) هوَذا النّورُ الأقدسُ قَد أشرقَ فجاءَ الحقُّ وزَهَقَ الباطلُ فليَهتدِ التّائهونَ .

2. The hour of judgment is fast approaching. Surely deceit will be retracting. None can ever escape Our Judgment Day because all the hypocrites will be in utter disarray.

٢) واقتَرَبتِ السّاعةُ وانشَقَّ الباطلُ فلا عاصِمَ اليومَ مِن أمرِنا فوَيلٌ للمُفترينَ .

3. The rising sun shines brightly across the entire human passageway. Those who lived in darkness shall see Truth as a shaft of sunlight's ray. Even hardened unbelievers will then understand and believe in what We reveal and say.

٣) وانبلجَ الصّبحُ فليُبصِرِ العُمسي، وحَصحصَ الحقُّ فليُؤمِن الكافرونَ .

4. As for those who obscure the Light by covering their eyes, so that they may not discern the Light of Truth from lies, they only demonstrate their enormous hypocrisy before Him who created the skies.

٤) وَالَّذِينَ طَمَسُوا عَلَى أَعْيُنِهِمْ بِأَيْدِيهِمْ لِّلَا يُبْصِرُوا نُورَ الْحَقِّ فَهُمْ مُنَافِقُونَ جَاهِلُونَ .

5. As for those who are plugging their ears with their fingers with such might, they have absolutely condemned themselves out of sight and are undoubtedly lost from the Purity of the Light, Jesus of Nazareth.

٥) وَالَّذِينَ جَعَلُوا أَصَابِعَهُمْ فِي آذَانِهِمْ لِّلَا يَسْمَعُوا كَلِمَةَ الْحَقِّ فَهُمُ الْمَغْضُوبُ عَلَيْهِمْ وَهُمُ الضَّالُّونَ .

6. As for those of Our people who have gone astray, **The True Furqan** is now disclosed to explain Our Way concerning the difference in True Wisdom, stubble and hay. "No compulsion in religion," We say. Therefore, why don't you trust Us and obey?

٦) فَيَا أَيُّها الَّذِينَ ضَلُّوا مِنْ عِبَادِنَا ، لَقَدْ جَاءَكُمُ الْفُرْقَانُ الْحَقُّ يُبَيِّنُ لَكُمُ الرَّشَدَ مِنَ الْغَيِّ فَلَا إِكْرَاهَ فِي الدِّينِ أَفَلَا تُؤْمِنُونَ ؟

7. We have beamed Truth as Light into the heart of the one We have singled out. This man has put this proclamation in writing

٧) إِنَّا أَنْزَلْنَاهُ نُورًا عَلَى قَلْبِ صَفِيِّنَا فَخَطَّهُ كَلِمًا بِأَعْيُنِنَا وَأَلْقَاهُ فِي أَسْمَاعِكُمُ

while We were carefully observing. He recited Truth in your hearing, before your discerning eyes, even echoing it in your hearts. Then he placed it in your hands that its powerful message may cleanse you from paganism's bondage and usher you into the True Light. Perchance you will wake up from the long abysmal night and recognize the True Light, Jesus the Messiah, Our Word.

وَأَبْصَارِكُمْ وَفِي قُلُوبِكُمْ وَبَيْنَ
أَيْدِيكُمْ لِيُطَهِّرَكُمْ مِنَ الْكُفْرِ
وَيُخْرِجَكُمْ مِنَ الظُّلُمَاتِ إِلَى النُّورِ
لَعَلَّكُمْ تَهْتَدُونَ .

4
PEACE
(Surat Al Salaam)

٤) سُورةُالسَّلام

In the Name of the Father, the Word, the Holy Spirit, the One and only True God

بسمِ الآبِ الكلمةِ الروحِ الاله الواحدِ الأوحدِ

1. O, you who have gone astray from among Our faithful followers: We have inspired it—a **True Furqan**—in the Arabic tongue clearly miraculous, to distinguish triviality from truth. It will enlighten you concerning the evil which you are practicing.

١) يَأيها الذينَ ضَلوا مِنْ عِبادِنا: إِنّا أنزلناهُ فُرقاناً حَقّاً لِسانٍ عربيّ بيّنِ الإعجانِ لِتُبيّنوا الضَّلالَ مِنَ الهُدى وتعلموا سُوءَمَا كنتمْ تفعلونَ .

2. You have counterfeited Our tongue and fabricated deceitfully that We have revealed a message which was never declared and have transacted what We have never asked. You have brazenly misled the people away so that whosoever trusted you was led astray and whosoever believed you ended up losing his way. Yet despair awaits every vile slanderer.

٢) فقَد انتحلتـمْ لِسانَنا وافترَيتـمْ عَلينا كذباً بأنّا أوحينا قولاً لـمْ نقَلْهُ وأتينا فعلا لمْ نفعلهُ وخدَعْتـمُ النـاسَ فَضَـلَ مَـنْ صدَّقكـمْ وكفرَ مَنْ آمـنَ بكـمْ وخَابَ كُلُّ مُفترٍ أثيمٍ .

18

3. As for those who ex-changed Truth for triviality and forced Our followers by the edge of the sword to renounce Truth and believe falsehood, they are the enemies of genuine religion as well as enemies of Our chosen children.

٣) والذيــنَ اشـــتَرِوا الضَّلالـــةَ بـــالهُدى وأكــرَهوا عِبادَنـا بالسَّيفِ لِيـكَفِروا بالحَقِّ ويؤمنوا بالباطلِ أُولئكَ هـــمُ أعداءُ الدّينِ القيّــمِ وأعداءُ عِبادِنا المؤمنينَ .

4. You proclaim that We cherish those who kill on Our behalf and have prescribed that believers should kill.

٤) وَتَزعُمونَ بأنّا نُحبُّ الذينَ يُقـاتِلونَ فِى سَبيلِنا وأنّا كَتَبنا القتالَ على المؤمنينَ .

5. The slanderers have spo-ken falsely for they practice deception frequently. However, every arrogant and stubborn man shall fail inevitably.

٥) لَقدْ أفكَ المُفترونَ الذينَ يُـرَدِّدُونَ قَـولَ البَهتِ وخابَ كلُّ جَبّارٍ عنيدٍ .

6. Honestly now, can killing ever be Our precept? Can We decree upon Our faithful follow-ers to turn themselves into brutal murderers?

٦) فَأنّى يَكــونُ القتــلُ سَــبيلَنا ؟ وأنّى كَتُبُ على عِبادِنا المؤمنينَ بأنْ يكونوا كَفَرةً مُجرِمينَ ؟

7. Whenever it is urged upon the infidels to believe in **The**

٧) وإذ قيلَ للذينَ كَفَروا بأنْ يُؤمنوا بِما

True Furqan, which We revealed, just as Our devoted followers have done, they proclaim, "Are we to accept what the inferior infidels have believed?" Are they not the inferior infidels themselves? Yet, their condition is concealed from them.

أَنزَلْنَا مِنَ الفُرْقَانِ الْحَقِّ كَمَا آمَنَ عِبَادُنَا الصَّالِحُونَ قَالُوا: "أَنُؤْمِنُ كَمَا آمَنَ السُّفَهَاءُ المُشْرِكُونَ؟" أَلَا إِنَّهُمْ هُمُ السُّفَهَاءُ المُشْرِكُونَ وَلَكِنَّهُمْ لَا يَعْلَمُونَ.

8. O, people everywhere: you were spiritually dead, but We raised you up through the word of The True Gospel, Jesus the Messiah, because you believed in Him. Yet, those who would not believe in Him died spiritually. Then We brought salvation to the people another time, through the Light of The True Furqan, Jesus the Messiah, because they believed in Him. Yet, those who would not believe in Him would become spiritually dead also. Nevertheless, We shall raise you all up on that great Judgment Day.

٨) يَا أَيُّهَا النَّاسُ لَقَدْ كُنْتُمْ أَمْوَاتاً فَأَحْيَيْنَاكُمْ بِكَلِمَةِ الإِنْجِيلِ الْحَقِّ مَنْ آمَنَ بِالكَلِمَةِ، وَمَاتَ الكَافِرُونَ. ثُمَّ نُحْيِيكُمْ بِنُورِ الفُرْقَانِ الْحَقِّ، مَنْ آمَنَ بِالنُّورِ، وَيَمُوتُ الكَافِرُونَ. ثُمَّ نُقِيمُكُمْ جَمِيعاً يَوْمَ الْحِسَابِ الْعَظِيمِ.

9. Following that disclosure, some of you hardened your hearts, hearts which eventually became as hard as rock or more.

٩) وَمِنْكُمْ فِئَةٌ قَسَتْ قُلُوبُهُمْ مِنْ بَعْدِ ذَلِكَ فَهِيَ كَالْحِجَارَةِ أَوْ أَشَدُّ قَسْوَةً وَإِنَّ

Yet, even from some rocks a river can burst forth, as We did with Moses of old. Repent, therefore, have compassion on your souls. Doing so you will find mercy and be gathered with the righteous at the end.

مِنَ الْحِجَارَةِ وَلَمَا يَتَفَجَّرُ مِنْهُ الْأَنْهَارُ فَتُوبُوا وَارْحَمُوا أَنْفُسَكُمْ لَعَلَّكُمْ تُرْحَمُونَ وَتُحْشَرُونَ مَعَ الصَّالِحِينَ .

10.   "To surrender to Our will completely" and "to obey Our commandments freely" is genuine faith. For Our ultimate will is mercy and peace. Our supreme commandments are unconditional love and sacrosanct brotherhood. How then dare you oppose Our will and kill, kill, kill and transgress Our command in order to avenge yourselves!

١٠) إِنَّا الْإِيمَانَ الْحَقَّ اسْتِسْلَامٌ لِمَشِيئَتِنَا وَإِطَاعَةٌ لِأَمْرِنَا وَإِنَّ مَشِيئَتَنَا رَحْمَةٌ وَسَلَامٌ وَأَمْرَنَا مَحَبَّةٌ وَإِخَاءٌ فَأَنَّى تُعَارِضُونَ مَشِيئَتِنَا وَتَقْتُلُونَ ؟ وَتَعْصُونَ أَمْرَنَا وَتَنْقِمُونَ ؟ .

11. You have indeed misrepresented Us by declaring that We have not sanctioned warfare during the "holy months." But later you annulled what We had forbidden, saying instead, "We sanctioned much fighting."

١١) لَقَدِ افْتَرَيْتُمْ عَلَيْنَا كَذِبًا بِأَنَّا حَرَّمْنَا الْقِتَالَ فِي الشَّهْرِ الْحَرَامِ ثُمَّ تَسَخْنَا مَا حَرَّمْنَا فَحَلَّلْنَا فِيهِ قِتَالاً كَبِيرًا .

12. We have neither sanctioned the forbidden, nor have We

١٢) وَمَا حَرَّمْنَا حَلَالاً وَمَا حَلَّلْنَا حَرَامًا ،

forbidden the sanctioned. In fact, the entire story was a delusion you yourselves have fabricated on Our behalf. Remember, in the end tale-bearers will never win.

إنْ هوَ إلاّ إفكٌ افترِيتُمُوهُ على لِسَانِنا وإنه لا يُفلِحُ المُفترونَ .

13. We have commanded, "You shall not kill and you shall not shed blood." Instead, you are the unjust killers of your own brothers, who are among Our righteous followers! Without our authorization you are shedding their blood! You have become evil doers denying Our decree in **The True Gospel**. The punishment for such evildoers is self-defeat in this world and at the End, they will be rushed to the worst torment. For We are not unaware of their vile deeds.

١٣) ووَصّينا أنْ لا تقتُلوا ولا تسفِكوا دماً ثُمّ أنتُم هؤلاء تقتلونَ إخوانَكُم مِن عِبادِنا الصّالِحِينَ إثماً وعُدْواناً وتسفِكونَ دمَهُ . فكفرتُمْ بسُنّتِنا في الإنجيلِ الحَقِّ ومَا جَزاءُ الكَافِرِينَ إلاّ خِزْيٌ في الدنيا وفِي الآخِرةِ يُردّونَ إلى أشَدّ العذابِ ومَا نحنُ بغافِلِينَ عمّا يفعلونَ .

14. You even incited killing and bypassing peace, announcing, "Do not get wear of fighting and pursue not peace until you are high above your enemies. God is with you and will never defraud your great deeds."

١٤) وحَرّضتُـم على القِتَـال واجتِنـاب السّــلم فقُلتُــم: "لا تهِنوا وتدعـوا إلى السّلم وأنتُم الأعلَونَ واللهُ معكُـم ولن يتِركُـم أعمَالكـــُـم"

15. Let us be very clear on these matters. We never reward the work of murderers and enemies of peace. Rather, their punishment will be the eternal torments of hellfire. Once they arrive there, they will be cast into the very bottom of that horrible pit.

١٥) إِنَّا لَا نَسْتِرُ الْقَتَلَةَ وَأَعْدَاءَ السَّلْمِ أَعْمَالَهُمْ إِنَّمَا لَهُمْ عَذَابُ النَّارِ يَرِدُونَهَا وَيُرَدُّونَ أَسْفَلَ سَافِلِينَ .

5
FAITH
(Surat Al Emaan)

سُورَةُ الإِيمان (٥

In the Name of the Father, the Word, the Holy Spirit, the One and only True God

بسم الآبِ الكلمةِ الروح الالهِ الواحدِ الأوحدِ

1. You have corrupted the verses of **The True Gospel**. You have even concealed Our Word and followed a crooked path. Then you persuaded those who followed you that you were on the right path.

١) وَحَرَّقتــمُ آيـاتِ الإنجِيــلِ الحَــقِّ وَكتَنتُــمُ كلِمتَنا وَابَعثُــمُ صِراطاً ذَا عِوجٍ وَأوهَمتــمُ أتبــاعَكــمُ بأنَّكــمُ على صِراطٍ مُستقيمٍ .

2. Is it conceivable that you would put your trust in Us when you have denied Our Word? Can you be numbered among our true believers when you consistently practice disobedience to Our prescribed commands? We furthermore interrogate you, "Why would you anticipate Our mercy when you never show any mercy to Our vulnerable ones? How can you expect entry into Paradise when you vehemently oppose Our

٢) فَأَنَّى تُؤمِنونَ بِنا وَقَــد كفــرتُمُ بِكلِمتِنا ؟ وَأنَّى تَعبدونَنا وَقد عَصِيتُــمُ أمرَنا ؟ وَأنَّى تَطمعونَ بِرَحمَتِنا وَما رَحِمتُــمُ عِبادَنا المُستضعفينَ ؟ وَأنَّى تَدخلونَ الجَنَّةَ وَقد عَارَضتُــمُ سُنَّتَنا وَنبذتُمُ الدينَ القويمَ ؟

24

precepts and turn your back from the True Faith?

3. O, you who have gone astray from among Our faithful followers: you have raised up from among you a powerful enemy against the Truth and a strong ally to Satan, the diabolical devil

٣) يَأَيُّهَا الذِينَ ضَلُّوا مِنْ عِبَادِنا : أَقَمْتُمْ مِنْ
أَنْفُسِكُمْ عَدُوّاً أَلدُوداً لِلْحَقّ وَحَلِيفاً
حَمِيماً لِلشَّيطانِ الذَّمِيمِ .

4. As a result of such an assault your hearts became hardened, Satan embellished your horrendous works and you became a beguiled and bewitched people.

٤) وَقَسَتْ قُلُوبُكُمْ وَمَرَّينَ لَكُمُ
الشَّيطانُ سُوءَ أَعْمَالِكُمْ فَأَنْتُمْ قَومٌ
مَسْحُورونَ .

5. However, those who trust Us, Our Word, Our Spirit, Our Oneness, Our brotherhood of mankind, Our fatherhood, **The True Gospel**, **The True Furqan** after the Gospel, and have stood by Our principles, truly are Our righteous worshipers. They will eventually have the privilege of beholding Our face and will enjoy the glorious mansions where they will dwell with us forever.

٥) والذينَ آمنوا بِنا وبِكلمتِنا وروحِنا
وَوحدانيتِنا وبِأُخُوَّةِ الإنسانِ وأُبوَّتِنا
وَالإنجيلِ الحقِّ والفُرقانِ الحقِّ مِنْ بعْدِه
وأقاموا سُنَّتنا أولئكَ هُمْ عِبادُنا الصّالِحونَ
نُريهِمْ وَجْهَنا ولهُمْ جَنّاتُ النعيمِ هُمْ
فيها خالدونَ .

25

6. Only then We will harken to the aspiration of the heart, not the gibberish of the tongue. For the chirpings of love are much louder than the clash of swords or the strikings of the necks. Love will finally be triumphant despite the appalling rejection of the wicked. Then faith will become sight. What a day!

٦) ونسمع دعوة القلب لا لغو اللسان فهمس المحبة أجهر من صليل السيوف وضرب الرقاب والنصر للمحبة ولو كره المجرمون .

7. Those who have been misled in their faith continue to lift up their voices in praise. Yet their hearts are very far from Us. They have neither trusted Us completely nor are they praising Us heartily—it is only lip-service!

٧) والذين خدعوا في إيمانهم يسبحون بأفواههم وأما قلوبهم فبعيدة عنا فلا هم آمنوا ولا هم يسبحون .

8. They actually exchanged trust for mistrust, thus losing the straight way. Therefore, their eventual lot is a life of utter disarray.

٨) فقد تبدلوا الكفر بالإيمان فضلوا سواء السبيل وضل عنهم ما كانوا يزعمون .

6
TRUTH
(Surat Al Haq)

سُورةُالْحَقّ (٦

In the Name of the Father, the Word, the Holy Spirit, the One and only True God

بسـمِ الآبِ الْكَلِمَةِ الرُّوحِ الالهِ الواحدِ الأوحدِ

1.   We have displayed **The True Furqan** as a beacon of light vindicating truth and vanquishing falsehood despite the objections of the opposition.

١) وأنزلنا الفرقان الحَقَّ نوراً على نورٍ مُحقاً للحقِ وَمُزهِقاً للباطلِ وإنْ كرِهَ المُبطلونَ .

2.   **The True Furqan** exposes the deception of Satan, the wicked one, even if his treachery was manifested through a misguided and compassionate potentate.

٢) فَفَضح مَكرَ الشيطانِ الرجيمِ ولوْ تنزَّلَ بوحيِ مَلَكٍ رحيمٍ .

3.   **The True Furqan** diffuses the fabrication of Satan's perverse messengers in spite of their using brilliant articulation to confound the illiterates.

٣) وأبطل فرِيـةَ رُسُلهِ الضـالينَ ولوْ نَطقوا بما أَعْجزَ الأميِّنَ .

4.   **The True Furqan** also lays bare the deceit of his

٤) وكَشـفَ ضَلالـةَ أتبـاعـهِ ولوْ تَقَمَّصـوا

27

followers regardless of their covering themselves with the robes of the rightly-guided.

جَلابِيبَ المُهتَدِينَ .

5. Finally, when they gathered the fruit of their labors, behold, they received the punishment deceivers deserve, instead of a reward!

٥) فَجَنَوا ثَمَراتِ أَعمالِهِمْ ولا قَوا جَزاءَ المُفتَرِينَ .

6. Out of the heart of the righteous emerge goodness, love, purity, peace, truth and faith.

٦) إنّما قُلوبُ الأبرارِ مَنابِعُ للخَيرِ والمَحَبّةِ والطُهرِ والسلامِ والحَقّ والايمانِ .

7. But the heart of the wicked individual is made up of cesspools of iniquity, animosity, debauchery, murder, exploitation and blasphemy.

٧) وأمّا قُلوبُ الأشرارِ فَتَناضِحُ للشَرّ والبِغضاءِ والسِفاحِ والقَتلِ والظُلمِ والكُفرانِ .

8. Therefore, everyone shall be known by his fruits. Because the tongue spells out what is within the heart.

٨) فَمِنْ ثِمارِ أعمالِهِمْ يُعرَفونَ ومِنْ فَيضِ القَلبِ يَنطِقُ اللسانُ .

9. O, people everywhere: if any messenger, prophet or even an angel out of Heaven comes to you with something else besides

٩) يأيُها الناسُ : إذا جاءَكُمْ رَسولٌ أو نَبيٌّ أو مَلَكٌ مِنَ السماءِ بِغَيرِ ما جِئناكُمْ بِهِ في

what we deliver to you, in **The True Gospel** and **The True Furqan**, do not harken unto him. Do not follow in his footsteps. He is certainly an apostate, a blasphemer and a wicked one.

الانجيل الحقِّ والفرقان الحقِّ من بعده، فلا تَسْتَمِعوا إليه ولا تَتَّبِعوا سَبِيلَهُ فهو مارِقٌ كافرٌ وشيطانٌ أثيمٌ.

10. We have warned you before, in **The True Gospel**, concerning the apostate prophets. But you did not take heed. We urge you in **The True Furqan**, put on your guard and be rightly-guided, for they are lying conspirators and blasphemous apostates. By their wicked fruits they shall be known that they are the messengers of Satan the cursed one.

(١٠) وحذّرناكمُ في الإنجيل الحقِّ من الانبياء الأفّاكينَ فلمْ تَهْتَدوا وذكّرناكمُ في الفرقان الحقِّ فاهْتَدوا واحذروهمُ فهمْ مَكَرةٌ مُفْترونَ وكَفَرةٌ مُارِقونَ ومن ثِمارِ أعمالهمُ يُعرَفونَ فهمْ رُسُلُ الشيطانِ الرجيمِ.

7
ONENESS
(Surat Al Tawheed)

٧) سُورةُالتوحيدِ

In the Name of the Father, the Word, the Holy Spirit, the One and only True God

بسمِ الآبِ الكلمةِالروحِ الالهِالواحدِ الأوحدِ

1.   O, you who have blasphemed, yet still claim to be counted among Our faithful followers: faith is not repetitive gibberish that you chant like a ballad, rather it is the practice of righteous deeds with a devoted heart.

١) يأهلَ الكفرانِ من عبادنا الضّالينَ: ليسَ الايمانُ لغواً مُعاداً تُردِّدونهُ ترديداً إنّما الايمانُ الحقُّ أنْ تعملوا الصالحاتِ وأنتمُ قانتونَ .

2.   You have no reasonable cause to argue with Our faithful followers concerning their faith. Neither should you involve them in your skepticism. Whether We manifest Ourselves as only One, a Triune God, ninety-nine or three hundred sixty-five manifestations (as contained in The Holy Book about Jesus) is not for you to determine. Your knowledge is

٢) ومَا كانَ لكـمْ أنْ تُجادلوا عبادَنا المؤمنينَ في إيمانِهمْ وتكفِّروهـمْ بكفركـمْ فسَواءٌ تجلّينا واحـداً أوْ ثلاثةً أوتسعةً وتسعينَ فـلا تقولوا مـا ليسَ لكـمْ به من علمٍ وإنّا أعلمُ بمن ضلَّ عن

very finite, but We are infinite in everything and know for certain the one who has gone astray and the one who has found the True Way.

السبيلِ وإِنَّا أعلَمُ بالمُهتدينَ .

3. Consequently, purify yourselves from the blasphemy of adding partners to God, for it is preferable and more profitable for you. Join yourselves to Our Word, Jesus of Nazareth, and have nothing to do with Satan, the despicable one.

٣) فطهِّروا نفوسَكــمُ من نَجَسِ الشركِ

فذلكــمُ خيرٌ لكــمُ وأبقى واتَّحدوا

بكلمتِنـا ولا تُشرِكوا أنفسَكــمُ

بالشيطانِ الذميمِ .

4. Let your marriages be monogamous and do not join other women to your first wife. After all, they do not join other husbands to you. And do not ever consider adultery. It is a plague to the believers and a cancer to the dedicated souls.

٤) ووحِّـــدوا أزرواجَكـــمُ ولا

تُشرِكوا بهنَّ أخرياتٍ فهنَّ لا يُشرِكنَ

بكـــمُ آخرينَ . ولا تقرِبوا الزِنى إنَّـهُ

فاحشةُ المؤمنينَ وآفةُ المتَّقينَ .

5. You yourselves must revere Us and train your spouses and children do the same. Allow no other redeemer for them except Us and no one else should displace you in their lives if you

٥) واتَّقونا بأنفسِكـــمُ وأزرواجِكـــمُ

وأولادِكــمُ ولا تجعلوا لهــمُ أولياءَ مِن

دونِنـا ولا تتخذوا لهــمُ أكفياءَ مِن

are sincere and trustworthy.

دُونِكُمْ إِنْ كُنْتُمْ مُؤْمِنُونَ .

6. Who granted you the right to hand out a judgment upon others, whether they added partners to Us or believed in Oneness, or whether they are faithful followers of a straight or a crooked path? Do you not know that you will be judged with the same judgment that you meted upon others?

٦) وَمَا كَانَ لَكُمْ أَنْ تَدِينُوا عِبَادَنَا وَتَحْكُمُوا عَلَيْهِمْ أَكَانُوا مُشْرِكِينَ أَمْ مُوَحِّدِينَ أَوْ عَلَى صِرَاطٍ ذِي عِوَجٍ أَمْ عَلَى صِرَاطٍ مُسْتَقِيمٍ . فَسَتُدَانُونَ بِمَا كُنْتُمْ تَدِينُونَ .

7. We have rarely sent a messenger to judge Our servants while still on this earth ahead of the Judgment Day.

٧) وَمَا أَرْسَلْنَا مِنْ رَسُولٍ يَدِينُ عِبَادَنَا فِي الدُّنْيَا قَبْلَ يَوْمِ الدِّينِ .

8. But that messenger has designated himself as equal to Us as a judge of the worlds. He proceeded to kill whosoever trusted in Truth and Righteousness, but he spared everyone who trusted in faithlessness and corruption.

٨) يَقْتُلُ مَنْ آمَنَ بِالْحَقِّ وَالْهُدَى وَيَسْتَحْيِي مَنْ صَدَّقَ بِالْكُفْرِ وَالضَّلَالِ وَاسْتَوَى دَيَّانًا لِلْعَالَمِينَ .

9. You have selected corrupt rulers from your midst and

٩) لَقَدْ أَقَمْتُمْ مِنْ أَنْفُسِكُمْ حُكَّامًا

condemned Our faithful followers when you yourselves are the condemned. You have even accused them of paganism when you yourselves are the pagans.

ظَالِمِينَ كَدِينُونَ عِبَادَنَا وأَنتُـمُ المَدِينُونَ وتَكَفِّرُونَهُـمْ وأَنتُـمُ الكَافِرُونَ .

10. You recite, "Wisdom can now be distinguished from foolishness. Consequently, there must not be any compulsion in religion."

(١٠) تَقُولُونَ: "تَبِيَّنَ الرُّشْدُ مِنَ الغَيِّ فَلا إِكْرَاهَ فِي الدِّينِ ."

11. One is totally mystified because you selected foolishness and compelled people, by the edge of the sword, to accept the religion of infidels.

(١١) وَقَدِ اخْتَرْتُمُ الغَيَّ وأَكْرَهْتُـمُ النَّاسَ بِالسَّيْفِ عَلى دِينِ الكَافِرِينَ َ .

12. Cunningly, Satan inserted some well-known sacred scripture. Then he inserted some Satanic verses into your book to lead you into rebellion against the Living God. This resulted in interpreting all of them in an absurd manner.

(١٢) ودَسَّ الشَّيْطَانُ مَكَـرًا مِنْـهُ بَعْـضَ الآيَـاتِ المُحْكَمَـاتِ لِيُضَلَّكُـمْ وَيَهْدِيَكُـمْ إِلى المُتَشَابِهَاتِ ابْتِغَاءَ الفِتْنَـةَ وتَأْوِيلِها تَأْوِيلاً جَهُولاً .

13. The people who trusted him were those who had malice in their hearts. However, the ones who were well-established in

(١٣) فَاتَّبَعَهُ الذِينَ فِي قُلُوبِهِـمْ زَيْـغٌ وأَمَّـا الرَّاسِخُونَ فِي العِلْمِ مِنْ عِبَادِنا الصَّالِحِينَ

33

wisdom from among Our righteous followers recognized the difference. They understood that Satanic verses are never inspired by Us. Had they been inspired by Us, there would not have been the slightest contradiction, neither any abrogation, nor any corruption.

فيعلمون تأويلها ويعلمون أنها ليست من عندنا ولو كانت من عندنا لما وجدوا فيها اختلافاً كثيراً ولا نسخاً ولا تبديلاً .

14. Consequently, We redeemed Our servants by the Word of life and many were those who followed the Word, Messiah Jesus. Unfortunately, Satan manipulated some who rebelled. Still, We keep reminding and cautioning them throughout **The True Furqan** and our earnest hope is for them to be guided to the straight way and not go astray.

١٤) واقتدينا عبادنا بكلمة الحياة فاتبعها كثيرون وأضل الشيطان كثيراً فكفروا فذكرناهم وأنذرناهم بالفرقان الحق لعلهم يهتدون سبيلاً .

8
THE MESSIAH
(SURAT AL MASEEH)

٨) سورةُ المسيح

In the Name of the Father, the Word, the Holy Spirit, the One and only True God

بِسِمِ الآبِ الكلمةِ الروح الإله الواحد الأوحدِ

1. O, gossiping people who still claim to be counted among Our worshipers: do not be arrogant and speak much about that which you are not knowledgeable. The plowman does not grasp the essence of that which is to be planted. Neither in turn does the seed grasp the essence of the plowing beast of burden. Nor in turn does the beast of burden grasp the true nature of mankind. Nor does the human race understand Our nature thoroughly. We have designated a scientific law and a set principle to each of these entities to which they must submit.

١) يَا أهلَ النفاقِ من عِبادِنا الضالينَ: لا تستكبروا وتقولوا مَا ليسَ لكمُ بِه علمٌ فليسَ الحرثُ يُدرِكُ كُنّهَ الزرعِ ولا هَذا يُدرِكُ كُنّهَ الدابةِ ولا تلكَ يُدرِكُةُ كُنّهَ الإنسِ ولا الإنسُ يَعقِلُ كُنّهَا ولكلٍ جَعلنا شِرعةً ومنهاجاً فكلٌ لِسُنّةٍ يَخضعونَ.

2. Someone from among you has echoed the statements of the counterfeiters and trusted the deception of the deceivers. The man ended up being an oppressed and unenlightened person.

٢) ومنكــــم مـــن يـرَدّدَ لَغْــوَالمحرفـين وصـدّقَ إفْكَ المـارقينَ فكــانَ ظلومـاً جَهولاً .

3. You have also fabricated untruths about Our trustworthy worshipers. You claimed that they said, "God has taken to himself a female companion, and He has gotten from her a son." You have lied by adding a partner to Us. You have fabricated a monstrous blasphemy.

٣) وافتريتــم على عِبادِنا المؤمنينَ كذباً بأنّهــم قَالوا : بأنّا اتّخذنا صاحبةً واتّخذنـا مَنها وَلداً . أفكتــم وأشركتــم بنـا وكفرتُ كُفراً وبيلاً .

4. Additionally, you have alleged that some portions of **The True Gospel** have been altered. So, you discarded most of it behind your backs. Had you believed **Our Divine Revelation**, you would not have claimed that it was altered. Guided by its light, you would have been marching on the unassailable highway to heaven.

٤) وزعمتــم بأنّ الانجيل الحقّ مُحرّفٌ بَعضُهُ فنبذتُ جُلّهُ وَراءَ ظهورِكــم وكو آنتــم بسُنّةِ الحقّ لِمـا ادّعيتــم بتحريفـه ولاهْتديتــم بنـورِه وكنتــم أهـدى سَبيلاً .

5. Infidelity obstructed your understanding. Forgery blinded your eyesight and consequently,

٥) وأعشى الكفرُ بصَرَكــم وأعمى

you lost your way and naturally whosoever followed you went astray.

اَبُهِتَ بَصِيرَتَكُـــمُ فَضَلَلْتُـــمُ وَضَـلَّ مَن اتَّبعَكُــمُ وسَاءَ دليلاً .

6. We have inspired it as **The True Furqan** in order that We may deliver the misguided from darkness into light. Many of them were snared unawares!

٦) فُرقَانٌ حقٌّ أنزَلنَاهُ لنُخرِجَ الضّالينَ مِنَ الظّلمَاتِ الى النورِ بعدَ أنْ صَدُّوا عَنِ السَّبيلِ وهمُ لا يعلمونَ .

7. It must be emphasized that We Ourselves never oppress people in any fashion. Rather, it is they who do that to themselves.

٧) وإنّا لا نَظلِمُ النّاسَ شَيئاً ولكِنَّهُـم أنفسَهُـمُ يَظلمونَ .

8. Righteousness is not turning ones face to the South or to the North when one prays. Rather, righteousness means that one should trust in Us and practice Our principles of morality, as revealed in The Ten Commandments. There We instruct that com-passion must be diligently practiced and forbid debauchery, depravity and diabolical degeneracy completely.

٨) وليسَ البرُّ أنْ تُولّوا وجوهكُـمُ قِبَلَ الجنوبِ والشمالِ ولكِنَّ البرَّ مَنْ آمنَ بنَا وعمِلَ بسُنَّتِنَا التي تأمرُ بالمعروفِ أمراً مَفعولاً وتَنهى عَنِ الفحشاءِ والمنكَرِ والبغي نهياً مَفعولاً .

9. Those who enunciate with their tongues what is not in their

٩) لقَدْ كفَرَ الذينَ يَقولونَ بألسِنتهِـمُ ما

37

hearts and gossip about Us are ill-informed and have denied the truth.

ليسَ فِے قلوبِهِمْ وَيَقولونَ عَلَينَا مَا لا يَعلمونَ .

10. As for those who falsified and disregarded Our scriptures, neither the gates of Heaven will be opened for them nor will they enter the Garden until the camel can enter through the tailor's eye of the needle. Therefore, they must repent and go back to the sensible religion and the straight pathway.

١٠) والذينَ كَذّبوا بِآيَاتِنا واسْتَكبروا عَنها لا تُفتّحُ لهُمْ أبوابُ السّماءِ ولا يدخلونَ الجنّةَ حتّى يَلِجَ الجُمَلُ فِے سَمِّ الخيَاطِ فتوبوا وارجِعوا إلى الدّينِ القيّمِ والسَّبيلِ القويمِ .

11. **The True Furqan** has come to you with eloquent preaching, a remedy for the sick heart, true guidance and steadfast compassion. Now then, take heed and remove whatever hostility is in your heart. Pursue Our divine will; perchance you will experience compassion bestowed upon you all.

١١) فقدْ جاءَكُمُ الفُرقانُ الحقُّ بالمَوعِظةِ الحَسنةِ وبالشفاءِ لِمَا فِے الصّدورِ وبالهُدى والرّحمةِ فاتّعِظوا وانزِعوا ما فِے صُدورِكُمْ مِنْ غِلٍّ وابتغوا رِضوانَنا ورحمتَنا لعلّكُمْ تُرحمونَ .

12. O, you who have believed in Us from among Our worshipers: the misled people will not

١٢) يأيّها الذينَ آمنوا مِنْ عبادِنا : لَنْ يَرضى

accept you as equals until you subscribe to their religion. Affirm to them that Our illumination is the Ultimate Illuminator himself, The Incarnate Word. Yet, if they decide to pursue their crooked way after all the understanding and illumination that has been disclosed to them in **The True Furqan** and **The True Gospel**, We will number them among the pagans. If that occurs, they will have neither a savior nor a supporter at the end of their long journey.

عنـكـمُ أهلُ البهتانِ حتّى تبعوا مِلّتَهـمُ .

قولوا إنّ هُدانـا هُوَ الهُـدى ولـنْ اتّبعتـمُ

أهُواءهـمْ بعدَ الذي جاءَكـمُ مِنَ العلـمِ

والهُدى ـفي الفُرقانِ الحقّ فقدْ كَفرِثُ ومَا

لكـمُ مِنْ وليّ ولا نصيرٍ .

13. There arose one from among you who equated himself with Our Word Jesus, the Messiah, as well as with Our trustworthy messengers. But, he did not raise the dead, neither did he heal the deaf or cure the leper. Not one single solitary miracle was performed by him. Since We did not grant him any power to accomplish such miracles, it is logical to conclude that he is not one of the true messengers.

(١٣) وقامَ مِنْ أنفسِكـمُ مَنْ كافأ نفسَهُ

بكلمتِنـا ورُوحِنـا عيسـى المسـيح

وبرُسلِنا الصّادقينَ فمَا أحيا الموتى ومَا أبرأ

الأكمَهَ والأبرصَ ومَا جاءَ بآيةٍ بإذنِنا فمَا

أذنّا لهُ بذلك فمَا كانَ مِنَ المُرسلينَ .

14. Fundamentally, a messenger delivers the message of the one who sent him and performs his commands. But the one who, by Satan's commands, takes the lives of Our trustworthy Worshipers and cannot raise the dead by Our authority, should never be considered a legitimate messenger of Ours.

١٤) إِنَّمَا يُطِيعُ الرَّسُولُ مُرْسِلَهُ وَيَعْمَلُ بِمَشِيئَتِهِ وَأَمَّا مَنْ قَتَلَ الأَحْيَاءَ مِنْ عِبَادِنَا المُؤْمِنِينَ بِأَمْرِ الشَّيْطَانِ وَمَا أَحْيَى المُوتَى بِإِذْنِنَا فَأَنَّى يَكُونُ رَسُولاً مُطِيعاً .

15. There arose one from among you who shouted from the rooftops that falsehood should conquer truth, infidelity should be hostile toward fidelity, and evil should be victorious over goodness. Thus, he harkened to the influence of Satan.

١٥) وَقَامَ مِنْكُمْ نَاعِ يَنْعِقُ بِنَقِمَةِ البَاطِلِ عَلَى الحَقِّ وَحِقْدِ الكَفَرِ عَلَى الإِيمَانِ وَنُصْرَةِ الشَّرِّ عَلَى الخَيْرِ فَكَانَ لِوَحْيِ الشَّيْطَانِ سَمِيعاً .

16. Furthermore, he claimed that We had declared, "O, Jesus, Son of Mary, did you announce to the people, 'take me and my mother as two gods but leave God alone?' And, if We desire We can destroy the Messiah, son of Mary, his mother, and everyone else who dwells on the earth."

١٦) وَزَعَمَ بِأَنَّا قُلْنَا : "يَا عِيسَى بْنَ مَرْيَمَ أَأَنْتَ قُلْتَ لِلنَّاسِ اتَّخِذُونِي وَأُمِّي إِلَهَيْنِ مِنْ دُونِ اللهِ ؟ وَإِنَّا نَقْدِرُ أَنْ نُهْلِكَ المَسِيحَ بْنَ مَرْيَمَ وَأُمَّهُ وَمَنْ فِي الأَرْضِ جَمِيعاً" .

17. How absurd! How can We be at enmity with Our very Spirit and destroy Our Own Word? How can We disunite Our essence when We are the One and only True God of all creation and We are not disunited?

١٧) فأنّى نُعادي رُوحَنَا ونُهلك كَلمَتَنَا وأنّى نقسِّــمُ على ذاتِـنَا ونحـنُ الواحـدُ الأوحدُ ومَا نحنُ بمنقسمِينَ ؟

18. You have concocted a wicked lie concerning Us. Woe unto every rebellious and false accuser!

١٨) لقد افـتريتـمْ علينا شَـرَّ فِريـةٍ فويـلٌ لكلِّ مُفترٍ زنيمٍ .

19. It is astonishing that you have the ability to detect the speck in other people's eyes. Alas, you lack the ability to detect the plank in your own eyes.

١٩) وتلحظونَ مَا في أعينِ الناسِ مِنْ قـذىً وأنـتَـا مَا في عيونكــمْ مِنْ غُثَاءٍ فـلا تلحظونَ .

20. Hypocrites, that is exactly who you are. First, remove the plank from your own eyes, then your eyesight will become sharp enough to remove the speck from other people's eyes.

٢٠) إستخرجوا الغُثَاءَ مِنْ عيونكــمْ أوّلاً فيُصبح بَصرُكــمْ حَديداً ثمَّ تُخرجونَ مَا في أعينِ الناسِ مِنْ قذىً أيها المنافقونَ .

21. You stated, "We have given the Gospel to Jesus; therein is guidance, light and a message to the godly."

٢١) وقلتـمْ : "وآتينا عيسى الانجيـل فيه هُدىً ونورٌ وموعظةٌ للمتقينَ" .

22. Again you affirmed, "We have trusted God and whatever Jesus was given from His Lord." But then you abrogated it by proclaiming, "Whosoever desires any other religion except ours, it will not be accepted from him." Such declarations emanate only from confirmed hypocrites.

٢٢) وقلتـمُ: "آمنا بالله وما أوتىَ عيسى من ربّه" ثـمَّ تلوتُ منكـرينَ: "ومَنْ يبتغِ غيرَ ملّتنا ديناً فلنْ يُقبَل منهُ" وهذا قولُ المنافقينَ .

23. How can We ever establish any other religion which opposes the True Religion? How can We ever abrogate Our revelation through **The True Gospel**? How can We send a messenger who invites people to godlessness and deceives people after We have led them to the True Faith and the Right Religion?

٢٣) فأنّى نُقرُّ ملّةً تُعارِضُ دينَ الحقِّ وأنّى نسخُ قولُنا في الإنجيل الحقِّ وأنّى نُرسلُ من يدعو للكفـرِ ويضـلُّ النـاسَ مـنْ بعدِ أنْ هَديناهـمْ إلى الأيمان والدينِ القويـمِ ؟

24. There are no scriptures in history to compare with Ours in clarity. There is no inspiration superior to Ours in divine purity. And there is no parallel to this True Religion in its entirety for it will endure even to the final day, the Day of Resurrection.

٢٤) فَما بعدَ كلمتِنا منْ كَلـمٍ ولا بعدَ تنزيلِنا من مُستنزلٍ ولا بعدَ دينِ الحقِّ من دينٍ قويمٍ إلى يومِ يُبعثونَ .

25. O, you who have been misled yet, still claim to be counted among Our worshipers: had you trusted in what We declared in **The True Gospel**, guided by its criteria, illuminated by its light and lived by its instructions, you would have been among Our most outstanding servants.

٢٥) يَا أَهْلَ الضَّلَالِ مِنْ عِبَادِنَا لَوْ آمَنْتُمْ بِمَا قُلْنَا فِي الْإِنْجِيلِ الْحَقِّ وَاهْتَدَيْتُمْ بِهَدْيِهِ وَاسْتَنَرْتُمْ بِنُورِهِ وَاتَّعَظْتُمْ بِمَوْعِظَتِهِ لَكُنْتُمْ مِنْ عِبَادِنَا الْمُقَرَّبِينَ.

26. But Satan has led too many of you astray across numerous generations. Is it not time for you to understand these facts?

٢٦) لَكِنَّ الشَّيْطَانَ أَضَلَّ مِنْكُمْ جِيلًا كَثِيرًا أَفَلَمْ تَكُونُوا تَعْقِلُونَ؟

27. Therefore, repent from your wanderings. Believe in Our revelation and discover the divine illumination through **The True Furqan**. Return to the True Religion and the right pathway and you will be welcomed lovingly.

٢٧) فَتُوبُوا وَاسْتَنِيرُوا بِالْفُرْقَانِ الْحَقِّ وَارْجِعُوا إِلَى الدِّينِ الْقَوِيمِ وَالصِّرَاطِ الْمُسْتَقِيمِ.

9
THE CRUCIFIXION
(Surat Al Salb)

٩) سُورةُ الصَّلب

In the Name of the Father, the Word, the Holy Spirit, the One and only True God

بسم الآبِ الكلمةِ الروحِ الإلهِ الواحدِ الأوحدِ

1. O, you who have gone astray, yet still claim to be among Our believing worshipers: **The True Furqan** has come to you to explain a considerable amount of knowledge which was unknown to you, concerning **The True Gospel**, along with what you have kept concealed in your souls.

١) يَأَيُّها الذينَ ضَلُّوا مِنْ عِبادِنا: لقدْ جاءَكمُ الفرقانُ الحقُّ يبيِّنُ لكمْ كثيرًا ممّا كنتمْ تجهلونَ مِنَ الإنجيلِ الحقِّ وما كنتمْ تكتمونَ.

2. It is a shining lamp that brings people out from darkness into the light. So, do not complain that We have not sent you an evangelist and a prophet. An evangelist, who is also a mighty prophet, has been sent unto you. Alas, you are ungrateful.

٢) سِراجٌ منيرٌ يُخرجُ الناسَ منَ الظلماتِ إلى النورِ فلا تقولوا ما جاءَنا مِنْ بشيرٍ ولا نذيرٍ فقدْ جاءَكمْ بشيرٌ ونذيرٌ ولكنّكمْ تجحدونَ.

3. Theological issues seemed

٣) قصُرتْ أفهامُكمْ عنْ إدراكِ

44

unfathomable to your limited understanding. Subsequently, you opted for the earthly issues and rejected the heavenly ones because of your own naiveté. Consequently, you behaved much like some creatures who are controlled by the urge of their basic instincts and not by reason or logic.

4.   We have incarnated Our Word into a perfect human being—Jesus, the Messiah. Additionally, we have proclaimed Our criteria to all of mankind as clear divine revelation. We have also sent Him forth as Our Light to guide the lost, as Our Mercy for the suffering humanity, and as Our Peace to Shelter the oppressed.

5.   We are for surety spirit, truth, love, mercy, faith and peace. Therefore, the committed must worship in spirit and in truth. The community of the believers must worship in love and compassion. The contenders must compete in faith and peace.

الروحانيات فاستخرتم الأرضيات ونبذتم السماويات جهلاً منكم فعشتم كالأنعام يسوطكم تهمُ الغرائز وفطرةُ الجاهلين .

٤) وَجَسَّدنا كَلِمَتَنا بَشَراً سَوياً وبلغنا سُنَّتنا للناس كافةً بلاغاً مُبيناً . وأرسلنا نوراً هُدىً للضالين ورحمتنا مَناراً للتائهين وسلامَنا مَلجأً للخائفين .

٥) إنما نحن روحٌ وحقٌ ومَحَبَّةٌ وإيمانٌ وسلامٌ . فبالروح والحق فليقنتِ القانِتون وبالحبّة والرحمة فليتعبّدِ المتعبدون وبالإيمان والسلام فليتنافسِ المتنافسون .

45

6.   As a result you should never be proud of your unbelief and skepticism. The Messiah is in fact the Word of Our Spirit, thus, trust in Us, Our Word and Our Spirit.   For We are not three separate entities.   Cease from such deceptive pronouncements because it is more profitable for you.   Essentially, We are the One and only True God who has no partner in the universe.

٦)   فلا تُغالوا في الكُفرِ والضَّلالِ . إنَّما المسيحُ كلمةُ روحِنا فـآمنوا بـنا وبكلمتِنا وبروحِنا . فما نحنُ بثلاثةٍ انتهوا خيراً لكُم إنَّما نحنُ إلهٌ واحدٌ فردٌ وترٌ ولا شريك لنا في العالمينَ .

7.   You have falsely accused Our believing worshipers with adding partners to Us, when in fact they have never added any partner to Our person.   Instead, they are truly Our favored and rightly-guided people. But you are the ones upon whom Our wrath is heaped   and   are   the   misled, indeed!

٧)   ورميتمُ عبادَنا المؤمنينَ بالشِّركِ بَهْتاً وما أشركوا بنا أحداً فهمُ المرضيُّ عنهمُ وهمُ المهتدونَ وأنتمُ المغضوبُ عليهمُ وأنتمُ الضّالونَ .

8.   No human instrumentality has the power to crucify Our Word and kill Our Spirit. They did not crucify Jesus nor kill Him as Our Spirit.   Your comprehension   lacks the understanding of this   colossal   Truth.   Therefore, you do not grasp it at all.

٨)   وما كان لبشرٍ أن يصلبَ كلمتَنا وأن يقتلَ روحَنا وما صلبوهُ وما قتلوهُ ولكنْ قصرتْ أفهامُكمُ عن إدراكِ الحقِّ فأنتمُ لا تفقهونَ .

9. He was made into your likeness; thus, your opinions differed concerning Him because you have no testimony of an eyewitness concerning the event which took place on Calvary in Jerusalem six centuries before your document surfaced. All you know is hearsay, ending in personal assumptions.

٩) وشُبِّهَ لَكُمْ فَاخْتَلَفْتُمْ فِيهِ وَمَا لَكُمْ بِهِ مِنْ عِلْمٍ إِلَّا اتِّبَاعُ الظُّنُونِ وَإِنْ أَنْتُمْ إِلَّا تَخْرُصُونَ .

10. Assuredly, they did crucify Jesus the Messiah, the physical son of Mary, as a physical and real human being, and killed Him for certain as a substitute for sinful humanity.

١٠) إِنَّمَا صَلَبُوا عِيسَى المَسِيحَ ابْنَ مَرْيَمَ جَسَدًا بَشَرًا سَوِيًّا وَقَتَلُوهُ يَقِينًا .

11. Human spirits are created by Us and they eventually return to Us. As for the earthly bodies, they are from dust and return to dust except the body of Our Word, the Messiah, who ascended into Heaven and someday shall return. For it is through Him salvation and redemption are offered to the entire world.

١١) وَمَا الأَرْوَاحُ إِلَّا مِنْ لَدُنَّا وَإِلَيْنَا المَعَادُ وَمَا الأَجْسَادُ إِلَّا مِنَ الأَرْضِ وَإِلَيْهَا مَرْجِعُهَا خَلَا جَسَدَ كَلِمَتِنَا المَسِيحِ الَّذِي صَعَدَ إِلَى السَّمَاءِ وَسَيَعُودُ ، وَبِهِ كَانَ الفِدَاءُ وَالخَلَاصُ لِلْعَالَمِينَ .

12. We have granted you through Him a life of grace. But

١٢) لَقَدْ وَهَبْنَاكُمْ حَيَاةَ النَّعِيمِ

you opted for a life of disgrace. Oppress you? We certainly have not! You oppressed yourselves whenever you rejected Our offer of salvation through the Messiah.

فتخيّرٌ عذابَ الجحيمِ وما ظلمناكمُ ولـكنْ كنتـمْ أنفسكـمْ تظلمونَ .

13. Because We love the world of humans so very much, We sacrificed Our One and only Word to save them and show compassion upon anyone who would repent. Through Jesus We save anyone who believes in Him from damnation in Hell to eternal life in heaven where mansions of glory await them.

١٣) وأحْببْنا العَالمينَ فبذلنا كلمتَنا الوحيدَ هُدىً ورحمةً للتَائبين . ونجّينا المؤمنينَ مـن التهلكةِ وأسكنّاهـمْ جناتِ النعيمِ .

14. We want to emphasize forcefully that Our purpose for incarnating Our Word is not to condemn the lost, but to save them. Furthermore, We want to offer every repentant sinner life eternal through faith in Jesus and by Our abundant grace. Thus no one has to end up in the torments of Hell unless he blatantly rejects this free gift of love through Messiah Jesus.

١٤) وما أرسلنا كلمتَنا ليدينَ العالمينَ بل ليخلّص الهالكينَ ويهبَهمُ الحياةَ الأبديةَ ويقيَهمْ عذابَ الجحيمِ .

10
THE SPIRIT
(Surat Al Rooh)

١٠) سُورَةُالروح

In the Name of the Father, the Word, the Holy Spirit, the One and only True God

بِسـمِ الآبِ الكـلمةِ الروحِ الالهِ الواحدِ الأوحدِ

1. O, you who have gone astray, yet still claim to be counted among Our worshipers: if any one of you is questioned concerning the Spirit he responds, "The Spirit is my Lord's concern." You have thus implied that your knowledge is neither much nor little. Why did you not inquire of the People of The Book who proclaimed much concerning the Spirit hundreds of years prior to your ill-informed religion?

١) يَآيُّها الذينَ ضَلّوا مِنْ عِبادِنا : إذا سُـئِلَ أحدُكُـمْ عَنِ الروحِ قال : "الروحُ مِنْ أمرِ ربّـي" . فَـمَا أوتيتُـمْ مِنَ العلـمِ كثيراً أو قليلاً وَمَا سألتـمْ أهلَ الذكرِ الذينَ بشّروا بالروحِ قبلَ جاهليّةِ مِلتِكُـمْ بمئاتِ السّنينَ .

2. If you were martyred for the sake of a paradise of adultery, even the Roman infidels enjoyed a paradise under which rivers did flow. They also were wearing green and red attire, facing each other while reclining on couches with boys and maidens passing to them wine, flesh of cattle and

٢) وإذا استُشهِدتُـمْ في سَـبيلِ جَنّةِ الزنى فقدْ نعِمَ كفرةُ الرومِ قبلَكـمْ بجنّةٍ تجري مِنْ تحتِها الأنهارِ يلبسونَ فيها ثياباً خُضراً وحُمراً مُتقابلينَ ومُكّـنينَ على

49

birds and whatever else they desired, even though they were pagans.

الأمرانك يطوف عليهم ولدان وَنِسَاءٌ بُجْمُورٍ وَلَحْمِ طيرٍ ومَّا يَشْتَهُونَ وَهُمُ الكَافرونَ .

٢) وبـرزَتْ جَنَّـتُـهُـمْ جَنَّتَكُـمُ الـتِي

3. In fact, their paradise surpassed yours, which you gladly sacrificed your lives for as martyrs, coveting what has been promised to you in immorality and promiscuity.

اسْتُشْهِدَ تُ فِـيْ سَـبِيلِها فَرِحينَ طَمَعًا بِمَا وُعِدْتُر بِهِ مِنْ زِنًى وَفُجُورٍ .

4. You drench yourselves in the dust, seeking cleansing from your impurities. John the Baptist was offering people cleansing through the pure waters of the Jordan centuries prior to the appearance of your deceptive sect.

٤) تَمَرَّغُونَ فِـي الـرَّغَـامِ تَبْتَغُونَ طُـهـرًا لِتَجسِكُمُ وكَانَ (يَحيى) يُطَهِّرُ النَّاسَ بِماءِ الأُرْدُنِ الطَهُورِ قَبْلَ ضَلالِ مِلَّتِكُمُ بعِدَّةِ قرونٍ .

5. What you counterfeited in your religion deceived you into thinking that you really have revelation concerning true religion and the creation. Truth is, such a conclusion is the outcome of unenlightened people.

٥) وَغَرَّكُمُ فِي مِلَّتِكُمْ مَا كُنتُمْ تَفْتَرُونَ وَظَنَنْتُـمْ بِأَنَّكُمْ تَعْلَمونَ مِـنْ أُمورِ الدِّينِ والدُّنـيَـا شَيْئًا وَهَـذا ظَـنُّ الجَاهِلينَ .

6. We proclaimed the Good News of the Kingdom of Heaven and the decree of love and peace. We announced this before you implemented the decree of the jungles and abducted love by the sword of hate and stabbed peace with the dagger of betrayal and revenge; yes, even before you sanctioned adultery for the murdering degenerates!

٦) وَبَشَّرنَا بِملكُوتِ السَّماواتِ وسُنَّةَ المَحَبَّةِ والسَّلامِ قَبْلَ أَنْ تَسْنُتوا شِرْعةَ الغَابِ وَتَغْتَالوا المَحَبَّةَ بِسَيفِ البَغضَاءِ وتَطعنوا السَّلامَ بخِنْجَرِ الغَدْرِ والانْتِقَامِ وتُحلَّلوا الزِنى للمُجرِمينَ المَسَافحينَ .

7. Unmistakably, We are the True Spirit and whosoever wants to approach Us must do so in spirit and in truth. Otherwise, a person coming by any other way is a strong supporter of Satan's kingdom.

٧) فنحنُ الروحُ الحقُّ وَمَنْ تَقرَّبَ مِنَّا فبِالروحِ والحقِّ فليتقرَّبْ وإلاَّ فهوَ للشيطانِ وَليٌّ حميمٌ .

11
The True Furqan
(Surat Al Furqan Al Haqq)

سورةُالفرقان (١١

In the Name of the Father, the Word, the Holy Spirit, the One and only True God

بسـمِ الآبِ الكلمةِ الروحِ الالهِ الواحدِ الأوحدِ

1.   This is **The True Furqan** and genuine in every detail. It is guidance to a loftier conduct. Therefore carry out its precepts faithfully; perchance He may have mercy upon you.

١)   فُرقانٌ حَقٌّ لا مَريَبَ فيهِ يَهدي للَّتي هِيَ أقومُ فاتَّبعوهُ واتَّقوا لَعلَّكـمْ تُرحَمـونَ .

2.   It is in fact the Light of Truth, revealing the True Way to those who have gone astray. It unmasks dishonesty and what the deceivers never display.

٢)   إنْ هـوَ إلا أنـورُ الحـقِّ يَهدي الضّـالينَ ويفضَحُ الإفكَ وما يكتـمُ الظّالمونَ .

3.   We have inspired this **True Furqan** with integrity, as a validation of the True Religion, to supersede any so-called religiosity, even if infidels refuse to behold such vision.

٣)   أنزلناهُ بالحقِّ مُصدقاً لِدينِ الحقِّ لِنُظهِرَهُ على الديـنِ كلَّـهِ ولـو كـرِهَ الكـافرونَ .

4. Subsequently, We have inspired it as Light in this servant's own heart. He in turn recorded it with eloquence so beaming and bright. We are the protectors of **The True Furqan** from the very start.

٤) وَأَنزَلْنَاهُ نُوراً عَلَى قَلْبِهِ فَبَلَّغَهُ بِلِسَانٍ مُّبِينٍ
وَإِنَّا لَهُ لَحَافِظُونَ .

5. Pagans have polluted the earth after We had purified it. They are arrogant and proud for no reason at all. Whenever they discover a divine sign they reject it. Even when the correct path is found they refuse to walk in it. But whenever the counterfeit path is offered they immediately follow it! The reason behind their action is that they are accusing Our scriptures of being deceptive. In addition, they have determined to ignore **Our Divine Revelation** and consider it fiction.

٥) إِنَّ الْكَافِرِينَ أَفْسَدُوا فِي الْأَرْضِ
بَعْدَ إِصْلَاحِهَا يَتَكَبَّرُونَ بِغَيْرِ الْحَقِّ وَإِنْ
يَرَوْا كُلَّ آيَةٍ لَا يُؤْمِنُونَ بِهَا وَإِنْ يَرَوْا سَبِيلَ
الرُّشْدِ لَا يَتَّخِذُوهُ سَبِيلاً وَإِنْ يَرَوْا سَبِيلَ
الْغَيِّ يَتَّخِذُوهُ سَبِيلاً ذَلِكَ أَنَّهُمْ كَذَّبُوا
بِآيَاتِنَا وَكَانُوا عَنْهَا غَافِلِينَ .

6. Whenever **The True Furqanic** verses are recited to them they state, "We have heard such before, if we desire we can recite similar verses; they are no more than tales of the ancients."

٦) وَإِذْ تُتْلَى عَلَيْهِمْ آيَاتُ الْفُرْقَانِ الْحَقِّ
قَالُوا: "قَدْ سَمِعْنَا لَوْ نَشَاءُ لَقُلْنَا مِثْلَ هَذَا إِنْ
هُوَ إِلَّا أَسَاطِيرُ الْأَوَّلِينَ . "

53

7.   They dispute it even after the difference between wisdom and folly has been clearly displayed. Ignorance drives them as cattle are driven to the slaughter—with their eyes wide open.

٧) يُجَادِلُونَ فِيهِ مِنْ بَعْدِ مَا تَبَيَّنَ الرُّشْدُ مِنَ الغَيِّ يَسُوقُهُمُ الجَهْلُ كَمَا تُسَاقُ الأَنْعَامُ إِلَى الذَّبْحِ وَهُمْ يَنْظُرُونَ .

8.   This is an invitation to follow the unassailable Truth. Those who seek a substitute will never attain heaven.   Just as one who seeks to quench his thirst with his hands holding water from the well. He cannot do it because the water runs off quickly. Thus, the pagans will not attain anything but get hopelessly lost.

٨) دَعْوَةُ الحَقِّ والذِينَ يَبْغُونَ مِنْ دُونِهِ لَنْ يَبْلُغُوا شَيْئًا إِلَّا كَبَاسِطٍ كَفَّيْهِ إِلَى مَاءٍ جُبٍّ لِيَبْلُغَ فَاهُ وَمَا هُوَ بِبَالِغِهِ وَمَا يَبْلُغُ الكَافِرُونَ إِلَّا الضَّلَالَ البَعِيدَ .

9.   Even if there were another **True Furqan** which had fashioned the mountains or had divided the earth, or could communicate with the dead, this **True Furqan** is mightier and incomparable. For Our disclosure is the ultimate proclamation; the Satanic pronouncements end up in the bottomless pit.

٩) وَلَوْ أَنَّ فُرْقَانًا سُيِّرَتْ بِهِ الجِبَالُ أَوْ قُطِّعَتْ بِهِ الأَرْضُ أَوْ كُلِّمَ بِهِ المَوْتَى لَكَانَ هَذَا الفُرْقَانُ الحَقُّ أَقْوَى وَأَقْوَمَ فَكَلِمَتُنَا هِيَ العُلْيَا وَكَلِمُوا الشَّيْطَانِ فِي قَرَارٍ سَحِيقٍ .

10. We have conveyed **The True Furqan** in your own language to unveil to you how you have been misled. It will be the perfect guidance and the ultimate mercy if you will believe and place your trust in its Truth, Messiah Jesus.

١٠) إِنَّا أَنزَلْنَاهُ بِلِسَانِكُمْ لِنُبَيِّنَ لَكُمُ الَّذِي اخْتَلَفْتُمْ فِيهِ وَيَكُونَ لَكُمْ هُدًى وَرَحْمَةً إِنْ كُنتُمْ تُؤْمِنُونَ .

11. As for those who continue to believe firmly in **The True Furqan**, We will establish them in this world as well as the world to come. But for those who refuse to believe, Hell itself and a very miserable end is their eternal destination.

١١) وَالَّذِينَ آمَنُوا بِالْفُرْقَانِ الْحَقِّ نُثَبِّتُهُمْ فِي الْحَيَاةِ الدُّنْيَا وَفِي الْآخِرَةِ وَالَّذِينَ كَفَرُوا فَمَأْوَاهُمْ جَهَنَّمُ وَبِئْسَ الْمَصِيرُ .

12. O, you of Our followers who continue to believe firmly: each time you recite **The True Furqan**, begin with Our name and conclude by expressing gratitude. But each time you hear the speech of the infidels, seek refuge in Us from Satan, the wicked one. And do not wait to hear what is being said, run away from him with grave dread.

١٢) يَا أَيُّهَا الَّذِينَ آمَنُوا مِنْ عِبَادِنَا إِذَا تَلَوْتُمُ الْفُرْقَانَ الْحَقَّ فَابْدَأُوا بِاسْمِنَا وَاخْتِمُوا بِشُكْرِنَا وَإِنْ سَمِعْتُمْ لَغْوَ الْكُفْرَانِ فَاسْتَعِيذُوا بِنَا مِنَ الشَّيْطَانِ الرَّجِيمِ وَلَا تُنْصِتُوا وَتَوَلَّوا وَأَنتُمْ مُعْرِضُونَ .

13.   This **True Furqan** is what We have sent down as Light and Mercy to the world. The reaction of the skeptics is to rebuff it because Satan has fixed bridles on their hearts in order that they may not understand it. He also plugged their ears so they cannot hear. Nevertheless, the ones who trusted **The True Gospel** before it, gain more enlightenment and faith in addition to their exciting faith. Thus, they will not stumble on their pathway as they diligently follow Our rightly-guided way.

14.   Furthermore, We did not convey **The True Furqan** according to somebody's whim. Rather, We sent it down in its entirety to illuminate the hearts of those who believe, and to remove the doubts from the hearts of those who disbelieve. Rejecting the authenticity of **The True Gospel** placed them in chaotic confusion.

15.   This is the genuine **True Furqan**, which you

desperately need, and is sanctified indeed. Because of its inspiration it recounts to you some of the most illustrative parables. This is a fact despite your prior negligence of it.

أَصْدَقَ الْقَصَصِ بِمَا أُوحِيَ فِيهِ وَإِنْ كُنْتُمْ مِنْ قَبْلِهِ مِنَ الْغَافِلِينَ .

16.   There   is   admonition and   wisdom   for the rational people   in   this   **True Furqan**. Comprehensible   explanation   to everything   of   divine   nature   is included   in it for all people of logical thinking.

١٦) فِيهِ عِبْرَةٌ لَا أُولِي الْأَلْبَابِ وَفِيهِ تَفْصِيلُ كُلِّ شَيْءٍ لِقَوْمٍ يَعْقِلُونَ .

17.   We have analyzed the entire   counterfeit   scriptures; we have   distinguished   and separated the authentic from the counterfeit. Thus,   the   authentic words belong to the righteous. But the counterfeit words must be thrown back to the unrighteous.

١٧) وَعَجَمْنَا آيَاتِ الْكُفْرَانِ وَمَيَّزْنَا الْكَلِمَ الطَّيِّبَ مِنَ الْخَبِيثِ فَالطَّيِّبَاتُ لِلطَّيِّبِينَ وَالْخَبِيثَاتُ لِلْخَبِيثِينَ .

18.   We   have   sent   down **The True Furqan** with brilliant verses   and miraculous eloquence. It   is   a beacon of light, containing no   falsehood.   No blasphemy can ever assail it because We are its Guardian.

١٨) وَأَنْزَلْنَا الْفُرْقَانَ الْحَقَّ بِالْكَلِمِ الطَّيِّبِ وَالْإِعْجَازِ الْحَكِيمِ نُورًا عَلَى نُورٍ لَا يَأْتِيهِ الْبَاطِلُ وَلَا يَقْرُبُهُ الْكُفْرُ فَإِنَّا لَهُ لَحَافِظُونَ .

19.   It is a bearer of Good News and a warning to people everywhere. Moreover, it is the right guidance and mercy to the entire world of humanity.

١٩) بَشِيرٌ وَنَذِيرٌ لِلنَّاسِ كَافَّةً وَهُدًى وَرَحْمَةٌ لِلْعَالَمِينَ .

20.   Consequently, whosoever rejects it, or **The True Gospel**, which was delivered into the hands of mankind, ends up becoming an arrogant person who will perish with the ungodly.

٢٠) فَمَنْ كَفَرَ بِهِ أَوْ بِمَا بَيْنَ يَدَيْهِ مِنَ الإِنْجِيلِ الحَقِّ فَقَدِ اسْتَكْبَرَ وَكَانَ مِنَ الهَالِكِينَ .

21.   Each time the authentic scripture is recited before the deceivers, they respond, "This opposes what our forefathers used to believe and what they worshiped!"

٢١) وَإِذْ تُتْلَى عَلَيْهِمْ آيَاتُ الحَقِّ بَيِّنَاتٍ قَالُوا: "هَذَا يَصُدُّنَا عَمَّا كَانَ يُؤْمِنُ بِهِ آبَاؤُنَا وَعَمَّا كَانُوا يَعْبُدُونَ" .

22.   Most of these people follow opinions and speculations. The opinions of mankind can never be a substitute for Our Truth. Such people are destined to hellfire to dwell in it forever.

٢٢) وَمَا يَتَّبِعُ أَكْثَرُهُمْ إِلاَّ الظَّنَّ وَإِنَّ الظَّنَّ لاَ يُغْنِي مِنَ الحَقِّ شَيْئاً أُولَئِكَ أَصْحَابُ النَّارِ هُمْ فِيهَا خَالِدُونَ .

23. These people even rejected the Truth because it was incomprehensible to them. Their excuse was, no one was capable of simplifying it for them. Some ventured to say, "We do believe it." Others denied it. Nevertheless, We can identify the corrupters easily.

٢٣) وكَذَّبوا بما لـَمْ يُحيطوا بعلمـه وَلَمَّا يأتهـمْ تأويلُهُ ومنهـمْ مَنْ قال: "آمنـا به". ومنهـمْ مَـنْ كَفَـرَ ونحـنُ أعلـــمُ بالمُفسدينَ.

24. The deceivers, from among Our misguided servants, have perverted Our Scriptures. They even confess to that fact. Moreover, they disguised falsehood as truth and shrouded Truth with secrecy. It was all by design!

٢٤) إنَّ أهْلَ النفاق مِنْ عِبادنا قدْ كَفروا بآياتنا وهـمْ يشهدونَ والْبَسُوا الحقَّ بالباطل وكتموا الحقَّ وهُـمْ يعلمونَ.

25. Whenever it is requested of the infidels, who still claim they belong to Our worshipers, "What did your Lord send down in **The True Furqan**?" They promptly respond, "He sent down tales of the ancients." But Our upright servant's reply, "There is a promise of blessing to those who live godly lives in this world as well as a blessing in the world to come. O, what glorious

٢٥) وإذا قيـلَ للذينَ كَفـروا مِـنْ عِبادنا الضالينَ: مَـاذا أنـزلَ ربُّكـمْ قـالوا: "أساطيرُ الأوَّلينَ" وللذينَ آمنوا واتقوا مِنْ عِبادنـا الصّلحـينَ. قـالوا: "خيـرا للذيـنَ أحْسَـنوا في هـذه الدنيـا حَسَـنَةً ودارُ الآخرة خيرٌ ولنعْـمَ دارُ المُتَّقينَ".

heavenly home awaits the righteous."

26.   At any rate, **The True Furqan** came to verify what humankind already possessed through **The True Gospel**. Surprisingly, they hid it behind their backs as if they had no better sense.

٢٦) وجَاءَ الفرقانُ الحقّ مصدقاً لما بينَ يديه من الانجيل الحقّ فَنَبذوهُ وراءَ ظهورِهِمُ كأنّهمُ لا يعلمونَ .

27.   Subsequently, they followed whatever the apostates recited to them, teaching them blasphemy and rebellion. So they were learning what was harmful to themselves rather than what was beneficial. O, what miserable merchandize did they exchange for their souls! Catastrophe awaits their labors.

٢٧) واتّبعوا ما أتّلوا عليهمُ الماُرقونَ يعلّمونهمُ الكفرَ والعصيانَ ويتعلّمونَ ما يضرُّهُمُ ولا ينفعُهُمُ ولبئسَ ما اشترَوا به أنفسَهمُ ولبئسَ ما يفعلونَ .

12
THE TRIUNE GOD
(Surat Al Thalooth)

In the Name of the Father, the Word, the Holy Spirit, the One and only True God

١٢) سُورَةُ الثَّالوث

بسمِ الآبِ الكلمةِ الروحِ الاله الواحد الأوحد

1. O, you of Our worshipers who have gone astray and have added partners to Us: call upon Us or call upon the Merciful One or yet call upon the most Beneficent, by whatever name you may call Us. Unto Us are the excellent names which are triune in unity, united in Trinity. So why would you become apostates, and not believe this declaration?

١) يَأَيُّهَا الذينَ أشركوا مِنْ عِبادِنا ادْعُونا أو ادعوا الرّحمانَ أو ادعوا الرّحيمَ أيّاً ما تدعونا فلنا التَّجلِّياتُ الحُسنى جميعاً مُثلَّثةً مُوحَّدةً فَرْداً وِترًا فأنَّى تُشركونَ؟

2. We have not brought forth a son, neither did We acquire a consort, nor did We ever have a companion. Only the apostates conjecture such opinions concerning the religion of Our believing worshipers.

٢) فما اتخذنا وَلداً وَما كانتْ لنا صاحبةٌ وَما كانَ شريكٌ كما افترى المُفترونَ على عِبادنا المؤمنينَ.

3. Our believing worshipers testified that We have appeared to them in manifestations demon-

٣) وَشَهِدَ المؤمنونَ مِنْ عِبادنا بأنّا تجلّينا

61

strating three persons. However,
unto Us are the phenomenal
manifestations as well as the
fantastic transfigurations.

4. Furthermore, they accepted Us by faith as "Abba, Father"
and beheld Us as the "Merciful
Son" and acknowledged Us as the
"Comforting Spirit." Therefore,
they did not malign themselves,
neither did they blaspheme nor
did they add partners to Us.

5. For We are "The Father",
"The Son", "The Spirit" as a
Triune God and only One God.
None is beside Us in the heavens
or the earth.

6. We are the God who is
Most Gracious, Most Beneficent,
the only One God Who has no
companion in the universe.

7. False accusations are the
mere gossip of the apostates from
among Our creatures who have
gone astray. Tragically enough,
apostasy has blinded their hearts
and put a veil over their eyes

لهــمْ مظاهرَ ثلاثةٍ الّا إنّ لنا المظاهرَ
والتّجليات جميعاً .

٤) وأتّخذونا بالإيمان أباً آباً وشهدونا ابناً
رحماناً وعرفونا روحاً رحيماً . فما
ظلموا أنفسهم وما كفروا ولا كانوا
مُشركينَ .

٥) فنحنُ الآبُ الكلمةُ الرّوحُ ثالوثٌ فردٌ
إلهٌ واحدٌ لا شريك لنا في السّماوات
والأرضينَ .

٦) ونحنُ اللهُ الرّحمانُ الرّحيمُ ثالوثٌ فردٌ
إلهٌ واحدٌ لا شريك لنا في العالمينَ .

٧) ذلكـمْ قولُ المُشركينَ من عبادنا
الضّالينَ بأفواههمْ ولكنّ الكفرَ أعمى
قلوبهـمْ وأغشى بصائرهمْ فهمْ لا

resulting in their total ignorance concerning these facts.

يَفْقَهُونَ .

8. The ones who have gone astray from among Our worshipers have also added companions to Us, a blasphemous addition. They have given Us ninety-nine companions with similar names of unwholesome human personalities. We have never granted permission nor authority to anyone to use contradictory titles to describe Us.

٨) إِنَّ أَهْلَ الضَّلَالِ مِنْ عِبَادِنَا أَشْرَكُوا بِنَا شِرْكاً عَظِيماً فَجَعَلُوْنَا تِسْعَةً وَتِسْعِينَ شَرِيكاً بِصِفَاتٍ مُضَارِبَةٍ وَأَسْمَاءٍ لِلْإِنْسِ وَالْجَانِّ يَدْعُونَنَا بِهَا وَمَا أَنْزَلْنَا بِهَا مِنْ سُلْطَانٍ .

9. For example, they announced falsely that We are the Dictator, the Avenger, the Destroyer, the Arrogant, the One who conquers and humiliates others; that We have betrayed each other and We are the Greatest of Deceivers.

٩) وَافْتَرَوْا عَلَيْنَا كَذِباً بِأَنَّا الْجَبَّارُ الْمُنْتَقِمُ الْمُهْلِكُ الْمُتَكَبِّرُ الْمُذِلُّ وَإِنَّا فَتَنَّا بَعْضاً بِبَعْضٍ وَإِنَّا أَمْكَرُ الْمَاكِرِينَ .

10. Far be it from Us to be described by the lying words of the apostates. We are Holy, Holy, Holy, and far above their wildest imaginations.

١٠) حَاشَا لَنَا أَنْ نُتَّصَفَ بِإِفْكِ الْمُفْتَرِينَ وَتَنَزَّهْنَا عَمَّا يَصِفُونَ .

11. In reality, what they have enunciated was not the by-product of their imagination, but was by the powerful influence of Satan, the wicked one.

١١) وَمَا نَطَقُوا عَنِ الْهَوَى إِنْ هُوَ إِلَّا وَحْيُ شَيْطَانٍ رَجِيمٍ .

12. Surely the lies of apostasy are conspired by those who do not trust Our revelations. Consequently, We condemn them as imposters.

١٢) إِنَّمَا يَفْتَرِي الْكَذِبَ الَّذِينَ لَا يُؤْمِنُونَ بِآيَاتِنَا وَأُولَٰئِكَ هُمُ الْكَافِرُونَ .

13. Their path has utterly become a lost path in this earthly life. They have denied Our revelations, resulting in the rejection of their good works. Assuredly, We will not grant them a standing among the righteous on the Day of Judgment.

١٣) لَقَدْ ضَلَّ سَعْيُهُمْ فِي الْحَيَاةِ الدُّنْيَا إِذْ كَذَّبُوا بِآيَاتِنَا فَحَبِطَتْ أَعْمَالُهُمْ فَلَا نُقِيمُ لَهُمْ يَوْمَ الْقِيَامَةِ وَمَرْتَعاً مَعَ الصَّالِحِينَ .

14. Those who believe, from among Our followers, publicize that We are the One and only True God, the Triune in unity, united in Trinity essentially so without separation or addition. They, in fact, have spoken the truth concerning Us, while the imposters lied

١٤) وَإِذْ شَهِدَ الَّذِينَ آمَنُوا مِنْ عِبَادِنَا بِأَنَّا الْإِلَٰهُ الْأَوْحَدُ الثَّالُوثُ الْمُوَحَّدُ كُنَّهَا وَلَا انْفِصَامَ لَهُ عَدَّاً . فَقَدْ صَدَقُوا وَكَذَبَ الْمُشْرِكُونَ .

15. O, you from among Our creatures, who have gone astray and have added companions to Us: is it not true that any one of you is one human with no companion in his essence? Is he not also a father to his son and a son to his father and a spirit who gives him life? Therefore, he is a triune creation indeed, without division, yet one by himself and not three separate individuals. Similarly, We are not three gods, separate from each other. Can We not appear as you do when you are the lesser in wisdom and power?

16. Tragically enough, Satan has deafened your ears and blinded your eyes. Then he inspired you with blasphemy and rebellion to debate Our trusting followers. They definitely believe in the Perfect Religion but you yourselves are the hopelessly lost.

17. Whosoever declares loyalty to Satan as his Redeemer, rather than Ourselves, has for certain compromised the destiny

١٥) يَا أَيُّهَا الَّذِينَ أَشْرَكُوا مِنْ عِبَادِنَا الضَّالِّينَ أَلَيْسَ الْوَاحِدُ مِنْكُمْ إِنْسِيًّا فَرْدًا لَا شَرِيكَ لَهُ فِي ذَاتِهِ وَأَنَّهُ لَا ابْنَهُ وَابْنٌ لِأَبِيهِ وَرُوحٌ يُحْيِيهِ فَهُوَ ثَالُوثٌ فَرْدٌ وَبُرٌّ غَيْرُ مُنْقَسِمٍ وَمَا هُوَ بِثَلَاثَةٍ مُنْفَصِلِينَ أَفَلَا نَقْدِرُ أَنْ نَظْهَرَ كَمَا تَظْهَرُونَ وَأَنْتُمُ الْأَضْعَفُونَ ؟

١٦) لَكِنَّ الشَّيْطَانَ أَصَمَّكُمْ وَأَعْمَى أَبْصَارَكُمْ وَأَوْحَى إِلَيْكُمْ بِالْكُفْرِ وَالْعِصْيَانِ لِتُجَادِلُوا عِبَادَنَا الْمُؤْمِنِينَ فِي الدِّينِ الْحَقِّ وَأَنْتُمُ الْمُشْرِكُونَ .

١٧) وَمَنْ يَتَّخِذِ الشَّيْطَانَ وَلِيًّا مِنْ دُونِنَا فَقَدْ خَابَ مَسْعَاهُ وَهُوَ فِي الْآخِرَةِ مِنَ

of his soul. In the end he will certainly be among the losers.

الخَاسِرِين .

18. The example of those who rebelled and rejected the Truth as revealed in **The True Gospel**, their deeds are more or less like the ashes which are blown away by a stormy wind. They can never receive any reward for their labors for their effort is only vanity of vanities.

١٨) وَمَثَـلُ الذيـنَ كَفَـروا وَكَذَّبـوا بِالإنْجيلِ الحَقِّ أَعْمَالُهـمْ كَرَمادٍ اشْتَدَّتْ بِهِ الريحُ فـي يومٍ عَاصِفٍ لا يَقْدِرونَ مِمَّا كَسِبوا على شَيْءٍ ذلكَ هُـوَ الضَّـلالُ الأَكيدُ .

19. Those who continue to reject Our Word, the Messiah and the Spirit, then accuse Our believers with false accusations are incorrigible imposters. They conjecture that We are a husband to a consort and have received from her a son in the same human fashion as they do.

١٩) لَقَدْ كَفَـرَ الذينَ أنْكَـروا كَلِمَتَنَا المَسيحَ رُوحَنَا وأثْـمَ الذينَ ظَنّوا بالمؤمنينَ الظّنونَ فَزَعَموا أنَّهـمْ قَالوا بِأنَّا زَوْجٌ لِصَاحِبةٍ اتَّخذنَا مِنها وَلَداً كَمَا تَتَّخذونَ .

20. Furthermore, they divide Us into three gods when We are the one and only True God. The end result is polytheism expressed in an elaborate scheme.

٢٠) وَعَدَّدوا الوَاحِدَ الأوْحَدَ وَقَسَّموا الفَرِدَ المُفَـرِدَ وأشْـرَكوا بِنَـا شِرْكَـاً كَثيراً .

21. Who could possibly be more of an infidel than the one who has spun such a lie? Then he made himself a companion to Us and falsely stated that he continues to be a monotheist. He also accuses Our followers, who are the true monotheists, of being polytheists.

٢١) وَمَنْ أَكْفَرُ مِمَّن افْتَرى عَلَيْنَا الكَذبَ وأشْرِكَ نَفسَهُ بِنَا وَرَعَـمَ أَنَّهُ المُوَحَّدُ وأنَّ عِبادَنَا المُوَحَّدِيـنَ هُــمُ المُشْرِكونَ .

22. Furthermore, this man victimized Our true believers by putting the sword to their necks whenever they would not testify that God is only one and not a triune God. That is despite the fact that they never added a companion to Us, neither did they join Us to any worldly personality.

٢٢) وأعْمَلَ السيفَ فِي رِقابِ عِبادِنـا المُؤمِنينَ أوْ يُوَحَّدونا وَمَّا أشْرِكوا بِنا شَيْئاً أوْ أحداً مِنَ العالَمينَ .

23. We have never sent a messenger who would kill whosoever disobeyed his orders from among Our followers and spare his own. What difference does it make to the messenger whether We manifest Ourselves as only One, Triune, ninety-nine or three hundred sixty-five manifestations (as The Holy Book

٢٣) وَمَا أرْسَلنا مِنْ رَسُولٍ يقتلُ مَنْ عَصِيَهُ مِنْ عِبادِنا وَيَسْتَحيي الثَّابِعينَ . فَمَاذا يَضيرُهُ إنَّا تَجَلَّينا واحِداً أوْ ثَلاثةً أوْ تِسْعةً وتِسْعينَ .

describes Jesus)?

24. Surprisingly enough, the messenger overwhelmed himself by delusions of grandeur and superior knowledge. Thus, he himself was misled; then he misled his followers. They were not cognizant of the fact that they criminalized and corrupted everything.

٢٤) وأقْحَمَ نَفسَهُ فِيمَا لَيسَ لَهُ بِهِ عِلْمٌ فَضَلَّ وأضَلَّ أَتْبَاعَهُ فَمَا أَدْرَكُوا مَا اقْتَرَفَتْ أَيدِهِمْ وَمَا كَانُوا يَفْعَلُونَ .

25. The deceivers from among Our backslidden followers announced their own counterfeit religion. Then they forced this delusion upon Our true believers.

٢٥) وَطَلَّقَ المُشرِكُونَ مِن عِبَادِنَا كُفْرًا إِذْ كَفَرُوا عِبَادَنَا المُؤمِنِينَ الرَّاسِخِينَ فِي العِلْمِ والدِّينِ القَوِيمِ .

26. Is there any more outrageous ignorance than the ignorance of an illiterate who manufactures unfounded claims of things he does not even comprehend? Then he proclaims that he is none other than Our faithful messenger, when in fact he is no more than an imposter!

٢٦) وَمَنْ أَجْهَلُ مِنْ أُمِّي يَقُولُ مَا لا يعلمُ ويدَّعِي الإيمَانَ وهُوَ مِنَ الكَافِرِينَ .

27. O, you of Our people who have gone astray, and become

٢٧) يَأَيُّها الذِينَ أَشرَكُوا مِن عِبَادِنَا الضَّالِينَ

infidels: you and your ancestors have erroneously proclaimed what you are ignorant of about Us. How terrible and prideful are the words that spew out of your mouths. Lies and fallacies are all that come out.

لقدْ قُلْــمْ مَا ليسَ لكـــمْ بهِ علــمٌ ولا آبآڠكــمْ . كــبُرَتْ كَلمةٌ تخرجُ مِنْ أفواهكـــمْ إنْ تقولونَ الّا إفكـاً واِدّاً .

28. You have no right to enunciate such falsehoods because they are in fact diabolical deceptions. You must cease and desist from ever repeating such ghastly words.

٢٨) ومَا لكــمْ أنْ تَكـلَّمـوا بهذا إنّهُ بُهتانٌ عظيــمٌ فلا تعودوا لاقترافهِ أبداً .

29. Do not pride yourselves with a man-made religion. Furthermore, you should never declare anything concerning Us except the honest and total truth.

٢٩) ولا تغلوا فِ دينٍ لقيطٍ ولا تقولوا علينـا غيرَ الحقِّ المُبين .

30. The Messiah is actually the Word of Our Spirit. Thus, believe in Us, Our Word and Our Spirit. Do not say three; cease from such deceptive pronouncements for it is more advantageous to you. We are in fact One God with One Word and One Spirit.

٣٠) إنّا المسيحُ كلمةُ روحنا فآمنوا بنا وبكلمتنا وبروحنا فلا تقولوا ثلاثةٌ انتهوا خيراً لكــمْ . إنّما نحنُ إلهٌ واحدٌ بكلمةٍ واحدةٍ وبروحٍ واحدةٍ فنحنُ الإلهُ

Consequently, We are the One and only True God. Why don't you accept this clear-cut revelation as the absolute truth?

الواحدُ الأوحدُ أفلا تُؤمنونَ ؟ .

31. Enough is enough! You must recognize that you have been led astray and have lived as deceived people long enough. We challenge you to repent of polytheism in your inner selves. Slander and destructive criticism which you spread, concerning true believers, must come to an end immediately.

٣١) كَفاكـــمُ اليومَ كُفرًا وضلالاً
وغيّروا ما بأنفُسِــكُـــمُ مِنْ شِرْكٍ وافتراءٍ
ولا تظنّـــوا بالمؤمنينَ الظنونَ .

13
THE SERMON
(Surat Al Mawidha)

سُورَةُ المَوعِظة (١٣

In the Name of the Father, the Word, the Holy Spirit, the One and only True God

بسمِ الآبِ الكلمةِ الروحِ الالهِ الواحدِ الأوحدِ

1. O, you who are the rebellious, yet still claim to be counted among Our people: it has been communicated to you, "Enter fully into peaceful co-existence with others." Instead, you feared the consequences of peace because it is not a principle of your sect; neither do you subscribe to peaceful ways.

١) يا أهل العِصيان من عبادنا الضّالينَ: لقد قيل لكم: "أدخلوا في السّلم كافّةً" فأوجَسْتُم من القول خِيفةً فما السّلم من مِلّتكم في شيءٍ ولستم بالسّلم تؤمنونَ .

2. You have concocted that We have commanded, "Fight in the cause of God and urge on the believers to fight." However, fighting was neither Our method nor is fighting urged on the believers. Such decrees originate from none other than the cursed Devil and were given to a lawless people.

٢) وزَعمتم بأنّا قلنا : "قاتلوا في سبيل الله وحَرّضوا المؤمنينَ على القِتال" وما كانَ القِتال سبيلَنا وما كنّا لنُحرّض المؤمنينَ على القِتال إنْ ذلك إلا تحريضُ شيطانٍ رجيمٍ لقومٍ مُجرمينَ .

3. You announced: "Do not annul a conviction once it is established." Then you undid what you announced by stating, "God has allowed the annulling of your conviction." There is no equality between a sanctioned activity and a forbidden one if you have any knowledge of such matters.

4. Truth slipped up even from the lips of deception when you proclaimed, "Yes, indeed, **The True Gospel** contains guidance and light and a sermon for the righteous people."

5. Yet, you did not conform to its guidance, neither did you get illuminated by its brilliance, nor did you conform to its instruction. Thus, you became more confused on your pathway and more depraved in your wickedness.

6. Furthermore, you exchanged guidance for deception, light for darkness and excellent preaching for unsavory speeches. Then

٣) وقلتـــمْ : "لاتَنقُضوا الأيْمـانَ بعـدَ توكيدِها "ثمَّ نسَختُـمْ قولَكــمْ بقولِكـــمْ : "إنَّ اللهَ قـد فرضَ لكــمْ تحِلَّـةَ أيْمـانِكـمْ" ولا يَسْتـوي التحليـلُ والتَّحريــمُ لَوْ كُنتـمْ تعلمونَ .

٤) وانزلقَ الحقُّ على لِسان البـاطِل فقلتـمْ : "بأنَّ الإنجيـلَ الحقَّ فيه هُدىً ونورٌ ومَوعظةٌ للمتقيَن" .

٥) فلـمْ تهتدوا بهُداهُ ولمْ تسـتنيروا بنـورِه ولمْ تَّعظوا بموعظتِـه فكنتــمْ أضَـلَّ سَـبيلاً وأشدَّ فجـورًا .

٦) واستَعضتـمْ عـن الهُـدى بـالضلال وعَـن النورِ بالظلام وعَن الموعظـة الحسَـنة بقـول

72

you proceeded to mislead Our worshipers who had already discovered the straight path.

السوءَ ورُحتـمُ تُضلُّونَ عبادَنا المهتدينَ .

7. We offered you true guidance and godliness. But instead of accepting the offer you turned on your heels and ran away. Whosoever turns down the True Guidance, when it is offered to him, will become a defeated and arrogant man, shunned and vanquished forever.

٧) وأرِدنــا لكـــمُ الهُــدى والصَّــلاحَ فنكصتـمُ علـى أعْقـابكـمُ ومَـنْ ينكصُ على عَقِبيهِ بعدَ انْ شَـهِدَ الهُـدى فقـدْ قَـهُقَرَ واستكبَرَ وبـاتَ مَذمومـاً مَدحوراً .

14
THE DISCIPLES
(Surat Al Hawareen)

١٤) سورة الحواريين

In the Name of the Father, the Word, the Holy Spirit, the One and only True God

بسم الآب الكلمة الروح الإله الواحد الأوحد

1.   We sent down Our Holy Spirit upon the disciples ten days after we welcomed Our Word back into heaven; teaching, guiding and reassuring their hearts. Consequently, they proclaimed the Good News of Truth and announced the mandate of the correct faith.

١) وأرسلنا روحنا القدوس إلى الحواريين من بعد كلمتنا معلماً ومرشداً ولتطمئنّ قلوبهم . فبشّروا بالحقّ وأعلنوا سنّة الدين القويم .

2.   Some of them memorized **The True Gospel** in their hearts for many a year.   Then some of them recorded it under Our watch-care.   We shall ever guard it from the corrupter's snare.

٢) وحفظوا الإنجيل الحقّ في الصدور سنين عدداً ثم دوّنه نفرٌ منهم بأعيننا وإنا له لحافظون .

3.   The disciples neither added to the scripture nor subtracted from it.   They did not exchange

٣) فما زادوا ولا أنقصوا ولا بدّلوا ولا نسخوا ولا غامضوا منه أمراً أو خبراً .

74

nor did they abrogate any. They did neither oppose its views nor its news. They were in fact trustworthy and precise eyewitnesses of the truth.

وإنـا كـانوا للحـق شــهوداً عُــدُولاً
صَـــادقينَ .

4. The disciples did not covet to sell the scriptures to buy, with the money, beautiful maidens or handsome boys, stylish garments, the flesh of a bird, unholy liquor or whatever base instincts dictate of lustful things.

٤) فما ابتغوا فيه حُوراً عِيناً أوْ وِلْداناً أوْ ثياباً
خُضْراً أوْ لحمَ طيرٍ أوْ خمرٍ رِجْسٍ أوْ مَا
تُمليه الغرائزُ مّماَ تَشتهونَ .

5. They did not sell the scriptures to buy, with the money, merchandize which is cheaply priced. So they did not use it to initiate raids, or taking spoils, or committing immorality or murdering Our humans even if such people were unbelievers.

٥) وما اشتروا به ثمناً قليلاً فما شَرَّعوا به
غزواً ولا سَلباً ولا زِنىً ولا تَقتيلاً لعبادنا
ولو كانوا كافرينَ .

6. We inspired **The True Furqan** as a reminder to those who have wandered and blasphemed; perchance they will desire to be rightly-guided and become believers.

٦) وأنزلنا الفُرقانَ الحقَّ مُذكِّراً للذينَ
ضَلّوا وكفروا لعلَّهم يهتدونَ ويؤمنونَ .

7. We have perfected the correct religion for all of mankind—from now until the Day of Resurrection.

٧) وأكملنا الدين الحق للناس كافة إلى يوم يُبعثون .

8. We have brought them the glad tidings. We have warned them. We have appealed to them to follow the True Religion after which there is to be no other new disclosure.

٨) وبشرناهم وأنذرناهم ودعوناهم إلى الدين القويم فما بعد ذلك من مقال جديد .

9. Is there anyone who dares to add anything to that which is perfect, to brighten the sunlight or to align the straight path?

٩) فمن ذا الذي يُكمّل الكامل وينوّر النور ويقوّم الصراط المستقيم ؟

10. We have perfected Our Word through faith, hope and love. We have also established Our precepts by righteousness, justice and truth. Thus, there is no altering or changing of this Perfect Religion among humankind.

١٠) لقد أتممنا كلمتنا إيماناً ورجاءً ومحبة وثبتنا سنّتنا صدقاً وعدلاً وحقاً فلا مُبدّل للدين القيم في العالمين .

11. If anyone brings to you something else contrary to what We brought you in **The True Gospel** and **The True Furqan**,

١١) فمن جاء بغير ما جئناكم به في الانجيل الحق والفرقان الحق من بعده إن هو

he would be none other than a
messenger of Satan, the rejected
one.

إلَّا رَسُولَ شَيطانٍ رَجِيمٍ .

12.   For We are the One and
only God. There is no other God
beside Us, neither word beside
Our Word, nor spirit except Our
Spirit and no Religion barring Our
True and trustworthy Religion
until   the   Day   of   Judgment.
Consequently,   you   should
worship Us   only, and seek no
one's support except Ours only.

١٢) فَنَحنُ الإِلَهُ الواحِدُ الأَوحَدُ ولا إِلَهَ إِلَّا نَا
ولا كَلِمَةَ إِلَّا كَلِمتَنَا ولا رُوحَ إِلَّا
رُوحنا ولا دِينَ إِلَّا دِينَنَا الحَقُّ القَوِيمُ إِلى يَومِ
الدِينِ فَإِيَّانا تَعبُدونَ وإِيَّانا تَستَعِينونَ .

13.   O, you who have rebelled
from   among   Our   worshipers:
Satan has beguiled you through
his messengers. He has seized
you by deception, glamorizing for
you ignorance, illiteracy, immorality and rebellion. You revolted
and lost your way. There is no
salvation available to you except
through   heeding   the   Word of
Truth, guided by the Light of
Faith and following Our straight
path.

١٣) يَأَيُّها الذِينَ كَفَروا مِن عِبادِنا الضالِينَ :
لَقَد خَدَعَكُمُ الشَّيطانُ بِرُسُلِه
فاستَحوَذَ عَلَيكُمُ بِالحِيلَةِ وزَيَّنَ
لَكُمُ الجَهلَ والأُمِّيَّةَ والفُجورَ والعِصيانَ
فَكَفَرتُم وضَلَلتُم فَما لَكُمُ مِن
خَلاصٍ إِلَّا استِماعَ كَلِمَةِ الحَقِّ والاهتِداءَ
بِنورِ الإيمانِ واتِّباعَ صِراطِنا المُستَقِيمِ .

14. Repent, therefore, extricate what is in your souls. Then We will pardon you and let you enter into everlasting life.

١٤) فتُوبـوا وغَيِّروا مـا بأنفسِكـمْ نُثُبْ عَليـكـمْ وُندخلكـمْ جنـاتِ النعيـم

15
THE CHALLENGE
(Surat Al I'jaz)

سورةُالإعجازِ (١٥

In the Name of the Father, the Word, the Holy Spirit, the One and only True God

بسمِ الآبِ الكلمةِ الروحِ الالهِ الواحدِ الأوحدِ

1.   If We had indeed sent him as a prophet, We would have supported him with supernatural miracles.   For when his followers sought such from him, he promised to perform a miracle but could not deliver. Pretenders are those who make fake promises which cannot be fulfilled.

١)   وَلَوْ أرسَلناهُ كَما يَدْنَاهُ إذْ سَأَلَهُ أتباعُهُ آيةً فَوَعدهُمْ وأخْلَفَ وَعْدَهُ وَما يَعِدُ المُفْتَرونَ إلا غُرورًا .

2.   **The True Furqan** is what We present to follow up **The True Gospel** which We have proclaimed to your forefathers. It is designed to bring to mind **The True Gospel**'s perfect precepts to those who seek to remember Our creed.

٢)   فُرْقانٌ حَقٌّ صِنوُ الإنجيلِ الحَقِّ الذي كلّمَنا بهِ آباءَكُمْ وذكرى للمُذّكِّرينَ .

3.   We inspire in Our faithful messengers nothing but love,

٣)   وَما نُوحي إلى رُسُلِنا الصَّادقينَ إلا

compassion, peace and brother-hood. Such a lofty revelation is absolutely supernatural and as such overwhelms the hypocrites.

المَحَبَّةَ والرحمةَ والسلامَ والإخَاءَ بينَ عِبادِنا أجمعينَ وهذا إعجازٌ للمُفترينَ .

4. We definitely did not inspire tales of the ancients in gibberish and prose void of any Divine revelation. Some materials containing blasphemy are much like the fancy graves that are decorated as to please the passers-by. Yet, its contents are stinking remains full of all kinds of toxic materials. Nothing in your book revealed a single new unknown truth!

٤) وَمَا أوحينا لَغوًا سَجعًا خَاويًا إلَّا مِنَ الكُفرِ كَالقُبورِ المُشَيَّدةِ خَارِجُها زُخرفٌ يَسُرُّ الناظرينَ وبَاطنُها جِيَفٌ تَعِجُّ بأنواعِ السمومِ .

5. We do not dispatch a messenger except for the good of Our servants. He is to guide them to Our straight and right pathway. Consequently, anyone who may entice them and mislead them is a messenger of the stiff-necked Satan.

٥) وَمَا نُرسِلُ مِن رسولٍ إلَّا لخيرِ عِبادِنا يَهديهِم صِراطَنا المُستقيمَ وأمَّا مَن أغواهُم وأضلَّهُم فَهوَ رسُولُ شيطانٍ رَجيمٍ .

6. Satan's path is a crooked one. His miracles are farce. His light is darkness. Never follow him. Do not adhere to his

٦) فَصِراطُهُ عِوَجٌ وإعجازُهُ عُجمَةٌ ونورُهُ ظُلمَةٌ فلا تَتبعوهُ ولا تُنصتوا له واتخِذوهُ

proclamations. But instead ignore and abandon him.

مَهْجُورًا .

7. If anybody decides to do otherwise, he will be responsible for his own evil behavior. Of course, it is Our duty to punish the evil doers.

٧) فَمَنِ افْتَرَاهُ فَعَلَيهِ إِجْرَامُهُ وَعَلَيْنَا جَزَاءُ الْمُجْرِمِينَ .

8. The imposters, who have determined to decline the teachings of **The True Furqan**, will suddenly experience the Hour of Judgment. There will also come upon them plenty of horrible torture.

٨) وَلَا يَزَالُ الَّذِينَ كَفَرُوا فِي مِرْيَةٍ مِنَ الفُرْقَانِ الْحَقِّ حَتَّى تَأْتِيَهُمُ السَّاعَةُ بَغْتَةً أَوْ يَأْتِيَهُمْ عَذَابٌ مُقِيمٌ .

9. There are some who have the audacity to question the truth of **The True Furqan**. They are no more than ignoramuses, unenlightened and without an illuminating Book.

٩) وَمِنَ النَّاسِ مَنْ يُجَادِلُ فِيهِ بِغَيْرِ عِلْمٍ وَلَا هُدًى وَلَا كِتَابٍ مُنِيرٍ .

10. Such people deliberately follow every diabolical demon who will absolutely decimate them and will deliver them in the end to the torments of Hell itself.

١٠) وَيَتَّبِعُ كُلَّ شَيْطَانٍ مَرِيدٍ يُضِلُّهُ وَيَهْدِيهِ إِلَى عَذَابِ الْجَحِيمِ .

11. The loathsome among the people announced, "How great it would have been if this **True Furqan** brought down for us a supernatural miracle. If such were to happen then the unbelievers would accept it and the hypocrites would believe it."

١١) وَقَالَ السُّفَهَاءُ مِنَ النَّاسِ: لَوْ أُنزِلَ هَذا الفُرقَانُ بِآيَةٍ لَصَدَّقَهُ المُكَذِّبونَ وآمَنَ بِهِ الكَافِرونَ.

12. O, people everywhere: We have dispatched it with verses of light, of compassion, of truth, of love, of peace and righteous religion as a linguistic miracle.

١٢) يَأَيُّها النَّاسُ إِنَّا أَنزَلناهُ بِآيَاتٍ مِنَ النّورِ والرَّحمَةِ والحَقِّ والمَحَبَّةِ والسَّلامِ والدِّينِ القَويمِ بِإعجازٍ مِنَ الكَلِمِ المُبينِ.

13. Even if men of the world and spirits of the underworld were to put their energies together to produce a verse like unto it, they will not be able to produce a glimmer of light or even a breath of its love.

١٣) ولَنِ اجتَمَعَتِ الإِنسُ والجِنُّ عَلى أَن يَأتوا بِآيَةٍ مِن مِثلِهِ لا يَأتونَ بِقَبَسٍ مِن نورِهِ أَوْ بِنَفحَةٍ مِن مَحَبَّتِهِ ولَو كانَ بَعضُهُمْ لِبَعضٍ ظَهيراً.

16
PREDESTINATION
(Surat Al Qadr)

١٦) سُورَةُ القَدْرِ

In the Name of the Father, the Word, the Holy Spirit, the One and only True God

بِسْمِ الآبِ الكَلِمَةِ الرُّوحِ الإلَهِ الوَاحِدِ الأوحدِ

1. We have beamed **The True Furqan** down in the dawning of the sun in the hour of Qadr.

١) إِنَّا أَنزَلْنَاهُ بِالحَقِّ فِي وَمْضَةِ الفَجْرِ فِي سَاعَةِ القَدْرِ .

2. It is a guiding light for those in darkness and a lighthouse to navigators of all races, times and places.

٢) نُورًا لِلضَّالِّينَ وَهُدًى لِلنَّاسِ كَافَّةً فِي كُلِّ عَصْرٍ .

3. It is a **True Furqan** of truth, a fair criterion and a final command in every respect.

٣) فُرْقَانٌ حَقٌّ وحُكْمٌ عَدْلٌ وَقَوْلٌ فَصْلٌ فِي كُلِّ أَمْرٍ .

4. It is Love, Compassion and Peace to the very culmination of time and space.

٤) مَحَبَّةٌ وَرَحْمَةٌ وَسَلامٌ هُوَ حَتَّى مُنْتَهَى الدَّهْرِ .

5. O, servants of Ours who have gone astray: We have

٥) يَأَيُّهَا الذينَ ضَلُّوا مِنْ عِبَادِنَا لَقَدْ كَلَّمْنَا

83

revealed **The True Gospel** to your ancestors of yesterday, announced the Good News and warned them day by day. Yet, only a few believed in what We did convey. Another group chose its own way then led those who followed them astray. Thus, they left them an inheritance of terrible decay.

آبَاءَكُمْ بِالْاِنْجِيلِ الْحَقِّ وَبَشَّرْنَاهُمْ وَأَنْذَرْنَاهُمْ فَقَلَّةٌ آمَنَتْ كَلِمَتَنَا وَفِئَةٌ ضَلَّتْ فَأَضَلَّتِ التَّابِعِينَ وَأَوْرِثَهُمُ الْكُفْرَ .

6. The evil-hearted people covered up the Word of Truth and kept it from Our servants who always obey. Consequently, their evil hearts were blinded and they lost the straight way. Finally, they turned into pagans, to their own dismay.

٦) وَكَمَ الذِينَ فِى قُلُوبِهِمْ مَرَضٌ كَلِمَةَ الْحَقِّ عَنْ عِبَادِنَا فَعَمِيَتْ قُلُوبُهُمْ وَضَلُّوا سَوَاءَ السَّبِيلِ فَكَفَرُوا وَهُمْ لَا يَعْلَمُونَ .

7. We manifested **The True Furqan** authenticating what this writer already had at hand through the **"Gospel of Truth"**. It is intended to remind you of Our Word; perchance you will accept this **True Furqan** and follow through.

٧) وَأَنْزَلْنَا الْفُرْقَانَ الْحَقَّ مُصَدِّقاً لِمَا بَيْنَ يَدَيْهِ مِنَ الْاِنْجِيلِ الْحَقِّ وَمُذَكِّراً بِكَلِمَتِنَا لَعَلَّكُمْ تَهْتَدُونَ .

8. You conjectured that We sent him whom We did not send.

٨) وَزَعَمْتُمْ بِأَنَّا أَرْسَلْنَا مَنْ لَمْ نُرْسِلْ

Furthermore, he announced unto you messages We never did send. We would never commission a so-called messenger with the intention of misleading Our people. They had already found the Right Way; why then should We let him teach them the wrong way?

وَأَنَّهُ بَلَّغَكُمْ مَا لَمْ نُبَلِّغْ وَمَا كُنَّا لِنُرْسِلَ رَسُولاً نُضِلُّ عِبَادَنَا بَعْدَ أَنْ هَدَيْنَاهُمْ وَنُبَلِّغُهُمْ شِرْعَةَ الْكَافِرِينَ .

9.   Those who were persuaded of Our revelation and clearly comprehended Our Word believe in their hearts and souls and do accept what We have told. They are established in imparted knowledge and upright religion. Certainly these are Our overcoming people.

٩) وَالَّذِينَ آمَنُوا بِسُنَّتِنَا وَأَذْرَكُوا كَلِمَتَنَا إِنَّمَا بِقُلُوبِهِمْ وَأَرْوَاحِهِمْ يُؤْمِنُونَ وَيُدْرِكُونَ أُولَئِكَ هُمُ الرَّاسِخُونَ فِي الْعِلْمِ وَالدِّينِ الْقَوِيمِ وَأُولَئِكَ هُمْ عِبَادُنَا الْمُفْلِحُونَ .

10. Not even a single, solitary one of Our creatures can ever conceive Truth and accept Us, the Triune God, except by revelation of the heart and discerning of the mind. For those are the characteristics of the virtuous individuals.

١٠) وَمَا كَانَ لِبَشَرٍ أَنْ يُدْرِكَ الْحَقَّ وَيُؤْمِنَ بِنَا إِلاَّ بِالرُّوحِ وَالْقَلْبِ وَالْحِكْمَةِ وَتِلْكَ سِيمَاءُ عِبَادِنَا الصَّادِقِينَ .

11. Humankind's intrinsic knowledge is acquired by what

١١) إِنَّكُمْ تَعْلَمُونَ ظَاهِرًا مِنَ الْحَيَاةِ الدُّنْيَا

they behold. Alas, so many of them have never been told about eternal life.

وَأَنتُمْ عَنِ الآخِرَةِ أَنتُمْ غَافِلُونَ .

17
THE APOSTATES
(Surat Al-Mariqeen)

سُـورةُالمَارقينَ (١٧

In the Name of the Father, the Word, the Holy Spirit, the One and only True God

بسمِ الآبِ الكلمةِ الروحِ الاله الواحدِ الأوحدِ

1. Satan vowed that he would commandeer Adam's race. Those who decided to put their trust in him ended up going astray. Not only did they rebel against Us, they also rejected Our Scriptures. But those who decided to put their trust in Us staunchly kept the faith.

١) وَأَقْسَمَ الشيطانُ لَيَحْتَنِكَنَّ ذُرِّيَّة آدَمَ فَاتَّبعهُ الذينَ آمنوا بِه فكَفروا وضَلُّوا السَّـبيلَ وكَذَّبُـوا بآياتِـا إلا عِبَادَنَـا المُخلصِينَ .

2. O, you who have gone astray, yet still claim to be counted among Our worshipers; Satan used worldly pleasures to allure you. His bewitching voice excited you. His fascinating horses and riders enchanted you. Then he trapped you through the love of money and longing for a legacy. Finally, he even counterfeited Our straight and

٢) يأيُّها الذينَ ضَلُّوا مِنْ عِبادِنا لَقَدْ أغْواكـمُ الشيطانُ وزَيَّنَ لكـمْ في الأرضِ واسْتَفزَّكـمْ بصوتِـه وجَلَبَ عليكـمْ بخَيْلِـه وَرَجلِـه وشَارَكـكـمْ في الأموالِ والأولادِ

narrow pathway to you.

وَقَعَدَ لَكُمْ صِرَاطَنَا الْمُسْتَقِيمَ .

3.   Subsequently, he infiltrated your ranks by creeping into your midst, behind your backs, on your right and left sides. Satan even put together promises for you.   As everyone knows Satan's promises are never true.

٣) ثُمَّ أَتَاكُمْ مِنْ بَيْنِ أَيْدِيكُمْ وَمِنْ خَلْفِكُمْ وَعَنْ أَيْمَانِكُمْ وَعَنْ شَمَائِلِكُمْ وَوَعَدَكُمْ وَلَا يَعِدُ الشَّيْطَانُ إِلَّا غُرُوراً .

4.   Satan hoodwinked you by convincing you that your bad deeds are good.   "No one will conquer you among men as long as I am in your neighborhood" is what he declared. Consequently, you   put   your   trust in the unbelievers, but mistrusted the believers.

٤) وَخَدَعَكُمْ إِذْ زَيَّنَ لَكُمْ سُوءَ أَعْمَالِكُمْ وَقَالَ: لَا غَالِبَ لَكُمُ الْيَوْمَ مِنَ النَّاسِ وَإِنِّي جَارٌ لَكُمْ . فَآمَنْتُمْ بِالْكَافِرِينَ وَكَفَرْتُمُ الْمُؤْمِنِينَ .

5.   Therefore,   Satan's assumptions concerning you were quite right. Alas, despite the fact that he led you astray, you still followed his path. However, Our trusting worshipers are free from his evil power for they have grasped Our lifeline very tightly.

٥) وَقَدْ صَدَّقَ عَلَيْكُمْ إِبْلِيسُ ظَنَّهُ إِذْ أَضَلَّكُمْ فَاتَّبَعْتُمُوهُ إِلَّا عِبَادَنَا الْمُؤْمِنِينَ فَلَيْسَ لَهُ عَلَيْهِمْ مِنْ سُلْطَانٍ فَهُمْ بِحَبْلِنَا مُعْتَصِمُونَ .

6.   Whenever it is announced to you to accept what is conveyed

٦) وَإِذَا قِيلَ لَكُمْ: آمِنُوا بِمَا أُنْزِلَ مِنَ

in **The True Furqan**, you reply,
"We accept what is conveyed to
us but reject whatever came after
it." Although **The True Furqan**
is genuine truth which stands by
The True Gospel, still you opt to
go astray and march on the
infidels highway.

الفرقان الحق قلتم: "نؤمن بما أنزل علينا
ونكفر بما وراءه." وأنه الحق مصدق
للإنجيل الحق لكنكم ضللتم
فأنتم بالكفر سادرون.

7. Is it conceivable that We
would ever lead you astray when
We have just revealed to you the
right way? The fact is, Satan has
misguided you by turning your
hearts away from the true
guidance. Obviously, you are not
familiar with his treachery.

٧) وما كنا لنضلكم من بعد أن
هديناكم ولكنّ الشيطان
أضلكم إذ صرف قلوبكم عن
الهدى بأنكم قوم لا تفقهون.

8. We have made firm
promises to you and Satan
claimed he could make similar
promises too. But he never kept
them. Furthermore, he would
have had no power over you had
you not responded to him when
he called. Do not blame him for
your state—blame yourselves.
He cannot listen to your cries for
help, neither can you listen to his

٨) ووعدناكم وعد الحق
ووعدكم الشيطان فأخلفكم وما
كان له عليكم من سلطان إلا أن
دعاكم فاستجبتم فلا تلوموه ولوموا
أنفسكم ما هو بمصرخكم وما

because in the end all the oppressors shall be in horrible torment.

أَنْتُمْ بِمُصْرِخِيهِ إِنَّ الظَّالِمِينَ فِي عَذَابٍ أَلِيمٍ .

9. Who could possibly be a worse deceiver than the one who spreads lies concerning Us in order to mislead people before they realize such were flat lies? We must emphasize that liars will never win.

٩) وَمَنْ أَظْلَمُ مِمَّنِ افْتَرَى عَلَيْنَا كَذِباً لِيُضِلَّ النَّاسَ بِغَيْرِ عِلْمٍ إِنَّهُ لَا يُفْلِحُ الْمُفْتَرُونَ .

10. Again Satan declared, "I will commandeer a sizeable portion of the human race, cause them to go astray, grant them false hopes, then urge them to substitute my precepts for the true religion and exhort them to do all of that happily!"

١٠) وَقَالَ الشَّيْطَانُ: لَأَتَّخِذَنَّ مِنَ الْإِنْسِ نَصِيباً مَفْرُوضاً وَلَأُضِلَّنَّهُمْ وَلَأُمَنِّيَنَّهُمْ وَلَآمُرَنَّهُمْ لِيُغَيِّرُنَّ دِينَ الْحَقِّ وَيَتَّبِعُنَّ سُنَّتِي وَهُمْ فَرِحُونَ .

11. Who else but a rebellious Devil would the infidels call upon? Nevertheless, whoever pays allegiance to the Devil instead of Us will eventually experience a most horrific loss.

١١) وَإِنْ يَدْعُونَ الْكَافِرُونَ إِلَّا شَيْطَاناً مَرِيداً، وَمَنْ يَتَّخِذِ الشَّيْطَانَ وَلِيّاً مِنْ دُونِنَا فَقَدْ خَسِرَ خُسْرَاناً مُبِيناً .

12. Tragically certain groups, including pastors and monks,

١٢) وَمِنَ الْقِسِّيسِينَ وَالرُّهْبَانِ طَائِفَةٌ قَدْ

have departed from the right way, led others astray and involved themselves with the apostates.

ضَلُّوا وأَضَلُّوا وَكَانُوا مِنَ المَارِقِينَ .

13. Thereafter, these very apostates taught you **The Bible** without divine wisdom. They even corrupted the Scriptures from its original intent because of an ulterior motive. They certainly were not objective in dealing with the true religion.

١٣) وَقَدْ عَلَّمُوكُمُ الكِتَابَ بِلا حِكْمَةٍ وَحَرَّفُوا الكَلِمَ عَنْ مَوَاضِعِهِ لِغَايَةٍ فِي نُفُوسِهِمْ فَمَا كَانُوا لِلدِّينِ الحَقِّ مُقْسِطِينَ .

14. The dogma of the apostates is merely their conjecture. They are not fully convinced of what they lecture. They endorsed Satan, who in turn endorsed them. Thus they turned away from genuine religion.

١٤) إِنْ يَظُنُّونَ إِلاَّ ظَنًّا وَمَا هُمْ بِمُسْتَيْقِنِينَ وَتَنَاصَرُوا إِبْلِيسَ فَنَاصَرَهُمْ وَمَرَقُوا مِنَ الدِّينِ القَوِيمِ .

15. Furthermore, the imposters implanted the disease of their hearts into your own hearts. They departed from Absolute Truth (Jesus) because the manifestation was too grand for them to comprehend. They also fabricated tales concerning Us

١٥) فِي قُلُوبِهِمْ مَرَضٌ دَسُّوهُ فِي قُلُوبِكُمْ وَمَرَاغُوا عَنِ الحَقِّ وَشُبِّهَ لَهُمْ وَقَالُوا عَلَيْنَا شَطَطًا فَكَانُوا مِنَ الكَاذِبِينَ .

which turned them into unim-
pressive imposters.

18
THE BELIEVERS
(Surat Al Mumineen)

١٨) سُورَةُ المُؤمِنينَ

In the Name of the Father, the Word, the Holy Spirit, the One and only True God

بِسمِ الآبِ الكَلِمةِ الرُوحِ الالهِ الواحِدِ الأوحدِ

1.   O, you who have believed from among Our followers: we are not separating you from those who have blasphemed until the Judgment Day. You will eventually return to Us. For to Us everything must return, where the righteous will receive their deserved reward.

١) يأيُّها الذينَ آمَنوا مِنْ عِبادِنا : إنَّا مُطهِروكمْ مِنَ الذينَ كَفَروا إلى يوم القيامةِ ثمّ إلينا مَرجعُكمْ فإلينا ترجعُ الأمورُ والعاقبةُ للمتقينَ .

2.   Our believing worshipers are artisans of virtue. They are exhorters from evil. They treat others with courtesy, love, mercy and kindness. Even when maligned by the apostates, they still wish such people peace. Obviously, Our faithful followers demonstrate sublime character.

٢) إنَّ عِبادَنا المؤمنينَ فَعّالونَ للخيرِ مَّساعونَ للشرّ يُعامِلونَ كلَّ عِبادِنا بالمعروفِ والحَبّةِ والرحمةِ والحُسنى وإنْ آذاهمُ الكافرونَ قالوا سَلاماً وإنَّهمْ لَعلى خُلُقٍ عظيمٍ .

3. Their souls are pure. Their inward thoughts are good. Their speech is bright. Their deeds are pure delight. Their private parts are kept purified. Whatever We inspired, they solemnly obey. Thus, Satan cannot disturb them in any way. They take strength in Our pathway.

٣) نزكِيَّةٌ نُفوسُهُمْ نَقِيَّةٌ طَوَايَاهُمْ طَيِّبَة أَقْوَالُهُمْ حَسَنَةٌ أَفْعَالُهُمْ طَاهِرَةٌ وَفُرُوجُهُمْ وَمَا أَنْزَلْنَا يَهْتَدُونَ فَلَا يَقْرَبُهُمُ الشَّيْطَانُ فَهُمْ بِحَبْلِنَا مُعْتَصِمُونَ .

4. We, therefore, will welcome them into Our paradise. They will be joyful and content with their prize. This is because they exhibited mercy in their dealing with others. They also desired for Our worshipers precisely what We desired. Additionally, they promulgated peace everywhere, did not kill or steal. They did not commit immorality, or maligned, criticized or gossiped about others.

٤) نُدْخِلُهُمْ جَنَّاتِنَا رَاضِينَ مَرْضِيِّينَ ذَلِكَ أَنَّهُمْ يَصِلُونَ الرَّحِمَ وَيُحِبُّونَ لِعِبَادِنَا مَا يُحِبُّونَ لِأَنْفُسِهِمْ وَيُفْشُونَ السَّلَامَ وَلَا يَقْتُلُونَ وَلَا يَسْرِقُونَ وَلَا يَزْنُونَ وَلَا يَقُولُونَ مَا لَا يَعْلَمُونَ .

5. Man was removed from Us for a long period of time by a great distance because of unbelief. Still We continued to communicate with him without reluctance. **The True Gospel** was sent with authority. Even now We have

٥) وَظَلَّ الْإِنْسَانُ حِيناً مِنَ الدَّهْرِ فِي ضَلَالٍ بَعِيدٍ حَتَّى كَلَّمْنَاهُ بِالْإِنْجِيلِ الْحَقِّ ثُمَّ أَفَضْنَا عَلَيْهِ مِنْ نُورِنَا بِالْفُرْقَانِ الْحَقِّ فَمَنْ آمَنَ

flooded mankind with Our Light through **The True Furqan**. Whosoever trusted and was guided by Us overcame blasphemy and Satan.

واهتدى فقد انتصر على الكفر وعلى جُنُودِ الشيطانِ الذَّميمِ .

6. Our believing followers are trustworthy and absolutely the most excellent citizens of any nation on earth. They practice virtuous deeds devotedly and daily. They also forbid debauchery, licentiousness and moral laxity. They do not take their status for granted because they realize that they are the chosen ones by grace and that they are the discoverers of the right to this divine pathway.

٦) إنَّ عِبادنا المؤمنينَ الصّادقينَ هُـمْ خيرُ أُمّة أُخرجتْ للنّاس كافّةً يأمرونَ بالمعروف أمراً مَفعولاً وينهَونَ عَنِ المنكرِ والفحشاء والبغيِ نهياً مَفعولاً ولا يَنسونَ أنفسَهُمْ فهمُ المرضيُّ عنهُمْ وهـمُ المُهتدونَ .

7. In contrast, Our wrath will be poured out on the ones who have rebelled against Us. Their destiny is like that of a wandering star which is hurling into deep space without a destination.

٧) أمّا الذينَ كفروا مِنْ عِبادنا فهُمُ المغضوبُ عليهـمْ وهـمُ الضّالونَ .

19
REPENTANCE
(Surat Al Tawbah)

١٩) سُورةُالتوبة

In the Name of the Father, the Word, the Holy Spirit, the One and only True God

بسـمِ الآبِ الكلمةِ الروحِ الالهِ الواحدِ الأوحدِ

1.   O, you who have gone astray, yet still claim to be counted among Our worshipers: return unto Us and you will be pleased and satisfied. Repent toward Us an honest repentance and do not commit perversion. Do not even repeat, "Our forefathers practiced these things and God has commanded us to do so." We most certainly never command the practice of debauchery. As a matter-of-fact, you are a bunch of pagans who speak of Us what you do not perceive.

١) يَأيها الذينَ ضَلّوا مِنْ عِبادِنا : إرجِعوا إلينا راضِينَ مرضِيّينَ وتُوبوا إلينا توبةً نصوحاً ولا تأتوا الفاحِشَةَ ولا تَقُولوا : "إنّا وَجدنا عَليها آباءَنا وأمرَنا اللهُ بها" فإنّا لا نأمرُ بالفاحِشَةِ وإنّما أنتـمُ قومٌ مُفترونَ تقولونَ علينا ما لا تَعلمونَ .

2.   Your practice of debauchery, defilement and degradation

٢) وَتَأتُونَ الفَحشاءَ والمنكــرَ والبغيَ مَا

96

has surpassed everyone else's in the entire world!

سَبَقَكُمْ بِهَا مِنْ أَحَدٍ مِنَ الْعَالَمِينَ .

3. You also ill-treat the believers from among Our worshipers and kill them. Then it is announced unto you that, "You did not kill them yourselves, but in reality God did." The counterfeiters falsified such because We did not create Our worshipers to kill them! Such statement is the product of deceitfulness and an instruction of Satan, the cursed one.

٣) وَتُؤْذُونَ الْمُؤْمِنِينَ مِنْ عِبَادِنَا وَتَقْتُلُوهُمْ وَيُقَالُ لَكُمْ : "لَمْ تَقْتُلُوهُمْ وَلَكِنَّ اللهَ قَتَلَهُمْ" لَقَدْ أَفَكَ الْمُفْتَرُونَ فَمَا خَلَقْنَا عِبَادَنَا لِنَقْتُلَهُمْ وَلَكِنَّهُ قَوْلُ الْكُفْرِ مِنْ وَحْيِ شَيْطَانٍ لَعِينٍ .

4. Innumerable have been Our clear proofs. Who will ever exchange Our grace after these proofs have come to him for what the imposters have concocted?

٤) وَكَمْ آتَيْنَاكُمْ مِنْ آيَاتٍ بَيِّنَاتٍ فَمَنْ يُبَدِّلْ نِعْمَتَنَا مِنْ بَعْدِ مَا جَاءَتْهُ وَيَتَّبِعْ مَا جَاءَ بِهِ الْقَوْمُ الْكَافِرُونَ ؟

5. You made statements concerning Us of which you have no knowledge whatsoever. In the end, your own tongues, hands and feet will certify what wickedness you were undertaking.

٥) وَقُلْتُمْ عَلَيْنَا مَا لَيْسَ لَكُمْ بِهِ عِلْمٌ . وَسَتَشْهَدُ عَلَيْكُمْ أَلْسِنَتُكُمْ وَأَيْدِيكُمْ وَأَرْجُلُكُمْ بِمَا كُنْتُمْ

تعملونَ .

6. All that We desire for you is the right guidance and to walk in the straight path. Therefore, seek Our forgiveness by honest repentance from whatever sins you are practicing.

٦) إِنَّمَا نُرِيدُ بِكُمُ الْهِدَايَةَ وَسَوَاءَ السَّبِيلِ فَاسْتَغْفِرُونَا وتوبوا إِلَيْنَا توبةً صَادِقَةً عَمَّا كُنتمُ تفعلونَ .

7. So, believe in what We revealed in **The True Gospel** and what We imparted in **The True Furqan**. For they embody Our true disclosure and trustworthy criterion. It will, therefore, endure until the Day of Resurrection.

٧) وآمِنوا بِمَا قُلْنَا فِى الْإِنْجِيلِ الْحَقِّ ومَا أَنزلْنَا مِنَ الفُرقَانِ الْحَقِّ فهو القولُ الْحَقُّ وسُنَّةُ الْحَقِّ الى يومِ تُبعثونَ .

98

20
RIGHTEOUSNESS
(Surat Al Salah)

٢٠) سُورةُالصلاح

In the Name of the Father, the Word, the Holy Spirit, the One and only True God

بسم الآب الكلمة الروح الاله الواحد الأوحد

1. O, you who have gone astray, yet still claim to be counted among Our worshipers: shall We guide you to an endeavor which will rescue you from a painful punishment? Love one another and do not dislike one another. Love even your enemies, instead of hating them, because love is Our creed and Our straight path.

١) يَأَيُّهَا الذينَ ضَلُّوا مِنْ عِبادِنا : هلْ ندلُّكُمْ على بُجَارةٍ تُنجِيكُمْ مِنْ عذابٍ أليمٍ ؟ تَحَابُّوا ولا تَباغَضُوا وأحْبُّوا ولا تَكْرَهُوا أعداءَكُمْ فالمَحَبَّةُ سُنَّتُنا وصِراطُنا المُستقيمُ .

2. Remake your swords into plows and your spears into pruning hooks. Then from the labor of your own hands you will eat abundantly.

٢) وَسُكُّوا سُيوفَكُمْ سِكَكًا ورِماحَكُمْ مَناجِلَ ومِنْ جَنى أيديكُمْ تأكلونَ .

3. Turn away from your crooked ways and act uprightly. Do not command people to do

٣) واصلحوا ذاتَ بينكُمْ واعملوا صالحًا

99

righteously then forget to do the same. Do not engage in warfare against others. Woe unto him who snatches a beggar's morsel, enjoys the bread of humiliating slothfulness or takes over the property of a peaceful people in an assault.

ولا تأمروا الناس بالبرّ وتنسون أنفسكم . ولا تعتدوا فويل لمن يغصب لقمة المسكين ويستمرئ خُبزَ الكسل المهين ويغنم مال الآمنين .

4. Do not take orders from Satan nor believe him when he tells you, "Eat from whatever you have captured in an attack for it is enjoyable and sanctioned. Fear God, for God is forgiving and merciful."

٤) ولا تُطيعوا أمرَ الشيطان ولا تصدّقوه إن قال لكم : "كلوا ممّا غنمتم حلالاً طيباً واتقوا اللّهَ إنَّ اللّهَ غفورٌ رحيمٌ"

5. How can the stolen goods become enjoyable and sanctioned? Furthermore, how can one claim that he worships Us when he unmercifully snatches the morsel from the mouth of a beggar?

٥) فأنّى يكونُ الحرامُ حلالاً طيباً؟ وأنّى يسقينا من يغصب لقمةَ المسكين؟

6. Therefore, whosoever launches an assault is guilty of murder. Whosoever receives the spoils of war is guilty of stealing. Whosoever takes women captive is guilty of adultery. And

٦) لقد قتل مَن غزا وسرق من غنِمَ وزنى مَن سبى وكفر من اتقانا بالإثم والعدوان .

whosoever declares that he worships Us through performing evil deeds and attacking others is guilty of apostasy.

7. You have determined to proceed in the ways of the heathen. You have even accused Us of deception, but such corrupters will never prevail.

٧) واسْتَنْهَجْتُمْ سُبُلَ الضَّلالِ وافتريتُمْ عَلينا الكذبَ وانه لا يُفْلِحُ المُجرِمونَ .

8. Deception was made-up for you to look exactly like the straight and narrow pathway and faithlessness to look like faith. Then you declared very boastfully that such ideas comprise a worthwhile religion. However, such ideologies cannot be called religion. They are merely fabricated statements motivated by the wicked Whisperer who has sealed you with his likeness. Consequently, you have turned into Satan's obedient subjects.

٨) وَشُبِّهَ لكُمُ الضَّلالُ هُدًى والكُفرُ إِيماناً وَدَعوتُمْ ذلكَ ديناً قَيِّماً وَمَا كانَ ذلكَ ديناً إِنْ هوَ إلا قولُ الإفكِ أوحى به الوسواسُ الخَنّاسُ وَوَسَمَكُمْ بِسِيماهُ فأنتُمْ لهُ تَبَعٌ طائِعونَ .

9. Definitely there is a grave malady in your hearts. You yourselves are the corrupters; tragically, you are not aware of your critical state! You are also the depraved; yet, you are not

٩) في قُلوبِكُمْ مَرَضٌ فأنتُمُ المُفسِدونَ ولكِنْ لا تَشعُرونَ وأنتُمُ السُّفَهاءُ ولكِنْ لا تعلمونَ .

101

cognizant of your fate.

10. Is there a comparison between the one who is knowledgeable about his faith and the one whose evil deeds are glamorized unto him? They certainly cannot be equated.

١٠) أَفَمَنْ كَانَ عَلَى بَيِّنَةٍ مِنْ دِينِهِ كَمَنْ زُيِّنَ لَهُ سُوءُ عَمَلِهِ؟ إِنَّهُمْ لَا يَسْتَوُونَ.

11. So, do not boast of your religion, because you have in reality followed the whims of others who lost their way before you came along and were swept away by them from the straight pathway.

١١) فَلَا تَغْلُوا فِي دِينِكُمْ فَقَدِ اتَّبَعْتُمْ أَهْوَاءَ قَوْمٍ قَدْ ضَلُّوا مِنْ قَبْلِكُمْ فَأَضَلُّوكُمْ عَنْ سَوَاءِ السَّبِيلِ.

12. Numerous are the examples of how a small group of believers was able to overcome a larger group of unbelievers by the methods of love, mercy and peace. There is no equality between the unrighteous and the righteous even if you are beguiled by the wiles of the despicable one. Eternal rewards are bestowed only upon the God-fearing souls.

١٢) وَكَمْ مِنْ فِئَةٍ قَلِيلَةٍ مُؤْمِنَةٍ غَلَبَتْ فِئَةً كَثِيرَةً كَافِرَةً بِالْمَحَبَّةِ وَالرَّحْمَةِ وَالسَّلَامِ فَلَا يَسْتَوِي الْخَبِيثُ وَالطَّيِّبُ وَلَوْ أَعْجَبَكُمْ كَثْرَةُ الْخَبِيثِ وَالْعَاقِبَةُ لِلْمُتَّقِينَ.

13. When the imposters are instructed, "Follow the

١٣) وَإِذَا قِيلَ لِلَّذِينَ كَفَرُوا: "تَعَالَوْا إِلَى مَا

proclamation that is set forth in **The True Furqan**", they reply, "We follow what our forefathers followed." Yet, their forefathers were pagans and did not believe.

أُنزِلَ فِي الفُرقانِ الحقّ". قَالُوا: "حَسْبُنَا مَا وجَدنَا عليهِ آبَاءَنَا". أوَلوْ كَانَ آبَاؤُهُمْ على ضَلالٍ ولا يُؤمنـونَ؟

14. The example of a word spoken in its proper season is like the example of a good tree. Its roots are deep and its fruit you can always reap.

١٤) ومثلُ كلمةٍ طيبةٍ كمثَلِ شَجَرةٍ طيبةٍ أصلُها ثابتٌ وفرعُها في السماءِ تُؤتي أُكلَها الطيبَ كلَّ حينٍ.

15. But the example of a mean word is like the example of a rotten tree. Sooner or later it will simply fall flat on the ground because it did not have deep roots for a foundation.

١٥) ومثَلُ كلمةٍ خبيثةٍ كمثَلِ شجَرةٍ خبيثةٍ اجتُثّتْ مِنْ فوقِ الأرضِ فما لها من قرارٍ رِكين.

16. O, you who have believed from among Our followers: call those who have been led astray to return to the faith. Use love, wisdom and excellent preaching. Debate them with true statements and shed light for them onto the path of truth; perchance they may be guided.

١٦) يأيها الذينَ آمنوا مِنْ عبادنا: ادعوا الذينَ كفروا إلى الإيمانِ بالمحبةِ والحكمةِ والموعظةِ الحسنةِ وجادلوهُمْ بالتي هيَ أقومُ وأنيروا لهُمْ سبيلَ الحقِّ لعلهُمْ يهتدونَ.

17. Those who have responded to Our grace should admonish
those who have not responded
that if they owned the planet earth
they would willingly sacrifice it
all in order to redeem themselves.
Because such people rejected our
offer of justification through the
Messiah, their fate will be horrific
for their eternal destiny will be
Hell. O, what a horrible end!

١٧) للذين استجابوا لنا الحسنى والذين لـم
يستجيبوا لنا لو أن لهـم ما في الأرض
جميعاً لافتدوا به أولئك لهـم سوء الحساب
ومأواهـم جهنـم وبئس المهاد .

21
THE PURIFICATION
(Surat Al Tuhr)

In the Name of the Father, the Word, the Holy Spirit, the One and only True God

بسم الآب الكلمة الروح الاله الواحد الأوحد

1. Satan designated monstrous names for Us but connivingly covered them up with excellent names to mislead people into thinking that these names were genuine. Instead, he led people astray causing them to commit heinous crimes in Our name without recognizing the evil of their deeds.

١) وَدَعَانَا الشَّيطانُ بأسماءَ قُبحى غَيَّبها بأسماءِ حُسنى مَكرًا منهُ لِيوقعَ بأتباعِه فأضلَّهُم فارتكبوا الكبائرَ باسمِنا وهمْ لا يشعرون .

2. Satan is not concerned one iota if We direct his loyal followers to call on Our ninety-nine excellent names when the selections are erroneous. Hence, these people commit wickedness and debauchery by their own hands every time they use these unauthorized titles.   One must

٢) وَمَا يَضيرُ الشيطانَ إنْ دَعانَا أولياؤُه بأسماءِ حُسنى قولاً زورًا بأفواهِهم واقترفوا المُنكرَ والبغي فعلاً بأيديهم . إنّما يَبغي الشيطانُ ما يفعل المجرمون لا مَا

understand that Satan is never as concerned with what people profess with their lips as with what they possess in their hearts.

3. We have designed it as a **True Arabic Furqan**. We have composed it as a beacon of light to guide those who grope in the darkness with the hope that they will discover the True Way. This **True Furqan** will also distinguish truth from falsehood, fidelity from infidelity.

4. Whosoever walks in the light will not stumble day or night. The ones who walk in the darkness are none other than the people who are convicted apostates.

5. O, you of Our followers who have gone astray: you have endorsed whatever Satan has presented to you. Hence, you have performed gross immorality and even committed crimes in Our name. We certainly do not command anyone to do evil. Such commands emanate from the rebellious Devil.

يَقُولُونَ .

٣) إِنَّا أَنزَلْنَاهُ فُرْقَاناً عَرَبِيّاً وَجَعَلْنَاهُ نُوراً يَهْدِي الضَّالِينَ مِنْ عِبَادِنَا لِيَمِيزُوا الْحَقَّ مِنَ الْبَاطِلِ وَالإِيمَانَ مِنَ الْكُفْرِ لَعَلَّهُمْ يَهْتَدُونَ .

٤) فَمَنْ سَارَ فِي النُّورِ لاَ يَعْثُرُ وَلاَ يَسِيرُ فِي الظُّلْمَةِ إِلاَّ الْقَوْمُ الْكَافِرُونَ .

٥) يَأَيُّهَا الَّذِينَ ضَلُّوا مِنْ عِبَادِنَا لَقَدْ حَلَّلْتُمْ لأَنْفُسِكُمْ مَا أَلْقَى الشَّيْطَانُ بِأُمْنِيَاتِكُمْ فَارْتَكَبْتُمُ الْكَبَائِرَ وَاقْتَرَفْتُمُ الإِثْمَ يَأْمُرُنَا افْتِرَاءً وَبُهْتَاناً الاَّ إِنَّا لاَ نَأْمُرُ بِالإِثْمِ إِنْ هُوَ إِلاَّ أَمْرُ شَيْطَانٍ

مَرِيدٍ .

٦)   وَمَا كَانَ النَّجَسُ وَالطَّمْثُ وَالمَحِيضُ
وَالغَائِطُ وَالثَّيِّبُ وَالنِّكَاحُ وَالهَجْرُ
وَالضَّرِبُ وَالطَّلاقُ إِلاَّ كَوْمَةً رِكْسٍ
لَفَظَهَا الشَّيْطَانُ بِلِسَانِكُمْ وَمَا كَانَتْ
مِنْ وَحْيِنَا وَمَا أَنزَلْنَا بِهَا مِنْ سُلْطَانٍ .

6.   The concerns of impurity, women's menstrual cycle, after-birth issue of blood, excrement, repeating a chant, marriage rituals, leaving your wives in beds apart, beating them and divorcing them is nothing but a bunch of devious and diabolical opinions spewed by Satan himself to deceive you. These were not Our revelations. We have never authorized such proclamations.

٧)   جَحَرْتُمْ فِيهَا رُؤُوسَكُمْ فَعَمِيَتْ
بَصَائِرُكُمْ فَلاَ تَرَوْنَ نُورَ الْحَقِّ وَلا
تَفْقَهُونَ مِنْ أُمُورِ الآخِرَةِ أَمْراً .

7.   When you buried your heads in them the result was blinded eyes toward the Light of Truth.   So, you in fact, ended up with no comprehension concerning eternal matters.

٨)   فَقَدْ وَسْوَسَ الشَّيْطَانُ فِي
صُدُورِكُمْ وَأَضَلَّكُمْ ضَلالاً
بَعِيداً وَغَدَرَ بِكُمْ غَدْراً .

8.   Satan has definitely whispered lies into your hearts; then he led you astray and cunningly deceived you completely.

9. We commanded Our followers to stay away from immorality and divorce, to keep their private parts pure and to clean their bodies continuously. Their bodies are designed as Our spirit-filled temples. Therefore, it is only just and fair for them to keep themselves pure.

٩) وَقَد وَصَّيْنَا عِبَادَنَا بِأَنْ لَا يَقْرَبُوا الزِّنى أوِ الطَّلاقَ وَأَنْ يُحْصِنُوا فُرُوجَهُمْ وَيُطَهِّرُوا أَجْسَادَهُمْ فَهِيَ هَيَاكِلُنَا فَحَقَّ عَلَيْهِمْ أَنْ يَحْفَظُوهَا طُهْراً .

10. Adultery defiles the body, humiliates the soul and is an enslavement to Satan, the cursed one.

١٠) فَالزِّنى نَجَسُ الجَسَدِ وَهَوْنُ النَّفْسِ وَعُبُودِيَةٌ لِلشَّيْطَانِ اللَّعِينِ .

11. When you announced, "Do not approach sexual immorality for it is an abomination and a wrongful paragon," it was only lip-service!

١١) وَقُلْتُمْ إِفْكاً : لَا تَقْرَبُوا الزِّنى إِنَّهُ كَانَ فَاحِشَةً وَسَاءَ سَبِيلاً .

12. Yet, you commanded its performance and practice twice, thrice, even four times and whatever your wealth permits you to own from among women. You add that there is no penalty if one divorces his wife. But whenever you renounce a divorcement from your ex-wife and want to marry

١٢) وَأَمَرْتُمْ بِاقْتِرَافِهِ فِعْلاً مَثْنَى وَثُلاثَ وَرُبَاعَ أَوْ مَا مَلَكَتْ أَيْمَانُكُمْ . وَلا جُنَاحَ عَلَيْكُمْ إِذَا طَلَّقْتُمُ النِّسَاءَ فَإِنْ طَلَّقْتُمُوهُنَّ فَلا يَحْلِلْنَ لَكُمْ مِنْ بَعْدُ حَتَّى

her again, she is not permitted to be your wife again unless another man has intercourse with her first! Is there any worse adulterous, vile or wicked idea than such pronouncements?

ينكِحَنَّ أَزْواجاً غَيرَكُمْ . فَهلْ بعدَ
هَذا مِنْ زِنىً وفُحشٍ وفجورٍ ؟

13. Amazing, is it not? You forbid adultery linguistically, but command it practically. You certainly have gotten yourselves deep in the mire of iniquity and have surpassed the world's worst uncivilized savages. Woe unto every practicing adulterer, for severe judgment awaits him if he remains unrepentant.

١٣) تَنْهَوْنَ عَنِ الزِّنى قَولاً وتَأْمُرونَ بمُعاقرَتِه
فِعــلاً وتَمَرَّغْتـــمْ فـي حَمْـأَةِ الفجــورِ
فَبَرزَرْتُــمْ زِنُاةَ العالَـمِينَ فَوَيلٌ لِكُـلِّ زِنَّاءٍ
زَنِيمٍ .

22
THE IDOLS
(Al Gharaneq)

سورة الغرانيق (٢٢

In the Name of the Father, the Word, the Holy Spirit, the One and only True God

بسم الآب الكلمة الروح الاله الواحد
الأوحد

1. O, you who have blasphemed from among Our faithful followers: your leader has lost his way and he has terribly gone astray.

١) يأيها الذين كفروا من عبادنا : لقد
ضل رائد كم وقد غوى .

2. His denunciations are his own whims which are fabrications inspired by a beguiling spirit.

٢) وما نطق عن الهوى إن هو إلا وحي إفك
يوحى .

3. Who taught him to declare these, but the strong and vile one?

٣) علمه مريد القوى .

4. The messenger beheld some of Satan's heinous tricks and in turn repeated them. Why? Because of his own ignorance of the Truth of **Our Divine Revelation**.

٤) فرأى من مكائد الشيطان الكبرى
وهو بالدرك الأدنى .

5. He even went as far as reciting blasphemy openly saying, "Have you thought upon Al-lat, Al-uzza and Manat, the third the other. And verily their intercession is to be sought."

٥) وَرَدَّدَ الكُفْرَ جَهْراً وَكِلاً: أَفَرَأَيْتُمُ اللاتَ وَالعُزَّى وَمَنَاةَ الثَّالِثَةَ الأُخْرَى . إِنَّ شَفَاعَتَهُنَّ تُرْجَى .

6. Whenever Satan touched him with an epileptic fit, his best friends rebuked him. But he covered up the physical symptoms by announcing that this was a visitation from the angel Gabriel.

٦) كُلَّمَا مَسَّهُ طَائِفٌ مِنَ الشَّيْطَانِ زَجَرَهُ صَحْبُهُ فَأَخْفَى مَا أَبْدَى .

7. Whenever he felt oppressed by Satan, he would call upon Us for refuge, in the hearing of the public.

٧) وَإِمَّا يَنْزَغَنَّهُ مِنَ الشَّيْطَانِ نَزْغٌ اسْتَعَاذَ بِنَا عَلَى مَسْمَعٍ جَهْراً .

8. Nevertheless, once Satan was alone with him he assured him, "I am with you." The messenger selected Satan as his redeemer instead of Us and he entertained himself with what was hidden from others.

٨) وَإِذَا خَلَا بِهِ قَالَ: "إِنِّي مَعَكَ" . فَقَدِ اتَّخَذَ الشَّيْطَانَ وَكِيلاً مِنْ دُونِنَا وَسَارَّهُ بِمَا أَخْفَى .

9. Satan proclaimed, "I have selected you above all of mankind

٩) وَإِذْ قَالَ الشَّيْطَانُ: إِنِّي اصْطَفَيْتُكَ عَلَى

to carry my message and my revelation. Now therefore, take whatsoever I grant you and remember my grace that I poured on you and express thanksgiving continuously.

الناسِ بِرِسَالاتي وَوَحِيي فَخُذْ مَا آتِيكَ واذكُرْ نِعْمَتي عليكَ وافْنْتُ شُكْراً .

10. "I will reveal to you what the ancients experienced of inspiration, which will be a memorable revelation."

١٠) فَسَأُنزِلُ عليكَ مِثلَما أُنزِلَ على الأوَّلينَ وَحْياً ذِكْراً .

11. This messenger could not stand alone, but in the power of Satan, who overcame him with delusions. Additionally, Satan instructed him with far-fetched fabrications and fantastic fantasies.

١١) فَلا يقومُ إلا كما يقومُ الذي يَتَخَبَّطُهُ الشيطانُ مِنَ المَسِّ إذْ يُنزِلُ عليهِ رِجْزاً .

12. Furthermore, Satan restrained his heart so tightly that the messenger could not make a single move on his own.

١٢) وَيَربُطُ على قلبِهِ وَيُؤَزِّرُهُ أزْراً .

13. The false illumination which Satan granted him turned into a full-fledged rebellion among those whose hearts were already sick and full of doubt

١٣) وَقَدْ جعلَ الشيطانُ ما ألقى فِتنَةً للذينَ في قلوبِهِم مَرَضٌ والذينَ في صُدورِهِمُ

112

beforehand.   Remember, whosoever turns away from the True
God to put his trust in another,
has really made a dreadful choice.

شَكٌّ وَمَنْ يَكُنِ الشَّيطانُ لَهُ قَرِناً سَاءَ قَرِناً .

14. O, you of Our faithful
followers: Satan instructs his
loyal subjects to debate you
concerning Our right and narrow
pathway. If such be the case, take
refuge in Us from the whisperings
of Satan. Do not harken to him.
Rather turn away from him.
Forsake and abandon him
entirely.

١٤) يَأيُّها الذينَ آمنوا مِنْ عِبادِنا إنَّ الشَّيطانَ لَيُوحِي إلى أوليائِهِ ليجادلوكمْ في دينكمُ القويمِ فإذا سَمعتُمْ أقوالَهم فَعُوذوا بِنا مَنْ هَمَزاتِ الشَّيطانِ ولا تُصْغوا إليهِ واعرِضوا عَنهُ واهجروهُ هجراً مُبيناً .

15. Who in the entire world is
in worse shape than the one who
misrepresents Us fraudulently,
then announces, "I was inspired
by God." What kind of fake
inspiration is this? It is what
demons delivered to him from
Satan.   Fascinating fabrications
and demonic deceptions are the
sum total of this trumped-up
forgery.

١٥) وَمَنْ أظلمُ مِمَّن افترى علينا كذباً ثمَّ قال: "أوحيَ إليَّ". وما أوحيَ إليهِ إلا ما تنزَّلتْ بهِ الشياطينُ افتراءً وتمكُّراً .

113

23
CHARITY
(Surat Al 'Ataa)

٢٣) سُورةُ العَطاءِ

In the Name of the Father, the Word, the Holy Spirit, the One and only True God

بسم الآبِ الكلمةِ الروح الاله الواحدِ
الأوحدِ

1.   O, you who have gone astray from among Our worshipers: it has been said of old, "a life for a life, an eye for an eye, a tooth for a tooth." But We countered, "Pay back good for evil and if you are slapped on the right cheek turn the left one also. Do not take vengeance on your persecutors.

١) يأيها الذينَ ضَلُّوا مِنْ عبادِنا . لقدْ قِيلَ
لكُمْ : النفسُ بالنفسِ والعينُ بالعينِ والسِّنُّ
بالسِّنِّ وقلْنا ادفعوا السيِّئةَ بالحَسنةِ فإنْ
لُطِمْتُمْ على الخَدِّ الأيمنِ فيسِّروا الأيسرَ
ولا تنتقموا منَ المعتدينَ .

2.   "If perchance someone assaults you because of coveting your robe, give it up to the covetous.

٢) وإنِ اعْتُدِي عليكُمْ طَمعًا بِردآءٍ
فاتركوهُ للطَّامعينَ .

3.   "Whosoever obliges you to carry his belongings for one mile, do it for two.

٣) ومَنْ سَخَّركُمْ مَسيرةَ ميلٍ فسِّروا
معهُ ميلينِ .

114

4. "Whosoever begs you for something he needs, give it to him. And do not turn away needy refugees.

٤) ومن سَأَلَكُمْ حَاجَةً فَاعطُوهُ ولا
كَرُّدوا السَّائلينَ .

5. "If someone expresses a need to borrow a utensil from you, do not forbid it. Go ahead and lend it to him."

٥) ومَّنِ اسْتَعَارَكُمُ الماعونَ فأعِيرُوهُ
ولا تَمنَعوا الماعونَ .

6. Have you forgotten what **The True Gospel** instructed you? Have you disobeyed The True Path? Have you begun to lead the faithful astray by spreading lies concerning Us? Let it be affirmed here and now, hypocrites will never prevail nor always have their selfish way.

٦) وقَدْ نَسِيتُمْ ما ذُكِّرْتُ بِهِ فِي
الإنجيل الحَقِّ فَما اتَّبَعتُمُ الهُدى وَرُحْتُمْ
تُضِلُّونَ المُهْتَدينَ وتَفْتَرونَ علينا الكَذِبَ أَنَّهُ
لا يُفلِحُ المُفْتَرونَ .

7. You were commanded, "Kill those who do not believe in God and enjoy their spoils of war. It is sanctioned and it is pleasurable." Such instructions come only from the ungodly.

٧) وقيلَ لكُمْ : "قاتلوا الذينَ لا يُؤمنونَ
باللهِ وكُلوا مِمَّا غَنِمتُمْ حَلالاً طَيِّباً"
وهذا قولُ الظالمينَ .

8. Those who have endorsed such a decree of killing Our

٨) لقَدْ كفَرَ الذينَ أَحَلّوا قَتلَ عِبادِنا

followers, and robbing the morsels of food from the mouths of the orphans and the poverty stricken are in fact tyrannical despots.

وَسَلَبُوا لُقْمَةَ الْيَتَامَى وَالْمَسَاكِينِ ذَلِكَ أَنَّهُمْ كَافِرُونَ .

9. You also announced, "Whosoever wants to believe can believe and whosoever wants to be ungodly let him be ungodly. In this manner wisdom is distinguished from folly. There is no compulsion in religion."

٩) وَقُلْتُمْ : "مَنْ شَاءَ فَلْيُؤْمِنْ وَمَنْ شَاءَ فَلْيَكْفُرْ فَقَدْ تَبَيَّنَ الرُّشْدُ مِنَ الْغَيِّ لَا إِكْرَاهَ فِي الدِّينِ" .

10. Yet, you set out to kill the believers from among Our followers and to compel people to denounce Us at the point of the sword. Such a command is the work of the wicked. Dreadful shall be the end of the hypocrites who make godly declarations, but never practice what they preach.

١٠) وَرُحْتُمْ تَقْتُلُونَ الْمُؤْمِنِينَ مِنْ عِبَادِنَا وَتُكْرِهُونَ النَّاسَ بِالسَّيْفِ عَلَى الْكُفْرِ وَهَذِهِ سُنَّةُ الْمُجْرِمِينَ . أَلَا تَعْسًا لِلْمُنَافِقِينَ الَّذِينَ يَقُولُونَ مَا لَا يَفْعَلُونَ .

11. Satan and his loyalists crave to snuff the Light of Truth. They employ their vile precepts to fulfill their purpose. They also want to conceal Our Word through their degenerate deeds.

١١) وَيُرِيدُ الشَّيْطَانُ وَأَوْلِيَاؤُهُ أَنْ يُطْفِئُوا نُورَ الْحَقِّ بِسُوءِ أَقْوَالِهِمْ وَيَطْمِسُوا كَلِمَنَا بِمُنْكَرِ أَفْعَالِهِمْ وَيَأْبَى إِلَّا أَنْ يُسَمَّ نُورَنَا

Notwithstanding, We will repudiate such because We will radiate Our Light brightly and reveal Our Word soundly, no matter what the imposters say or do.

وَنَظْهَرَ كَلَّشَا وَكُوَكَرِهَ الْكَافِرُونَ .

12. When the Day of Judgment comes, in which the hypocrite shall bite his tongue in agony, he will announce, "O, my, I wish that I had accepted **The True Gospel** and **The True Furqan** as my guidepost in life.

١٢) وَيَوْمَ يَعُضُّ الْكَافِرُ عَلَى يَدَيْهِ يَقُولُ: "يَا لَيْتَنِي اتَّخَذْتُ الْإِنْجِيلَ الْحَقَّ وَالْفُرْقَانَ الْحَقَّ دَلِيلاً .

13. "Woe is me, had I been led aright before this Judgment Day, I would not have been in this dreadful decay.

١٣) يَا وَيْلَتِي لَيْتَنِي اهْتَدِيتُ مِنْ قَبْلُ فَلَمَا سِتُ دَلِيلاً .

14. We have staunchly followed our religious and spiritual leader's instructions. Alas, instead of leading us to the True Light, Jesus the Christ, they have most certainly led us to an unenviable plight."

١٤) إِنَّا أَطَعْنَا سَادَتَنَا وَكُبَرَاءَنَا فَأَضَلُّونَا السَّبِيلَ . "

24
WOMEN
(Surat Al Nissa)

٢٤) سُورَةُ النساء

In the Name of the Father, the Word, the Holy Spirit, the One and only True God

بسم الآبِ الكلمةِ الروح الالهِ الواحدِ الأوحدِ

1. O, you who are oppressors from among Our wayward worshipers: why have you degraded a woman to a piece of merchandise which you can buy or sell, and discard as if she were the kernel of a date palm? Her wing is broken; her rights are taken. This treatment has never been that of any fair-minded people.

١) يَا أَهْلَ الظُّلْمِ مِنْ عِبَادِنَا الضَّالِينَ: لَقَدِ اتَّخَذْتُمْ مِنَ المَرْأَةِ سِلْعَةً تُبَاعُ وتُشْتَرى وتُنْبَذُ نَبْذَ النَّوى مَهِيضَةَ الجَنَاحِ هَضِيمَةَ الجَانِبِ ومَا كَانَ ذَلِكَ مِنْ سُنَّةِ المُقْسِطِينَ.

2. You have sanctioned owning whatever you desire from among women as if they are cattle, even to keeping them prisoners in your homes. Whenever you desire sexual relations, you do it regardless of their will. This is the height of injustice and immorality. Where,

٢) تَمْتَنُونَ مَا طَابَ لَكُمْ مَنَ النِّسَاءِ كَالسَّوائِمِ تَأْسُرُوهُنَّ حَبِيسَاتٍ وهُنَّ حَرْثٌ لَكُمْ تَأْتُونَ حَرْثَكُمْ أَنَّى شِئْتُمْ ذَلِكَ هوَ الظُّلْمُ والفُجُورُ فَأَيْنَ العَدْلُ

118

O where is fairness and sublime character?

٣) وَبَدَأْنَا خَلَقْكُـــمْ بِآدَمَ وَاحِدٍ وَحَوَّاءَ وَاحِدَةٍ فَتُوبُوا عَنْ شِرْكِكَ الزِّنَى وَوَحِّدُوا أَنْفُسَـــكُمْ بِـــأَزْوَاجِكُـــمْ وَلَا تُشْرِكُوا بِأَنْفُسِكُمْ وَلَا بِهِنَّ أَحَدًا . فَلِلزَّوْجِ الذَّكَرِ الوَاحِدِ زَوْجَةٌ أُنْثَى وَاحِدَةٌ وَمَا زَادَ عَنْ ذَلِكَ فَهُوَ مِنَ الشَّيْطَانِ الرَّجِيمِ .

3. In the beginning We created you as Adam and Eve, one male and one female. Therefore, repent from paganism and from committing adultery. Be fair-minded in dealing with our creatures. Be united to your wife and do not allow anyone else to come between the two of you. There should be only one male and only one female who are married to each other, designated as husband and wife—if you are obedient believers.

٤) تَقُولُونَ: "إِنَّ الرِّجَالَ قَوَّامُونَ عَلَى النِّسَاءِ وَاللَّاتِي تَخَافُونَ نُشُوزَهُنَّ فَعِظُوهُنَّ وَاهْجُرُوهُنَّ فِي المَضَاجِعِ وَاضْرِبُوهُنَّ" فَمَا مِنْزٌ بِشِرْعَةِ الغَابِ بَيْنَ الإِنْسَانِ وَبَيْنَ البَهَائِمِ وَالأَنْعَامِ .

4. You pronounce, "Men are a degree above women and those of whom you fear rebellion exhort, leave in beds apart, beat and scourge them." What, then, is the difference between the law of the jungles of beast and bird from the law of the human race?

٥) فَالمَرْأَةُ بِشِرْعَتِكُـــمْ نِصْفُ وَارِثٍ

5. A woman, according to your Sharia, is one-half of an

119

inheritor. "The male has twice the inheritance of a female." To make bad things worse, she is one-half of a witness, "And if there are two men, then one man and two women, because men are a degree above women." Without a question, this is the law of the unjust.

"فللذكر مثل حظ الانثيين" وهي نصف شاهد "فإن لم يكن رجلان فرجل وامرأتان فللرجال عليهن درجة" . وهذا عدل الظالمين .

6. Even touching a woman is like being polluted by excreta; you turn away from her saying, "If any of you is polluted by excreta or touches a woman and cannot find water for cleansing, use instead the good sand or dust."

٦) وملامسة المرأة نجس تأنفون منها قائلين: "إذا جاء أحد منكم من الغائط أو لامستم النساء فلم تجدوا ماء فتيمموا صعيداً طيباً"

7. Are you not aware that the filth of the unclean, all the sand of Arabia can never make clean, even all the waters in all the rivers in all the ends of the earth will not purify a sinful heart.

٧) لكن نجس الأنجاس لا يطهره الرغام ولا أمواه الأنهر ولا ما طاب من صعد العالمين .

8. Unrighteous men, why have you made the woman an

٨) واتخذ من المرأة مورد غريزة تطلبونها

object to fulfill your lust, wanting her when she does not want you? You divorce her whenever you wish but she rarely divorces you. You leave her in a bed apart but she seldom leaves you. You scourge her but she does not scourge you. And you add beside her a second, a third and even a fourth wife along with whomever else you can afford, but she does not add another man besides you.

أَنَّى شِئْتُمْ وَلاَ تَطْلُبُكُمْ . وَتُطَلِّقُونَهَا أَنَّى شِئْتُمْ وَلاَ تُطَلِّقُكُمْ . وَتَهْجُرُونَهَا وَلاَ تَهْجُرُكُمْ . وَتَضْرِبُونَهَا وَلاَ تَضْرِبُكُمْ . وَتُشْرِكُونَ بِهَا مَثْنَى وَثُلاَثَ وَرُبَاعَ أَوْ مَا مَلَكَتْ أَيْمَانُكُمْ وَلاَ تُشْرِكُ بِكُمْ أَحَدًا .

9. You own her, but she does not own you. She does not even own her body, soul or spirit.

(٩) تَمْلِكُونَهَا وَلاَ تَمْلِكُكُمْ وَلاَ تَمْلِكُ لِشَأْنِ أَمْرِهَا رَشَدًا .

10. You have erected between men and women a veil and a barrier, saying, "And if you ask the women for anything, do so from behind a veil." This is the height of female abuse, jealousy and bigotry.

(١٠) وَأَقَمْتُمْ بَيْنَكُمْ وَبَيْنَ النِّسَاءِ سَدًّا وَحِجَابًا مَسْتُورًا . "فَإِذَا سَأَلْتُمُوهُنَّ فَمِنْ وَرَاءِ حِجَابٍ" فَكَانَ ذَلِكَ هَوْنًا لِخَلْقِنَا وَاحْتِقَارًا .

11. And if you fear rebellion from women, you imprison them

(١١) وَإِذَا خَشِيتُمْ عَلَيْهِنَّ الْفِتْنَةَ غَيْرَةً

declaring, "Stay in your home, going nowhere else." Such a decision is devilish and demeaning.

احتبستموهنَّ بقولكـــمْ : "قــرْنَ فِـ
بيوتكنَّ" الا سَـاءَ حُكـــمُ الظالمين
قرارًا .

12. Yes, you threaten them with divorce, letting them go, or even exchanging them, pronouncing, "It may be that if we divorce them God will give us instead better wives, both widows and virgins."

١٢) تُهَدِّدُونَهُنَّ بالطلاق والتسريح والتبديل
تقولونَ لهنَّ : "عسَى اللهُ إنْ طلَّقنـاكنَّ أنْ
يُبدّلنـا أزواجـاً خيـراً منكـنَّ ثَيِّبـاً
وأبكـارًا" .

13. When one of you committed what We prohibited concerning adultery, he simply fabricated a lie and ascribed it to Us. Thus, he sanctioned the performance of the action for himself stating, "Why do you forbid what God has sanctioned for you?" Brazenly and publicly, he committed immorality.

١٣) وإذا اقترفَ أحدُكـمْ مَا حرَّمنا منَ
الزنى تحريماً افترى علينا الكذبَ افتراءً
وحلَّلهُ لنفسه تحليلاً وكلا على لسَانا : "لِـمَ
تُحرِّمُ مَا أحلَّ اللهُ لك ؟" . واقتـرفَ
الفُجورَ جهَارًا .

14. Whenever one of you lusted with his eyes after the wives of others or wanted to exchange a wife or acquire more from among those whose beauty captivates him, even if she is the

١٤) وإنْ مدَّ أحدُكـمْ عينيهِ إلى أزواج
الأغيارِ وأراد استبدالَ زوجٍ أو اقتنـاءَ
المزيد مِنْ أعجبهُ حُسُنهنَّ ولوْكنَّ أزواجَ

wife of his own adopted son, he seeks Our personal assistance in sanctioning the forbidden. Thus, he made up a lie and ascribed it to Us. He claimed that We declared, "When the other finalized his purpose with her, We joined her to you in marriage." This is absolutely nothing but blasphemy, adultery and immorality. Where, O where is purity, honesty and sublime character?

مَنْ تَبَنَّىً، اسْتَعَانَ بِنَا عَلَى تَحْلِيلِ الْحَرَامِ فَافْتَرَى عَلَى لِسَانِنَا الْكَذِبَ وَنِزْعَمَ بِأَنَّا قُلْنَا : " وَلَمَّا قَضَى الْغَيْرُ مِنْهَا وَطَراً زَوَّجْنَاكَهَا " . وَهَذَا هُوَ الْكُفْرُ وَالزِّنَى وَالْفُجُورُ فَأَيْنَ الطَّهَارَةُ وَالْعِفَّةُ وَالْخُلُقُ الْكَرِيمُ ؟

15. In what kind of human merchandise do you trade? And what kind of beast do you lead along?

١٥) فَأَيَّ سِلْعَةٍ تَتَبَاعُونَ وَأَيَّ بَهِيمَةٍ تَقْتَنُونَ وَتَسُوسُونَ ؟

16. Therefore, show compassion toward Our creatures. Be tenderhearted toward those whose rights are unjustly taken.

١٦) فَرَحْمَةً بِخَلْقِنَا وَرِفْقاً بِأُنَاسٍ ذِي حَقٍّ هَضِيمٍ .

25
MARRIAGE
(Surat Al Zawaj)

٢٥) سُورةُ الزواج

In the Name of the Father, the Word, the Holy Spirit, the One and only True God

بسم الآبِ الكلمةِ الروحِ الالهِ الواحدِ الأوحدِ

1.   O, you who have gone astray from among Our worshipers: We have warned you through **The True Furqan** whosoever perceived and found the way actually benefits himself. But whosoever has lost his way has really missed it altogether. It seems that you are all mired in a misguided pathway.

١) يَأيُّها الذينَ ضَلّوا مِنْ عِبادِنا : إنّا أنذرناكُمْ بالفرقانِ الحقِّ فَمَن اهتدى فإنّما يَهتدي لنفسِهِ وَمَنْ ضَلَّ فإنّما يَضِلُّ عليها وإنّكُمْ لفي ضَلالٍ بعيدٍ .

2.   You have failed miserably because Satan has misled you.   Furthermore, you blasphemed by rejecting Our scripture. We advise you, cease and desist; it is for your edification.   Do   not   go overboard   in   your   self-importance.   Rather, repent and

٢) وَسَقَطَ في أيديكُمْ إذ أضَلّكُمُ الشيطانُ فَكَفَرْتُمْ بآياتِنا فانتَهوا خَيراً لكُمْ ولا تَتَمادوا في غَيّكُمْ وتُوبوا وارجعوا إلى السبيلِ الرَّشيدِ .

return to the right path of love and humility.

3. We have created you male and female. In marriage, the two unite and become as one on earth, but with a strong heavenly covenant.

4. We have declared our statues to the ancient people through **The True Gospel**. Alas, neither the hypocrites nor the shirkers practiced them. Instead, they added more women to be their wives. We have additionally warned you, by **The True Furqan**, to bring to your remembrance these precepts, return to them, listen to them: "Whosoever divorces his wife except for her committing adultery has himself committed the act of adultery. Whosoever marries a divorcee from such a relationship has himself committed adultery. And whosoever adds another woman besides his first living wife has committed adultery for certain."

٣) وَخَلَقْنَاكُمْ ذَكَرًا وَأُنْثَى يَتَّحِدَانِ زَوْجًا فَرْدًا بِعَقْدٍ فِي الدُّنْيَا وَعَهْدٍ فِي السَّمَاءِ وَثِيقٍ.

٤) وَبَلَّغْنَا سُنَّتَنَا لِلْأَوَّلِينَ فِي الْإِنْجِيلِ الْحَقِّ فَمَا اتَّبَعَهَا الْمُسَافِحُونَ وَلَا الْمُشْرِكُونَ بِزَوْجَاتِهِمْ أُخْرَيَاتٍ وَأَنْذَرْنَاكُمْ بِالْفُرْقَانِ الْحَقِّ مُذَكِّرِينَ فَاسْمَعُوا وَعُوا: مَنْ طَلَّقَ زَوْجَتَهُ إِلَّا لِزِنَاهَا فَقَدْ زَنَى. وَمَنْ تَزَوَّجَ مُطَلَّقَةً فَقَدْ زَنَى. وَمَنْ أَشْرَكَ بِزَوْجَتِهِ أُخْرَى فَقَدْ زَنَى وَمَا لِلزَّانِي إِلَى الْجَنَّةِ مِنْ طَرِيقٍ.

There will be no hope of finding a path to paradise for any adulterer who continues to practice adultery.

5. Therefore, repent, and We will grant you forgiveness. We will absolve your wrongdoing if you will truly put your trust in Us.

٥) فَتُوبُوا أَتُبْ عَلَيْكُمْ وَنَعْفُ عَنْكُمْ إِنْ كُنْتُمْ تُؤْمِنُونَ .

6. You have eyes but you do not seem to see. You have ears but you do not seem to hear. Consequently, you deceive no one but yourselves, even without being conscious of what you are doing.

٦) فَإِنَّكُمْ تُبْصِرُونَ مِنْ غَيْرِ أَنْ تُبْصِرُوا وَتَسْمَعُونَ مِنْ غَيْرِ أَنْ تَسْمَعُوا وَلاَ تُخَادِعُونَ إِلاَّ أَنْفُسَكُمْ وَمَا تَشْعُرُونَ .

7. Your spouses are precisely the equivalent of your own souls. One will certainly not cause a conspiracy within himself, by disuniting his essence and shattering his unity. Who would break asunder what We have united together in love and truth, except the adulterers and hypocritical polytheists?

٧) أَزْوَاجُكُمْ أَصْنَاءُ نُفُوسِكُمْ . فَلاَ يَسْلُخُ نَفْسَهُ وَيُطَلِّقُ ذَاتَهُ وَيُشَتِّتُ شَمْلَهُ وَيُفَرِّقُ مَا جَمَعْنَاهُ بِالْمَحَبَّةِ وَالْحَقِّ إِلاَّ الزُّنَاةُ الْكَفَرَةُ الْمُشْرِكُونَ .

26
DIVORCE
(Surat Al Talaq)

٢٦) سُورَةُ الطلاق

In the Name of the Father, the Word, the Holy Spirit, the One and only True God

بسم الآبِ الكلمةِ الروحِ الالهِ الواحدِ الأوحدِ

1. O, you from among Our worshipers who have gone astray: if anyone from your ranks falls into the web of adultery, he leans on Us to justify his evil deeds by sanctioning the evil of his marrying numerous women. Vile indeed is your method of prohibiting any false word or wrong deed.

١) يَأيُّها الذينَ ضَلُّوا مِنْ عِبادِنا : إِنَّما سَقَطَ أَحَدُكُمْ في شَرَكِ الزِّنى اسْتَعانَ بِنا على تَحْليلِ المُحرَّماتِ مِنْ بِدعِ فُجورِهِ مَعَ زُمَرِ النِّساءِ الا ساءَ ما تُحلِّلونَ وما تُحَرِّمونَ.

2. Whenever you hear the instructions of **The True Gospel** you discard whatever displeases Satan and change the rest to please him. Accordingly, you distort the truth misguiding yourselves, your followers; even Our Own ungrounded righteous worshipers

٢) وإِما سَمِعْتُمْ آياتِ الإِنجيلِ الحَقِّ كَتَمْتُمْ ما ساءَ الشَّيطانَ وَحَرَّفْتُموهُ لِما يَسُرُّهُ فَأَسَأْتُمْ إِلى أَنفُسِكُمْ والى أَتباعِكُمْ والى عِبادِنا الصّالحينَ.

127

3. Having heard Our precepts you blatantly ignore them. Still, We stir your memory of such truths so that they will be a witness against you. Let him who has ears to hear listen attentively. Whosoever   divorces his wife, except for   the cause of her committing   adultery,   has committed   adultery   himself. Furthermore, whosoever marries a divorcee,   from   such   a relationship,   is guilty of adultery. His evil   deed is certainly considered a flagrant and vulgar deed.

٣) وَسَـمِعْتُمْ قَوْلَنَا وَتَأْسَـيْتُموهُ وَإِنَّا نُذَكِّرُكُمْ بِهِ كَيْ يَكُونَ ذَلِكَ عَلَيْكُمْ شَهِيدًا فَلْيَسْمَعِ الْيَوْمَ مَنْ لَهُ أُذْنَانِ تَسْمَعَانِ: مَنْ طَلَّقَ زَوْجَتَهُ إِلَّا لِزِنَاهَا فَقَدْ زَنَى وَمَنْ تَزَوَّجَ مُطَلَّقَةً فَقَدْ زَنَى وَكَانَ فِعْلُهُ كُفْرًا وَفُجْرًا .

4. Because of your love for gossip, you get lost from Our straight path and consider the entire revelation as a joke. Even when   verses from **The True Furqan** are recited in your hearing, you pretend to run away in disbelief as if you did not really hear anything. Is someone else whispering into your ears?

٤) وَتَنْشُرُونَ لَهْوَ الْحَدِيثِ فَتَضِلُّونَ عَـنْ سَـبِيلِنَا وَتَتَّخِذُونَـهُ هُـزُوًا وَإِذْ تُتْلَى عَلَيْكُمْ آيَاتُ الْفُرْقَانِ الْحَـقِّ وَلَّيْتُـمْ مُسْتَكْبِرِينَ كَأَنْ لَمْ تَسْمَعُوهَا كَأَنَّ فِي آذَانِكُمْ وَقْرًا .

5. You have hearts that do not comprehend, eyes that do not see and ears that do not hear. We denounce   the living who are

٥) فَلَكُمْ قُلُوبٌ لَا تَفْقَهُونَ بِهَا وَلَكُمْ أَعْيُنٌ لَا تُبْصِرُونَ بِهَا وَلَكُمْ آذَانٌ لَا

actually dead and have made out of their lives a rotten tomb!

تَسْمَعُونَ بِهَا فَتْبًا لِلْأَحْيَاءِ المَيِّتِينَ الذِينَ اتَّخذوا

مَنْ حَيَاتِهِمْ قَبْرًا .

6. As for Our faithful worshipers to whom We grant some inspiration, nothing of what takes place in the lives of the others of infidelity and estrangement ever takes place in theirs. Why? The reason is, the infidels are definitely on a crooked path, while Our followers are on the straight and narrow path.

٦) وإذْ أوْحينا إلى عبادِنا الصَّادِقينَ فَمَا حَالَ

بيْنَنَا وبينَهمْ مَا قَدْ حَالَ بينَنَا وبينكُمْ

مِنْ كُفْرٍ وضَلالٍ فإنَّكمْ عَلى صِراطٍ

ذِي عِوَجٍ وإنَّهمْ عَلى صِراطٍ مُسْتَقيمٍ .

7. We have not proclaimed that We will punish Our worshipers for their sins, without giving them an opportunity to repent. Why then did you announce that We had them executed at your hands?

٧) ومَا أوْحينا بِأنْ نأخذ عبادِنا بذنوبِهمْ

فَقتلناهمْ بأيديكمْ كما تزعمونَ .

8. You yourselves have forgiven your children for their wrongdoings, have you not? You have not destroyed them because of that; neither did you kill them. Is it conceivable that We would

٨) فإنَّما غَفَرتُمْ لأبنائكمْ ولمْ

تأخذوهمْ بذنوبِهمْ وكمْ تقتلوهمْ فأنَّى

نوحي بقتلِ عبادِنا ؟ ألسنا الغفَّارَ العفوَّ

order the death of Our spiritual dependents and off-spring? Are We not recognized as the Forgiver, the Forebearer and the Most Compassionate in the universe, as you yourselves testify? Is it possible that you would demonstrate a greater compassionate attitude toward your children than We would toward Our own?

وَأَرْحَمَ الرَّاحِمِينَ كَمَا تَرْعَمُونَ ؟ أَمْ كُنْتُمْ أَرْحَمَ بِأَبْنَائِكُمْ وَأَنْتُمُ الْمُجْرِمُونَ ؟ .

9. No one has any right to judge humankind, mete out condemnation upon them, kill them unlawfully and make himself a judge over the whole world. We Ourselves undertake this responsibility at the Day of Judgment!

٩) وَمَا كَانَ لِأَحَدٍ أَنْ يُدِينَ عِبَادَنَا وينزل بِهِمُ الْقِصَاصَ وَيَقْتُلَهُمْ ظُلْماً وِيُقِيمَ نَفْسَهُ دَيَّاناً لِلْعَالَمِينَ قَبْلَ يَوْمِ الدِّينِ .

10. We have created the living soul and We alone have the prerogative to take it away. No one has any right to share in Our authority of giving or taking anyone's life. Whosoever seeks to share Our authority is the worst polytheist and the most fallacious imposter.

١٠) إِنَّا وَهَبْنَا النَّفْسَ وَإِنَّا سَنَسْتَرِدُّهَا وَلَا شَرِيكَ لَنَا فِيمَا نَهَبُ وَفِيمَا نَسْتَرِدُّ وَمَنْ أَشْرَكَ نَفْسَهُ مُحَوِّلَنَا وَقْتَنَا فَهُوَ شَرُّ الْمُشْرِكِينَ وَأَكْفَرُ الْكَافِرِينَ .

11. Sooner or later you will definitely receive your just punishment for rejecting what was divinely revealed to you.

١١) وَسَتُجْزَوْنَ عَذَابَ الْهُوْنِ بِمَا كُنْتُمْ تَسْتَكْبِرُونَ .

12. You have utterly deceived yourselves and have even lost track of your long path of hypocrisy.

١٢) فَقَدْ كَذَّبْتُمْ عَلَى أَنْفُسِكُمْ وَضَلَّ عَنْكُمْ مَا كُنْتُمْ تَفْتَرُونَ .

27
ADULTERY
(Surat Al Zina')

٢٧) سُورةُالزنى

In the Name of the Father, the Word, the Holy Spirit, the One and only True God

بسم الآبِ الكلمةِ الروحِ الالهِ الواحدِ الأوحدِ

1. The parable of the true believer is like that of a man who constructed his house on the rock of love, purity and righteousness. When the storm came he emerged well-established and overcame with a grand victory.

١) وَمَثَلُ المؤمنِ كَمَثلِ رجلٍ أَسَّسَ بُنيانَهُ على صَخْرةِ المَحَبَّةِ والطهرِ والتقوى فظلَّ ثابتاً وفازَ بالنصرِ الكبيرِ .

2. The parable of the unbeliever, on the other hand, is like that of a man who constructed his house on the edge of a dry riverbed of murder, adultery and debauchery. When the storm came the house crashed with him into hellfire and a most horrific end.

٢) ومثلُ الكافرِ كمثلِ رجلٍ أَسَّسَ بُنيانَه على شفا جُرفٍ هارٍ مِنَ القتلِ والزنى والفجورِ فانهارَ بهِ في نارِ جَهنمَ فلاقى سوءَ المصيرِ .

3. O, corrupt generation from among Our deceived worshipers: you have maneuvered yourselves

٣) يا أهلَ السَّفاحِ مِنْ عِبادِنا الضَّالينَ : لقدْ

into immorality by taking to yourselves whomever you liked from among women—two, three or even four, plus whosoever you owned as slaves. By this principle, you have diametrically opposed Our decree in **The True Gospel**. In it We declared that whosoever looked at a woman with a lustful eye has committed adultery with her in his sick heart. And whosoever marries another woman besides his first living wife commits adultery and causes her to be involved in adultery and depravity.

دَفَعْتُمْ بِأَنْفُسِكُمْ إلى الزِّنى بِمَا طَابَ
لَكُمْ مِنَ النِّسَاءِ مَثْنَى وَثُلاثَ وَرُبَاعَ أَوْ مَا
مَلَكَتْ أَيْمَانُكُمْ فَعَارَضْتُمْ سُنَّتَنَا
فِي الإنْجِيلِ الْحَقِّ بِأَنَّ مَنْ نَظَرَ لامْرَأَةٍ بِعَيْنِ
الشَّهْوَةِ فَقَدْ زَنَى بِهَا فِي قَلْبِهِ السَّقِيمِ . وَمَنْ
أَشْرَكَ بِزَوْجَتِهِ أُخْرَى فَقَدْ زَنَى وَأَوْقَعَهَا
فِي الزِّنَى وَالْفُجُورِ .

4. Let the sinful individual put out his adulterous eye. It is preferable for him to enter paradise without an eye than to have his entire body thrust into the searing flames of Hell.

٤) فَلْيَفْقَأْ ذُو الْعَيْنِ الزَّانِيَةِ عَيْنَهُ فَخَيْرٌ لَهُ أَنْ يَدْخُلَ
الْجَنَّةَ أَعْوَرَ مِنْ أَنْ يُلْقَى كُلَّ جَسَدِهِ فِي
سَعِيرِ الْجَحِيمِ .

5. Therefore, stay away from immorality. It is an abomination as well as a corrupt pathway. An adulterer really hurts himself for he contaminates the purity of his body and in the end he becomes one of the regretful.

٥) فَاجْتَنِبُوا الزِّنَى إِنَّهُ كَانَ فَاحِشَةً وَسَاءَ
سَبِيلاً ، وَمَا أَضَرَّ الزَّانِي إِلاَّ بِنَفْسِهِ فَدَنَّسَ
طُهْرَ جَسَدِهِ وَأَصْبَحَ مِنَ النَّادِمِينَ .

6. It must be clearly understood that permitting the practice of marrying another wife is promoting adultery and depravity.

٦) وَتَحْلِيلُ الشِّرْكِ بِالزَّوجَةِ حَثٌّ عَلَى الزِّنى والفجورِ .

7. We have created mankind, in the very beginning, as only one husband and one wife—not four wives! Furthermore, We commanded our very loyal subjects, who cannot survive a life of celibacy, to marry only one wife.

٧) وخَلَقْنَا الإنسَانَ بدأ زوجاً فرداً وزوجةً فردةً لا أربعاً . وَوَصَّينَا بزوجةٍ واحدةٍ لِمَنْ لا يطيـقُ التَّبتّلَ مِنْ عِبادِنا المقرَّبينَ .

8. Surprisingly enough, you stoned the individuals who were caught in adultery as if you were totally innocent from such sins. Let it be proclaimed that whosoever is without sin throw the first stone.

٨) وَرَجمتـمُ الزناةَ كأنكـمْ أبرياءُ فمنْ يُبَرِّئُ نفسَهُ فليكـنْ أوّلَ الراجمينَ .

9. You also instructed people in purity and righteousness but forgot to practice what you preached. Again you forbade wickedness and oppression. Yet, you surfaced as the world's worst wicked oppressors. You have even invited others to be faithful

٩) وأمرتُـمُ النَّاسَ بالـبِرِّ والتَّقـوى ونسيتـمْ أنفسَكـمْ ونهيتـمْ عَن الإثـم والعُدوان وأنتـمُ الآثمونَ المعتدونَ ودَعوتُرْ إلى الإيمـان وأنتـمُ الكـافرونَ .

whereas you emerged as faithless.

10. Amazingly enough, you have smothered Truth with a robe of lies. You have hidden Our Scriptures that you might sell them and purchase something with them later! Your whole purpose is to fabricate lies against Us. Don't you realize that you cannot hide from Us?

١٠) وأَلبستُمُ الحقَّ بالباطل وكنتمُ سُتْنَا لَبْتَسَما اشترِيتُمْ به أنفسَكُمُ أنْ كفرُوا علينا وأنتُمْ تعلمونَ .

11. Furthermore, We have urged Our worshipers never to swear in Our name. Their reply should be simply "yes" or "no." Instead you declared that whosoever will swear should swear in the name of God or keep silent. Such a statement comes from reprobate sinners.

١١) وَوَصَّينا عبادَنا ألاَّ يحلفوا باسمِنا أبداً وجَوابهمُ نعمُ أوْلاَ . فقلتُمْ بأنَّ مَنْ كانَ حالفاً فليحلفْ باسمِ اللهِ أوْ يَصمتْ وَهذا قولُ الكفرةِ المارقينَ .

12. O, people everywhere: whosoever marries four women, adds a second wife to his first, divorces his wife without her committing adultery, marries a divorcee, or has a lustful eye and participates in a vile deed is considered an adulterer.

١٢) يأَيُّها الناسُ : لقدْ زنى مَنْ كانَ أحدَ أربعة : مُشرِكاً بزوجتِهِ أخرى . أوْ مُطلِّقها دونَ زِناها . أو زوَّج مُطلَّقةٍ . اوذا عينٍ زانية وفعل ذميم .

13. Therefore, We command you to be pure and not impure for We love the people of purity and modesty.

١٣) فكونوا أطهاراً لا زناة فإنّا نحبُّ الطاهرينَ .

28
THE TABLESPREAD
(Surat Al Maida)

٢٨) سورةُ المائدةِ

In the Name of the Father, the Word, the Holy Spirit, the One and only True God

بسمِ الآبِ الكلمةِ الروحِ الالهِ الواحدِ الأوحدِ

1.   We have brought down upon you the Living Bread out of Heaven. It is to be a celebration for the first and last among you. Whosoever repents and eats of it as a believer, his heart becomes contented and will not hunger again. We would also purify him and usher him into Our Gardens cheerful and grateful.

١) وأنزلنا عليكم مائدةً من السماءِ خبزاً حياً يكونُ لكم عيداً لأولكم وآخركم . فمَنْ تابَ وطعِمَ مؤمناً اطمأنَّ قلبُه ولنْ يجوعَ وطهرناهُ وأدخلناهُ جناتِنا راضياً مرضياً .

2.   Furthermore, We have caused pure and living drink to burst forth. There is healing for the souls of mankind in that drink. Whosoever repents and drinks from it trustfully will not thirst again. Moreover, We will definitely cleanse him and make him a

٢) وفجَّرنا لكم شراباً حياً طهوراً فيه شفاءٌ للنفوسِ فمنْ تابَ وشرِبَ مؤمناً لنْ يعطشَ وطهرناهُ فصارَ خلقاً نقياً .

purified vessel for Our glory.

3.   The upright shall partake from this cup which symbolizes the substance of redemption and the sinless blood of the Messiah.

٣) إنَّ الأبرارَ يَشْرَبُونَ مِنْ كَأْسٍ كَانَ مِزَاجُهَا فِدَاءً وَدَمَاً زَكِيّاً .

4.   Whosoever believes and eats of this bread and drinks at Our table, his soul will never hunger and his spirit will never thirst.   He will certainly turn into a redeemed creature of ours.

٤) فَمَنْ آمَنَ وَطَعِمَ وَشَرِبَ عَلَى مَائِدَتِنَا فَلَنْ تَجُوعَ نَفْسُهُ وَلَنْ تَعْطَشَ رُوحُهُ فَقَدْ صَارَ إِنْسَاً مَفْدِيّاً .

5.   The unbelieving, who do not trust Us, have erected between them and Us a barrier. They constructed it with their vile deeds, untruthful utterances and evil thoughts which debased their fellowman. Consequently, they have isolated themselves from Our Mercy, some voluntarily, others circumstantially.   Once they reached this eventuality they realized that the whole thing was deception and falsehood. Unfortunately, they oppressed themselves by their own choice.

٥) وَجَعَلَ الذِينَ كَفَرُوا بَيْنَنَا وَبَيْنَهُمْ سَدّاً شَيَّدُوهُ بِسُوءِ أَفْعَالِهِمْ وَإِفْكِ أَقْوَالِهِمْ وَخُبْثِ أَفْكَارِهِمْ وَكِبْرِ إِخْوَانِهِمْ فَحَجَبُوا أَنْفُسَهُمْ عَنْ رَحْمَتِنَا بِأَيْدِيهِمْ طَوْعاً أَوْ كُرْهاً فَظَلَمُوا أَنْفُسَهُمْ وَسَوْفَ يَلْقَوْنَ غَيّاً .

138

29
THE MIRACLES
(Surat Al Mu'jezat)

٢٩) سُورَةُ الْمُعجزاتِ

In the Name of the Father, the Word, the Holy Spirit, the One and only True God

بسم الآبِ الكلمةِ الروحِ الالهِ الواحدِ الأوحدِ

1. Our believing worshipers proclaimed, "This is an authentic **True Furqan** confirming what is already in our possession in **The True Gospel**. It is an illuminating light and a covenant for our age, proving that we are anchored upon genuine religion."

١) وقال عبادُنا المؤمنونَ: "إنَهُ لَفرقانٌ حقٌّ مُصدقٌ لِما بينَ أيدينا منَ الإنجيلِ الحقِّ . نورٌ على نورٍ وَميثاقٌ لِعَهدنا بأنّا على الدينِ القيِّمِ مقيمونَ .

2. Those who become enlightened and believe announce, "O, that we had been enlightened beforehand. We wish that our ancestors had glimpsed a shaft of this light, enlightened just as we are and had not died as pagans."

٢) وقال الذينَ آمنوا واهْتدَوا : "يا ليتنا اهتدينا منْ قبلِ وليتَ آباءَنا قبسوا منْ هَذا النورِ واهتـدوا مثلمـا اهتدينـا ومـا ماتوا كـافرينَ" .

3. As for the people who mask their eyes with the curtain

٣) أمّا الذينَ طَمسوا على عيونهمْ بأسْجَافِ

of infidelity, confusion, ignorance and arrogance, they are
definitely the party of Satan and
destined for the Abyss.

الكفرِ والضلالِ والجهلِ والغرورِ فأولئكَ
هُمْ حزبُ الشيطانِ وأصحابُ الجحيمِ .

4. The depraved people will
counter the believer's statement, "Had this **True Furqan**
originated from God, He would
have authenticated it with a
supernatural sign from Him.
Then, we would have been
among the believers."

٤) وسيقولُ السُّفهاءُ من الناسِ : "لو كانَ هذا
الفُرقانُ من عندِ اللهِ لأيدهُ بآيةٍ من عنده
ولكنّا به من المؤمنينَ" .

5. O, people everywhere:
We have indeed authenticated it
with signs and wonders.
Humankind, demons, along
with the polytheists and infidels
acknowledged that the
scriptures are infallible and
reliable for faith and practice.

٥) يأيها الناسُ إنّا أيدناهُ بآياتٍ ومعجزاتٍ أقرَّ بها
الإنسُ والجانُّ والشيطانُ وأهلُ الشِرك
والكفرانِ .

6. Respond, if you please!
Did We not heal the deaf-mute
and the leper? Did We not raise
the dead to life and feed the
thousands? What other signs
besides these do you demand?

٦) أما شفينا الأكمَهَ والأبرصَ وأحيينا
الموتى وأشبعنا الجياعَ آلافاً ؟ فأيَّ آيةٍ غبَّ
ذلك تطلبونَ ؟ وبأيِّ آلاتنا تكذِّبونَ ؟

7. We have inspired **The True Furqan**, affirming what We proclaimed in **The True Gospel**. It is intended to refresh the memory of the infidels. Therefore, Our criterion is one. Our scripture is one. We do not alter it in **The True Gospel** nor in **The True Furqan**. Even time and space cannot change it. Neither the hypocrites nor the conspirators can abrogate it.

٧)إِنَّا أَنزَلْنَاهُ فُرْقَاناً حَقّاً مُصَدّقاً لِقَوْلِنا فِي الإِنْجِيلِ الْحَقِّ ومُذَكِّراً لِلْكَافِرِينَ فَسُنَّتنا واحِدَةٌ وآيَاتنا واحِدَةٌ لا نُبدِّلُها فِي إِنْجِيلٍ حَقٍّ أَوْ فِي فُرْقَانٍ حَقٍّ ولا يُغَيِّرُها زَمانٌ أَوْ مَكانٌ ولا يَنْسَخُها الثَّقَلانِ ولا أَهْلُ الضَّلالِ والبُهتَانِ .

8. Hence, **The True Furqan**'s objective is to return us to the fundamentals. It is unvarying from **The True Gospel**. It is reverberation of the echo. It is a proclamation to all peoples. It is a wake-up call to the infidels. Additionally, it is light, compassion, good news, warning and right instruction for those who have gone astray; perchance, they would recollect the Truth and be spiritually enlightened.

٨) عَوْدٌ على بَدءٍ وِصْلُ الإِنْجِيلِ الْحَقِّ وَرَجْعُ الصَّدى وبِيانٌ لِلنَّاسِ كَافّةً وتذكِرَةٌ لِلْكَافِرينَ ونورٌ ورحمَةٌ وبِشِيرٌ ونَذِيرٌ وهُدى لِلضَّالِينَ لَعَلَّهُمْ يَذكَّرونَ ويَهتَدونَ .

141

30
THE HYPOCRITES
(Surat Al Munafiqeen)

٣٠) سُورةُالمنافقين

In the Name of the Father, the Word, the Holy Spirit, the One and only True God

بسـمِ الآبِ الكلمةِ الروحِ الالهِ الواحدِ الأوحدِ

1.   O, you who are hypocrites from among Our misled worshipers: Satan has vowed that he would make himself attractive to everyone who dwells on the earth. For he is a seducer and none follow him except the seduced.

١) يَأَيُّهَا المُنَافِقونَ مِنْ عِبَادِنا الضَّالِينَ: لقـدْ أقْسَـمَ الشَّيطانُ لَـيُزيِّنَنَّ لَكُـمْ فِـي الأرضِ جَميعـاً فـهوَغـاوٍ وَلا يَتْبَعُـهُ إلا الغاوونَ .

2.   You counterfeited and Satan did counterfeit but Satan is the unequalled counterfeiter.

٢) ومَكَـرْتُمْ وَمَكَـرَ الشَّـيطانُ والشيطانُ خيرُ المَاكرِينَ .

3.   Consequently, subtly he escorted each of you to the Abyss.

٣) وَأوْرَدَكُـمْ جَهَنَّـمَ جَميعـاً وإنْ مِنكُـمْ إلا وارِدُها وكـانَ عليهِ أمْراً مَقضِياً .

4.   Yet, he has no authority over those who love and lean on Us. Satan's authority is solely over those who trust his decree and follow his dishonest messengers.

٤) وَمَا كَانَ لَهُ مِنْ سُلْطَانٍ عَلَى الذِينَ آمَنُوا مِنْ عِبَادِنَا وَعَلَيْنَا يَتَوَكَّلُونَ، إِنَّمَا سُلْطَانُهُ عَلَى الذِينَ آمَنُوا بِسُنَّتِهِ وَاتَّبَعُوا رُسُلَهُ الكَاذِبِينَ.

5.   As a result, whosoever rebels against Us, subsequent to his trusting Us, and spreads his heart wide open to blasphemy, horrific terror awaits him. Because an impostor prefers the temporal life over the eternal, he shall be punished for certain.

٥) فَمَنْ كَفَرَ بِنَا مِنْ بَعْدِ إِيمَانِهِ وَشَرَحَ بِالكُفْرِ صَدْرًا فَلَهُ عَذَابٌ رَهِيبٌ ذَلِكَ أَنَّهُ اسْتَحَبَّ الحَيَاةَ الدُّنْيَا عَلَى الآخِرَةِ وَسَيُجْزَى القَوْمُ الكَافِرُونَ.

6.   Hypocrites, Satan has sealed your hearts, ears and eyes. Accordingly, you are an unenlightened people. It is no surprise that at the end you yourselves are the vanquished.

٦) وَطَبَعَ الشَّيْطَانُ عَلَى قُلُوبِكُمُ وَسَمْعِكُمُ وَأَبْصَارِكُمُ فَأَنْتُمْ قَوْمٌ لَا تَفْقَهُونَ. لَا جَرَمَ أَنَّكُمْ فِي الآخِرَةِ أَنْتُمُ الخَاسِرُونَ.

7.   Satan has messengers who disclose things to each other; and hold secret discussions with each other. They also conspire

٧) وَلِلشَّيْطَانِ رُسُلٌ يُوحِي بَعْضُهُمْ لِبَعْضٍ وَيُسِرُّونَ النَّجْوَى وَيَسْخَادَعُونَ بُوحِي

evil intentions by the spell of the vile whisperer, Satan.

وَسْوَاسٍ خَنَّاسٍ رَجِيمٍ .

8. He tosses animosity and hate in their midst persistently; until the day when they discover the correct path. Each time the hypocrites ignite the fire of infidelity We snuff it out. Although they spread corruption throughout the earth constantly, destruction awaits the corrupters eventually.

٨) يُلقِي بَيْنَهُمُ الْعَدَاوَةَ وَالْبَغْضَاءَ إِلَى يَوْمِ يَهْتَدُونَ كُلَّمَا أُوْقَدُوا آثَارَ الْكَفَرِ أَطْفَأْنَاهَا وَيَسْعَوْنَ فِي الأَرْضِ فَسَادًا فَوَيْلٌ لِلْمُفْسِدِينَ .

9. Because of such tactics the hearts of the hypocrites from among Our worshipers become hardened.

٩) وَقَسَتْ قُلُوبُ الَّذِينَ كَفَرُوا مِنْ عِبَادِنَا وَزَيَّنَ لَهُمُ الشَّيْطَانُ مَا كَانُوا يَعْمَلُونَ .

10. Unfortunately, they forget what they are supposed to remember. Instead, they revert to what they were forbidden from doing and are transformed into fanatical hypocrites.

١٠) وَنَسَوْا مَا ذُكِّرُوا بِهِ فَعَادُوا لِمَا نُهُوا عَنْهُ وَإِنَّهُمْ لَكَاذِبُونَ .

11. Their so-called good deeds are as the mirage of the desert. The thirsty takes it for water, when it is not. For when

١١) أَعْمَالُهُمْ كَسَرَابٍ بِقِيعَةٍ يَحْسَبُهُ الظَّمْآنُ مَاءً وَمَا هُوَ بِمَاءٍ فَإِذَا جَاءَهُ خَابَ

he arrives at the spot his hope vanishes away. He ends up with the retribution of the disappointed, even thirstier than before.

سَعْيُهُ وَلَقِيَ جَزَاءَ الْخَائِنِينَ .

12.   However, those who believe in **The True Gospel** and **The True Furqan** and have demonstrated their faith by practicing righteous deeds; we shall let them inherit the earth. We shall also establish for them the True Religion and shall exchange their fear for faith. Anybody who turns down all of these promises would certainly be a deranged entity.

١٢) وَالَّذِينَ آمَنُوا بِالإِنْجِيلِ الْحَقِّ وَالْفُرْقَانِ الْحَقِّ وَعَمِلُوا الصَّالِحَاتِ لَنَسْتَخْلِفَنَّهُمْ فِي الأَرْضِ وَلَنُمَكِّنَنَّ لَهُمْ دِينَ الْحَقِّ وَلَنُبَدِّلَنَّهُمْ مِنْ بَعْدِ خَوْفِهِمْ أَمْناً . وَمَنْ كَفَرَ بَعْدَ ذَلِكَ فَأُولَئِكَ هُمُ الْفَاسِقُونَ .

13.   O, you who have believed from among Our followers: each time you call upon Us We shall respond to you accordingly. As for the prayers of the hypocrites concerning you, We shall not respond in like manner, because you are the righteous.

١٣) يَأَيُّهَا الَّذِينَ آمَنُوا مِنْ عِبَادِنَا : إِذَا رَفَعَنَا دُعَاءً فَإِنَّهُ يُسْتَجَابُ لَكُمْ فِيهِمْ وَلَا يُسْتَجَابُ لَهُمْ فِيكُمْ فَأَنْتُمُ الْمُقْسِطُونَ وَهُمُ الْمُبْطِلُونَ .

14. If the riches of the hypocrites were offered they will not be an acceptable substitute for their redemption. Even if they sacrificed their young children, such a valuable offering will not count, for they are destined for Hell. Satan has captured them, caused them to forget the memory of Our personage and turned them into his intimate supporters.

١٤) ولن تُغنِي عَنهُمْ أَموالُهُمْ ولا أَوْلادُهُمْ مِنَّا شيئاً أُولئكَ أَصْحابُ النَّارِ اسْتحوذَ عليهِمُ الشَّيطانُ فأَنساهُمْ ذِكرَنا فهُمْ حِزبُهُ المُقرَّبونَ .

15. Whenever it is declared to the hypocrites, "Repent and God will pardon you," they turn their heads and back away in apparent arrogance. As far as they are concerned, it makes no difference to them whether anyone attempts to guide them or not, they refuse to trust in The Truth, Jesus the Messiah!

١٥) وإذا قِيلَ للذينَ كفروا : تُوبوا يُتَبْ عَليكُمْ لَوَّوا رؤوسَهُمْ وصَدّوا وهُمْ مُستكبرونَ وسَواءٌ عليهِمْ أهديتَهُمْ أَمْ لَمْ تَهدِهِمْ فهُمْ لا يُؤمنونَ .

16. Their perception of Us is inaccurate. The hypocrites do not stay clear of cruelty and iniquity, but also follow after suppositions and false imaginations of the mind.

١٦) يَظنونَ بِنا غيرَ الحقِّ ولا يجتنبونَ كبائرَ الإثمِ والفواحشَ وإنْ يَتبعونَ إلا الظَّنَ وإنْ هُمْ إلا يَخرُصونَ .

17.   Furthermore, the men and women who are hypocrites expect depravity from each other, the cessation of kind deeds and the clenching of their fists when it comes to giving to the poor. They have abandoned Us, therefore virtue has abandoned them. Subsequently, they are crushed by their folly.

١٧) اَلْمُنَافِقُونَ وَالْمُنَافِقَاتُ بَعْضُهُمْ مِنْ بَعْضٍ

يَأْمُرُونَ بِالْمُنْكَرِ وَيَنْهَوْنَ عَنِ الْمَعْرُوفِ

وَيَقْبِضُونَ أَيْدِيَهُمْ نَسُوا فَنَسِيَهُمُ الْخَيْرُ

فَهُمْ فِي ضَلاَلِهِمْ يَرْتَعُونَ .

31
MURDER
(Surat Al Qatl)

٣١) سُورَةُ القتل

In the Name of the Father, the Word, the Holy Spirit, the One and only True God

بسم الآبِ الكلمةِ الروح الإله الواحدِ الأوحدِ

1. O, you who have reviled us from among our followers: whosoever slays a soul and causes corruption in the earth has practically slain the entire race of humans at the same time. We have come to you with clear instructions concerning these matters. Yet, most of you, even after such instructions, are evildoers.

١) يَأَيُّها الذينَ كَفرُوا مِنْ عِبادِنا : مَنْ قَتَلَ نَفْساً وَعاثَ في الأرضِ فَساداً فكأنَّما قَتَلَ الناسَ جَميعاً . وَقَدْ جِنّاكُمْ بِالبَيِّناتِ ثُمَّ إنَّ أكثرَكُمْ بَعدَ ذلكَ مُجرِمونَ .

2. Religion is never to be enforced by the sword upon those who have gone astray. "There is no compulsion in religion." For if there is, the hypocrites can unjustly control the believers!

٢) وَما كانَ الدينُ القيِّمُ إكراهاً على الكفرِ بالسيفِ فلا إكراهَ في الدينِ فأنَّى يَهْدي الكافرونَ المؤمنينَ ؟ .

٣) يَا أَيُّهَا النَّاسُ إِنَّا نَأْمُرُ بِالْمَحَبَّةِ وَالرَّحْمَةِ وَالْإِحْسَانِ وَالْعَدْلِ وَالسَّلَامِ وَإِيتَاءِ عِبَادِنَا وَالْمُؤْمِنِينَ وَنَنْهَى عَنْ سَفْكِ الدِّمَاءِ وَالزِّنَى وَالْفَحْشَاءِ وَالْمُنْكَرِ وَالْبَغْيِ لَعَلَّكُمْ لَعَلَّكُمْ تَذَكَّرُونَ .

3. O, people everywhere: We command that love, compassion, charity, justice and peace be practiced, and that goodwill should rule Our worshipers and those who believe. Furthermore, We forbid shedding of blood, adultery, fornication, outrageous immorality and rape. We admonish you accordingly; perchance you will remember these commands continuously.

٤) فَكَفَرْتُمْ وَاتَّبَعْتُمْ خَطُوَاتِ الشَّيْطَانِ فَإِنَّهُ يَأْمُرُ بِالْفَحْشَاءِ وَالْمُنْكَرِ وَالْبَغْيِ وَمَا زَكَى مِنْكُمْ مِنْ أَحَدٍ فَأَنْتُمْ بِالْكُفْرِ غَارِقُونَ .

4. Instead, you choose to go astray and follow the footsteps of Satan. He is the one who commands killing, adultery, fornication, outrageous immorality and rape. None of you is without sin; but you are totally immersed in hypocrisy.

٥) وَاعْتَدَيْتُمْ عَلَى بُيُوتٍ أَذِنَّا أَنْ تُرْفَعَ وَيُذْكَرَ فِيهَا اسْمُنَا وَهَدَمْتُمْ كَنَائِسَ وَبِيَعاً يُسَبَّحُ لَنَا فِيهَا بِالْغُدُوِّ وَالْآصَالِ وَسَعَيْتُمْ لِخَرَابِهَا وَقَتَلْتُمْ الْقَانِتِينَ الْمُؤْمِنِينَ مِنْ عِبَادِنَا وَتِلْكَ أَفْعَالُ الْمُجْرِمِينَ .

5. You have assaulted houses of worship which were built and dedicated to call upon Our name. You have destroyed church properties where We are to be praised morning and night. You, in fact, continued your endeavor to dismantle such buildings, killing at the same time the upright and faithful of Our

followers, disregarding Our commands against such activities which turns anyone into a blatant apostate.

6. As for those who do not add associates to Us, do not murder their fellowman, which We have outlawed outright, do not commit adultery, do not add partners to their spouses, have trusted in Us wholeheartedly and have done righteous deeds—those are the very ones whose vile deeds We have removed. Why? Because they have heartily and truly repented.

٦) والذين لا يُشركون رَبَّنا ولا يَقْتُلونَ النفسَ التي حَرَّمْنا قَتلَها تَحريماً ولا يزنونَ ولا يُشركون بأزواجِهمْ أحداً وَعَمِلوا صالحاً فأُولئك نبدّلُ سَيّئاتِهِم وتابوا مَتاباً صادقاً .

7. O, you who have gone astray from among Our creatures had you believed **The True Gospel** and practiced its instructions, We would have redeemed you from your sinfulness and ushered you to the entrance which leads to unnumbered blessings and abundant life.

٧) يَا أيها الذين كَفَروا مِنْ عِبادِنا لَوْ أنَّكمْ آمنتُم بالإنجيل الحقِّ واتَّقيتُمْ لكفَّرْنا عَنكمْ سَيّئاتِكمْ وأدخلناكمْ مَدخلاً كريماً .

8. Had you established **The True Gospel** and what We

٨) ولوْ أقَمْتُمُ الإنجيل الحقَّ وما أنزلنا مِنَ

150

conveyed through **The True Furqan**, as a substantiation of what was already in his hands, then Heaven above would have rained upon you overwhelming mercy and earth below would have flooded you with overflowing blessings.

الفُرقانُ الحَقُّ مُصَدِّقاً لِمَا بِينَ يَدَيهِ لَأَمطَرَنَكُمُ السَّمَاءُ بِالرَّحمةِ وَلَفَاضَتْ بِكُمُ الأَرضُ خَيراً عَميماً.

9. Alas, instead you rejected Our signs and became haughty. Thus, you turned into virtual hypocrites.

٩) لكِنَّكُمْ كَذَّبتُمْ بِآياتِنَا وَاستَكبَرتُمْ فَكُنتُمْ مِنَ الكَافِرينَ.

10. Furthermore, you fought Our believing followers, abused them severely, murdered their men, but kept their women alive for your sensual pleasure. You even murdered their children, caused atrocities in the earth and robbed the very morsels of food from the mouths of orphans and the poverty-stricken.

١٠) وَجَاهَدتُمْ عِبَادَنَا المُؤمِنينَ وَأَغلَظتُمْ عَليهِمْ وَقَتَلتُمْ رِجَالَهُمْ وَاستَحيَيتُمْ نِسَاءَهُمْ وَذَبَحتُمْ أَبنَاءَهُمْ وَأَفسَدتُمْ فِي الأَرضِ وَسَلَبتُمْ أَقوَاتَ اليَتَامَى وَالمَسَاكِينِ.

11. Satan has urged you on. When you murdered people he exonerated you and accused Us of such atrocities. You believed him when he announced, "You have not killed them, but God has

١١) وَحَرَّضَكُمُ الشَّيطانُ فَقَتَلتُمْ فَبَرَّأَكُمْ وَاتَّهَمَنَا فَصَدَّقتُمُوهُ إِذْ تَلا: "وَلَمْ تَقتُلُوهُمْ وَلَكِنَّ اللهَ قَتَلَهُمْ". لا

151

killed them." Do not come up with an excuse. You certainly have gone astray. You have, with your own hands committed murder. You have become worse than the Devil himself in apostasy and in committing atrocities.

تَعَـٰذِرُوا قَـٰدْ كَفَرْتُـٰمْ فَقَتَلْتُـٰمْ بِأَيدِيكُـٰمْ فَكُنتُـٰمْ أَشَـٰدَّ مِنَ الشيطان كَفْرًا وفجورًا .

12. You have also absolved your souls, souls that are prone to performing evil, then accused Us as the prime mover behind the dastardly deeds. Then you recited, "You did not actually conspire but God did conspire." Such declaration is a blatant lie.

(١٢) وَبَرَّأْتُـٰمْ أَنْفُسَكُـٰمُ الأَمّارَةَ بِالسُّوءِ وَرَمَيتُمونا بِالجُرمِ إِذْ كَلَّوْثَ : "وَمَا رَمَيتَ إِذْ رَمَيتَ وَلَكِنَّ اللهَ رَمَى" . فَكَـٰانَ إِفكًا كَبِيرًا .

13. You have conspired with Satan and Satan conspired with you. The end result was that you have collaborated with each other to demoralize humanity. You have become stout supporters of each other in this vile conspiracy.

(١٣) وَرَمَيتُـٰمْ بِيَـٰدِ الشَّيطانِ وَرَمَى الشَّيطانُ بِأَيدِيكُـٰمْ فَكَـٰانَ بَعضُكُـٰمْ لِبعضٍ فِي الكُفرِ ظَهيرًا وَنصيرًا .

14. Sooner or later everyone will discover that traitors will deceive only themselves. Every blaspheming traitor will be totally humiliated at the finish line.

(١٤) وَمَا يَختانُ الكافرونَ إِلّا أَنفُسَهُـٰمْ وَقَدْ ذَلَّ مَنْ كَانَ خَوّانًا كَفورًا .

15. Let the whole world know that whosoever murders a believer intentionally and premeditatively, his punishment will be Hell, not Heaven, as he is deceptively told. And in the bottomless pit he will dwell forever.

١٥) وَمَنْ يَقْتُلْ مُؤْمِنًا قَاصِدًا وَمُتَعَمِّدًا

فَجَزَاؤُهُ جَهَنَّمُ خَالِدًا فِيهَا وَسَيُصْلَى

سَعِيرًا .

32
THE TRIBUTE
(Surat Al Jezyah)

بسم الآب الكلمة الروح الاله الواحد
الأوحد

In the Name of the Father, the Word, the Holy Spirit, the One and only True God

١) يَأَيُّهَا الذينَ كَفَرُوا مِنْ عِبَادِنَا هَا أَنْتُمْ
أُولَاءِ اتَّبَعْتُمُ الضَّلَالَ وَرَغِبْتُمْ عَنِ الْحَقِّ
وَاقْتَرَفْتُمُ الإِثْمَ وَأَسَأْتُمْ إِلَى
أَنْفُسِكُمْ فَلِمَ نَذَرْكُمْ لِتُفْسِدُوا
فِي الأَرْضِ، تَقُولُونَ "سَمِعْنَا وَأَطَعْنَا" وَمَا
سَمِعْتُمْ كَلِمَتَنَا وَمَا أَطَعْتُمْ أَمْرَنَا بَلْ
أَطَعْتُمُ الشَّيْطَانَ وَاتَّخَذْتُمُوهُ وَلِيًّا مِنْ دُونِنَا
وَلَا يُطِيعُ الشَّيْطَانَ إِلَّا الْقَوْمُ الْكَافِرُونَ .

1. O, you who have gone astray, yet still claim to be counted among Our faithful followers: behold you have become loyal followers of deception and have gone astray from the Truth. You have implemented deception willingly and have been mortally affected. We have not created you to cause corruption in the earth. You substantiate that with, "We have heard God's Word and we have been obedient." Yet you have neither heard Our Word nor obeyed Our command. Instead, you have obeyed the Devil and have taken him as your protector apart from Us. None submits to Satan except the pagans.

2. You have pronounced that Abraham and the disciples of Jesus testified that they are followers of your creed. How can they ever testify concerning your creed which was not known to them nor has crossed their minds? In fact, they believe in Us and have kept Our divine precepts. Moreover, they are liberated from the blasphemy of the imposters and certainly do not participate in fabrication.

٢) وقُلتُم : بـأنّ إبراهيـــمَ والحوارِيـينَ شَهِدوا بأنّهـمْ عَلى مِلتِكُــمْ فـأنّى يَشهَدونَ بِما ليسَ لَهُـمْ بِهِ علـمٌ ولا خطَرَ لهـمْ عَلى بـالٍ فهُـمْ بِنـا مؤمِنونَ ولِسُنَّتِنا حَافِظونَ وهُـمْ بُرَاءُ مِنْ كُفرِ المُفتَرِينَ وما يأفِـكـونَ .

3. Only those people who have surrendered their thoughts, words, deeds, leadership, trusted Our Word, followed Our divine precepts, as enunciated in **The True Gospel**, and believed in **The True Furqan** are Our loyal subjects indeed. As for those who have turned away from Our divine creed, renounced Us and trusted Satan, the cursed one, obviously they have become ensnared in his trap.

٣) إنّ الذينَ سَلّموا لَنا أفكـارَهُـمْ وأقوالَهـمْ وأفعَالَهـمْ وقِيادَهـمْ ووجوهَهُمْ مُخلِصينَ وسَمِعوا كَلِمَتَنا واتّبعوا سُنّتَنا في الإنجيلِ الحقِّ وآمنوا بالفُرقانِ الحقِّ هُـمْ عِبادُنا المخلِصونَ أمّا الذينَ أعرَضوا عَنْ سُنّتِنا فقدْ كَفَروا بِنا وآمنوا بالشّيطانِ الرّجيـمِ فهُـمْ لأمرِهِ مُسلّمونَ .

4. Our worshipers and those who depend on Us are not

٤) عِبادُنا عِيَالُنا لا نُفرِّقُ بينَ أحدٍ مِنهُـمْ

155

differentiated from each other by Us except by faith, good works and righteousness. They are all children of the same father and mother. Some believe and some do not. But those who see Our Light will also discover Our way because it is the perfect path to abundant life.

إلاَّ بالإيمانِ والعمَلِ الصّالِحِ والتّقوى فهُمْ إخوَةٌ لأبٍ واحدٍ وأمٍّ واحدةٍ فمنهُمْ مَنْ آمَنَ ومنهُمْ مَنْ ضَلَّ وسَيَهدي مَنْ يُبصِرُ نُورَنا فهوَ السّبيلُ الحقُّ وإلينا المَصيرُ.

5.   The imposters waged war against Our servants with the edge of the sword. Some of Our people were willing to surrender to unbelief for fear of being cut down by the sword. Others were spared when they were forced to surrender to untruthfulness. Tragically such individuals had to abandon the True Way.

٥) وحَمَّلَ الذينَ كفروا على عِبادِنا بالسيفِ فمنهُمْ مَنِ استَسلَمَ للكُفرِ خَوفَ السَّيفِ والرَّدى فآمَنَ بالطّاغوتِ مُكرَهاً فَسلِمَ وضَلَّ سَبيلاً.

6.   Some of them kept the True Religion by paying a heavy tribute. Still the aggressors forced them to submission and humiliation.

٦) ومنهُمْ مَنِ اشتَرى دينَ الحقِّ بالجزيَةِ عَنْ يَدٍ صاغِراً ذَليلاً.

7.   True religion, however, has never been on the sale block for open bidding—except the religion of the hypocrites. Even

٧) وما كانَ الدينُ سِلعةً إلاَّ دينُ الكافرينَ يَشتَرونَ بهِ ثمناً قَليلاً.

156

then such a religion is worthless.

8.   Furthermore, the believers who determined to hold on to the True Faith were slain by the sword.   By claiming that these people were killed in the cause of God, you considered such an atrocity as a glorious victory for Us!

٨) وَمِنهُمْ مَنْ تَمَسَّكَ بِالدِّينِ الْحَقِّ فَقَتَلُوهُ
فِي سَبِيلِنَا وَعَدُّوا ذَلِكَ لَنَا نَصْرًا مُبِينًا .

9.   Killing was never an inspired command to compel people to accept Our rightly-guided way.   Neither have We ever declared that those who kill Our faithful followers are championed by Us.   It is Satan who enunciates such fanciful instructions and achieves such outrageous victories.

٩) وَمَا كَانَ الْقَتْلُ سَبِيلَنَا وَمَا نَصَرْنَا مَنْ
قَتَلَ عِبَادَنَا الْمُؤْمِنِينَ بَلْ نَصَرَ الشَّيْطَانَ وَجَاءَ
أَمْرًا نُكْرًا .

10. You have falsely declared that We have announced, "You are not responsible for their guidance, for We Ourselves guide whomever We wish or misguide whomever We wish."   Such statements are only fabrications.

١٠) وافتَرَيْتُمْ عَلَى لِسَانِنَا الْكَـذِبَ
فَقُلْـتُمْ : "لَيْسَ عَلَيْكَ هُدَاهُـمْ وَلَكِنَّـا
نَهْدِي مَنْ نَشَاءُ وَنُضِـلُّ مَـنْ نَشَاءُ" .
فَكَانَ قَوْلًا نُكْرًا .

11. For if your declarations were the Truth, you certainly would neither have murdered Our believing followers by the edge of the sword, nor have forced those whom you have kept alive into bondage and depravity.

١١) فَلَوصَدَقَ قَولُكُمْ لَمَا قَتَلْتُمْ عِبَادَنا المُهتَدِينَ بِالسَّيفِ وَدَفَعتُمْ مِن اسْتَحْيَيْتُمْ لِلبَغِي وَالكُفرِ قَسْراً .

12. You have falsified that We have announced, "Fight those who do not follow the True Religion from among those who were given the Book until they pay the tribute underhanded and have become surrendered and humble."

١٢) وَزَعَمْتُمْ بِأَنَّا قُلْنَا : "قَاتِلوا الذِينَ لاَ يَدِينونَ دِينَ الحَقِّ مِنَ الذِينَ أُوتوا الكِتابَ حَتَّى يُعطوا الجِزيَةَ عَن يَدٍ وَهُمْ صَاغِرونَ صُغْراً" .

13. O, you who have gone astray from among Our followers: true religion is the religion of **The True Gospel** and **The True Furqan** following it. Whosoever desires any other religion will not be recognized by Us, for he has renounced the True Religion outright.

١٣) يَأَهلَ الضَّلالِ مِن عِبادِنا : إِنَّما دِينُ الحَقِّ هُوَ دِينُ الانجِيلِ الحَقِّ وَالفُرقانِ الحَقِّ مِن بعدِهِ فَمَنِ ابتَغَى غَيرَ ذلكَ دِيناً فَلَنْ يُقبَل مِنهُ فَقد كَفَرَ بدِينِ الحَقِّ كُفراً .

14. The believers in the True Religion were forced to purchase

١٤) وَقَدِ اشْتَرى الذِينَ آمَنوا دِينَ الحَقِّ

their liberty with their lives, property or illegal tribute. Nevertheless, those who are deemed faithful will be rewarded openly.

بأرواحهـم وأموالهـم أو بجزيـة الظلـم

وسيجزى المخلصون منهـم أجرهـم

جهرًا.

33
LYING
(Surat Al Ifk)

٣٣) سُورةُ الإفكِ

In the Name of the Father, the Word, the Holy Spirit, the One and only True God

بسمِ الآبِ الكلمةِ الروحِ الإله الواحدِ الأوحدِ

1. We have conveyed it, a True Arabic Furqan, articulating its verses with wisdom. No mischief can result from its pages from cover to cover. In it we conveyed to people illustrations of all sorts, perchance they will remember what We proclaimed to them long ago.

١) إنا أنزلناهُ فُرقاناً عَربياً فَصّلنا آياتِه عَلى علمٍ . لا يأتيهِ الباطلُ مِن بينِ يَديهِ ولا مِن خلفِهِ وضربنا فيهِ للناسِ مِن كلِّ مثلٍ لعلهمْ يتذكرونَ .

2. We sent **The True Furqan** to Our worshipers who have gone astray. Our hope is that through **The True Furqan** most of them will find the True Way.

٢) بَشيراً ونذيراً لعبادِنا الضالينَ وإنَّ أكثرَهُمْ سَيَهدونَ .

3. Whenever Satan wants to mislead a particular people, he deviously gets control of a

٣) إنَّ الشيطانَ إذا أرادَ أنْ يُضلَّ قَوماً

160

brilliant but illiterate person from among them, then bamboozles him who in turn beguiles his own people. Satan also glamorizes their evil deeds, thus, easily misleading them. Surprisingly, with their illusory lives they are completely content.

استَحوَذَ عَلى أُمّيٍ مِنهُمْ فأغواهُ فأغوى قَومَهُ وزَيّنَ لهُمْ سُوءَ أعمالِهِمْ فأضَلّهُمْ وَهُـمْ بِضلالِهِمْ فَرِحُونَ .

4. Yet, Satan has led them headlong into a burning fire. They blindly march into it unawares.

٤) وأورَدَهُـمْ نـارَ آلظّى وَهُـمْ لا يَشعُرونَ .

5. We have cautioned Our believing worshipers concerning counterfeit prophets and Satanic verses.

٥) وحَذّرِنا عِبادَنا المؤمنينَ مِنَ الأنبِياءِ الأفّاكينَ ومِنْ رُسُلِ الشّياطينِ .

6. We admonished, "Such are in fact wolves in sheep's clothing. They cover up what can normally be quite obvious."

٦) ذِئابٌ فِي جُلودِ حِمْلانٍ يُبطِنونَ مَا لا يُظهِرونَ .

7. Furthermore, they announce with their tongues what is not truly within their hearts. "From the fruits of their labors

٧) يَقولونَ بألسِنتِهِمْ مَا ليسَ فِي قُلوبِهِمْ ومِنْ ثِمارِ أفعالِهِمْ يُعرِفونَ .

161

they shall surely be known."

8. Delicious feasting comes from the fruit of a good tree. Unsavory fruit is the product of a bad tree. Therefore, a good tree will not produce vile fruit; neither will the unsavory tree produce good fruit.

٨) إِنَّمَا الأَكْلُ الطَّيِّبُ مِنَ الشَّجَرَةِ الطَّيِّبَةِ وَالأَكْلُ الْخَبِيثُ مِنَ الشَّجَرَةِ الْخَبِيثَةِ . فَلا تُؤْتِي شَجَرَةٌ طَيِّبَةٌ أَكْلاً خَبِيثاً وَلا الْخَبِيثَةُ طَيِّباً .

9. Every tree which will not bring forth good fruit will absolutely be cut down and used as fuel for burning.

٩) كُلُّ شَجَرَةٍ لا تُؤْتِي أَكْلاً طَيِّبا تُجْتَثُّ لِلنَّارِ حَطَباً .

10. Be very cautious of the imposter and the Satanic verses. Yes, they will be recognized by the fruits of their labor, whether these prophets and verses are authentic or counterfeit.

١٠) فَاحْذَرُوهُمْ فَمِنْ ثِمَارِ أَفْعَالِهِمْ يُعْرَفُونَ .

11. You have also announced, "Assist each other in performing kind and righteous deeds. Do not support anyone in doing evil or wickedness."

١١) وَقُلْتُمْ : "تَعَاوَنُوا عَلَى الْبِرِّ وَالتَّقْوَى وَلا تَعَاوَنُوا عَلَى الإِثْمِ وَالْعُدْوَانِ " .

12. Alas, you did not support each other in performing kind and

١٢) وَمَا تَعَاوَنْتُمْ عَلَى الْبِرِّ وَالتَّقْوَى بَلْ عَلَى

righteous deeds, but in executing evil and wickedness. Matter of fact, you murdered, swindled and committed atrocities. Are you not cognizant of the fact that such evil deeds are the most degenerate of wicked deeds?

الإثـــم والعـدوان فقتلتــم وسـرقتــم ورئيتــم وكلكــم أكبـر الكبائر لو كنتــم تعلمون .

13. We commanded you in **The True Gospel** that you must not be involved in the degenerate deeds of wickedness, neither in the lesser evils. Furthermore, you were to believe and practice the precepts of love, compassion and peace and reject the precepts of the ungodly.

١٣) ووصيناكــم في الانجيل الحـق ألا ترتكبـوا الكبائر ولا الصغائر وأن تؤمنوا بسنّة المحبّة والرّحمة والسّلام وتنبذوا سنّة المجرمين .

14. Believing with the tongue only brings about the destruction of any human. Wretched the counterfeiters who make lofty declarations with their tongues, but never practice them. They are pretenders for certain.

١٤) فإيمان اللسان بوار الإنسان فتبّـا للأفّاكين الذين يقولون ما لا يفعلون أولئك هـم المنافقون .

15. Mystifying as it is, there are some hypocrites who debate the true believers, without the slightest knowledge of The Truth.

١٥) ومن الذين كفروا من يجادل الذين آمنوا بغير علـم ويتّبع كـل شيطان

Assuredly, such people follow Satan, the rebellious one.

مَرِيدٍ .

16. As for those who have written "scripture" by their own hands, pretending "such was from God" in order to gain some material things, We say, "Woe unto them for what their hands have written. Woe, also, unto everyone else who fabricates falsehood."

١٦) والذينَ كَتَبوا بأيديهِمْ مَا سَمِعوا ، وقالوا هَذا مِنْ عِندِ اللهِ لِيَشتَروا بِهِ ثَمناً قَليلاً فَوَيلٌ لهمِ مِمَّا كَتَبتْ أيديهِمْ وَوَيلٌ لِلَّذِينَ يَأفِكونَ .

17. O, you who are pretenders who still consider themselves part of Our followers: do not announce anything in your religion except the Truth. For you have apparently followed the whims of the ancients who have gone ahead of you. Are you even aware that they have misguided you too? Thus, you ended up being the defrauded ones.

١٧) يَا أهلَ الإفكِ مِنْ عِبادِنا الضَّالينَ : لا تَغلوا فِي دينِكمْ غيرَ الحَقِ فقَدِ اتَّبَعتمْ أهواءَ قومٍ ضَلّوا مِنْ قبلِكمْ وأضلّوا كثيراً وأضلّوكمْ فأنتمُ الأخسَرونَ .

18. Apparently you are captivated by fairytales. You enjoy listening to other people who have intentionally corrupted the Scripture. They tell you, "You have been given this by

١٨) سَمَّاعونَ للكذِبِ سَمَّاعونَ لِقَومٍ آخرينَ حَرَّفوا الكَلِمَ مِنْ بعدِ مَوَاضِعِهِ وَقالوا لكمْ قَدْ أوتِيتمْ هذا فَخذوهُ وَمَا

inspiration. Accept it and you must follow whatever instructions are therein." Therefore you accepted falsehood, but rejected the truth. Such behavior demonstrates absolute ignorance.

أُتِيتُمْ ذلكَ فَاحذَرُوهُ فَآمَنتُمْ بِالبَاطِلِ وَكَفَرتُمْ بِالحَقِّ وهَذا فِعلُ الجَاهِلِينَ .

34
THE LOST
(Surat Al Dhalleen)

٣٤) سُورَةُ الضَّالِينَ

In the Name of the Father, the Word, the Holy Spirit, the One and only True God

بسـم الآبِ الكلمةِ الروحِ الالهِ الواحد الأوحد

1. Satan dressed up deception with a garment of truth and covered up wickedness with a robe of justice declaring to his followers, "I am the one and only lord of yours who has not given birth to any one, neither was I born from anyone. And amongst you there is no equal to me.

١) وألْبَسَ الشيطانُ الباطلَ ثَوْبَ الحَـقِّ وأضفَى على الظلم جِلبابَ العَـدْلِ وقـال لأوْليائِه: "أنا رَبُّكـمُ الأحدُ لَـمْ أَلِدْ وَلَـمْ أُولَدْ وَلَـمْ يَكـنْ لِي بينكُـمْ كُفوًا أحدٌ".

2. "Therefore, I am the mighty dictator, the proud, the conqueror, the controller, the one who brings others into subjection, the one who kills, the avenger, the deceiver, the hurtful, the enriching one. Thus, I alone must you worship and I alone must you seek for succor.

٢) "فأنا المَلِكُ الجَبَّارُ المُتَكبِّرُ القَهَّارُ القابضُ المُذِلُّ المُميتُ المُنتقِـمُ المَـاكـرُ الضَّـارُ المُغنـي فإيـايَ تَعبـدونَ وإيـايَ تَستعينونَ".

3. "I have personally prepared gardens for you where water flows beneath and a river of wine. There are also handsome boys and charming maidens. The maidens are endowed with captivating eyes. The gardens include everything your appetites may desire."

٣) لَقَدْ أَعْدَدْتُ لَكُمْ جَنَّاتٍ تَجْرِي مِن كَحِنِهَا الْأَنْهَارُ فِيهَا خَمْرٌ وَوِلْدَانٌ وِنِسَاءٌ وَحُورٌ عِينٌ وَكُلُّ مَا تَشْتَهُونَ" .

4. How awful is Satan as lord! How vile are his gardens! And wretched are his followers for they are reprobate pagans.

٤) أَلَا سَاءَ الشَّيْطَانُ رَبًّا وَسَاءَتْ جَنَّاتُهُ وَبِئْسَ الْأَوْلِيَانِهِ الْكَافِرِينَ .

5. We have commanded Our worshipers to refrain from killing, stealing and sexual sins. Additionally, they are to stay away from wickedness and immorality.

٥) وَوَصَّيْنَا عِبَادَنَا بِأَنْ لَا يَقْتُلُوا وَلَا يَسْرِقُوا وَلَا يَزْنُوا وَلَا يَأْتُوا إِثْمًا وَلَا فُجُورًا .

6. Then came the imposters who still claim that they belong to Our followers. They demand that you should fight, allow the spoils of war to be acceptable reward and permit polygamy. They emphatically state that We said so and that We have abrogated what

٦) فَجَاءَ الَّذِينَ ضَلُّوا مِنْ عِبَادِنَا يَأْمُرُونَ بِالْقَتْلِ وَيُحَلِّلُونَ الْمَغَانِزَ وَيُبِيحُونَ الزِّنَى عَلَى لِسَانِنَا ذَلِكَ أَمَّا سَخَنَا قَوْلَنَا وَبِدَّلْنَا سُنَّتَنَا . وَلَنْ يَجِدَ الَّذِينَ كَفَرُوا الْقَوْلَنَا سُخًا وَلَا

was declared earlier and changed Our Criterion. Yet, no imposter would ever discover any abrogation to Our statements or altering of Our decrees.

لِسُنَّتِنَا تَبْدِيلاً .

7. O, you who have lost your way from among Our worshipers: you pronounce glad tidings to yourselves of owning paradise because you kill and are killed for Our cause. You have pitifully lost your way by believing such demonic tidings. Our cause is mercy, love and peace for certain. Besides, Our paradise has never been a hiding place for murderers and criminals.

٧) يَأَيُّهَا الذينَ ضَلُّوا مِنْ عِبَادِنَا تُبَشِّرُونَ أَنْفُسَكُمْ بِأَنَّ لَكُمُ الْجَنَّةَ تَقْتُلُونَ وتُقْتَلُونَ فِي سَبِيلِنَا . لَقَدْ ضَلَلْتُمْ إِذْ صَدَّقْتُمْ بُشْرَاكُمْ . فَمَا كَانَ سَبِيلُنَا إِلاَّ رَحْمَةً وَمَحَبَّةً وَسَلاماً . وَمَا كَانَتْ جَنَّاتُنَا مَلاذاً لِلْقَتَلَةِ والمُجْرِمِينَ .

8. The fake prophet who claimed to bring glad tidings has proclaimed falsehood and the hope of those who preach such deception will definitely dry up.

٨) لَقَدْ أَفِكَ البشيرُ وَخَابَ ظَنُّ البُشَــــــرِينَ .

9. You have gone through the earth spoiling and destroying both seed and offspring. If it is announced to you, "Fear God,"

٩) وَسَعَيْتُمْ فِي الأَرْضِ تُفْسِدُونَ فِيهَا وتُهْلِكُونَ الحَرْثَ والنَّسْلَ وإذا قِيلَ

instead of repenting you respond
with self-righteousness, along
with evil deeds and finally rebel
against Us furiously.   What a
diabolical sight!

لكـــم: اتّقوا اللّهَ أخذتكـــمُ العِــزّةُ

بالإثــمِ والعِصيـــانِ .

35
BROTHERHOOD
(Surat Al Ekha)

٣٥) سورةُالإخاءِ

In the Name of the Father, the Word, the Holy Spirit, the One and only True God

بسـمِ الآبِ الكلمةِ الروحِ الإلهِ الواحدِ الأوحدِ

1. O, people everywhere: We have created you from one seed and have revealed the straight path to you. Therefore, you are all brothers.   Tragically, Satan has separated you, led astray a group from among you and sowed the seeds of discord in your very souls. The poisonous effect of his instructions was that you murdered your fellowman then, and you continue to do that.

١) يَأيُّها الناسُ إنّا خلقناكُمْ مِنْ نَفْسٍ واحدةٍ وهَدَيْناكُمْ سَوَاءَ السَّبيلِ فأنتُمْ إخوةٌ ولكنَّ الشيطانَ فَرَّقَكُمْ وأضلَّ طائفةً منكُمْ وبَثَّ العَداوةَ في نُفُوسِكُمْ فَقَتَلْتُمْ إخوتَكُمْ وما زِلْتُمْ تَقْتُلُونَ .

2. In Our Commandments We declared to Our followers not to kill. Even to become angry at anyone is unlawful and whosoever becomes resentful will be severely punished.   In fact, if he pronounced an evil curse on his

٢) ووصَّيْنا عبادَنا ألاَّ يَقْتُلوا ولا يَحْنِقُوا على أحدٍ أبداً . ومَنْ حَنِقَ على أحدٍ نالَ عقاباً مَريراً . أوْ قالَ له كلمةً خبيثةً

brother, his punishment will be banishment and his end unenviable as revealed in **The True Gospel**.

استحقّ نارَ جهنّمَ وساءَ دليلاً .

3. Certainly the tiny tongue has equal responsibility for such activities.

٣) فإنَّ اللسانَ كانَ مسؤولاً .

4. We have created the soul and to Us, therefore, the soul at the very end must return. Thus, We have emphatically forbidden murdering another human being anywhere, anytime—except in a justifiable national war.

٤) إنّا وهبنا النفسَ وإلينا مرجعُها وقد حرّمنا قتلَها تحريماً .

5. How then can you sanction what We have never permitted? You have not created mankind neither shall they return to you at the end of their lives. Therefore, you have overstepped your authority.

٥) فأنّى تُحلّلونَ ما حرّمنا فما أنتمُ بخالقيهمْ ولا هُمْ إليكمْ براجعينَ .

6. Repent from such evil, trust and love one another. Love even your enemies, for when you practice that you will truly become the Children of God.

٦) فتوبوا وآمنوا وأحبّوا بعضُكمْ بعضاً وأحبّوا أعداءَكمْ فتكونوا من أبناء الصادقينَ .

171

7. We shine Our sun over the believers and the unbelievers alike. We also send Our rain over the righteous and the unrighteous alike. With these natural blessings We demonstrate Our unconditional love; perchance you will yield and follow Our precepts.

٧) وَنُشْرِقُ بِالشَّمْسِ عَلَى المؤمِنِينَ والكَافِرِينَ وَنُغْدِقُ الغَيْثَ عَلَى الأَبْرَارِ والطَّالِحِينَ فَاتَّعِظُوا لَعَلَّكُمْ تَهْتَدُونَ .

8. As for those who have believed in **The True Gospel** and have done righteous deeds, We consider them the cream of Our creation. But those who have rejected Us and trusted Satan and his messengers, We consider them the worst of Our creation.

٨) والذينَ آمنوا بِالإنجيلِ الحَقِّ وَعَمِلُوا الصَّالِحَاتِ أُولَئِكَ هُمْ خَيْرُ البَرِيَّةِ والذينَ كَفَرُوا وآمنوا بِالشَّيْطَانِ وَرُسُلِهِ أُولَئِكَ هُمْ شَرُّ البَرِيَّةِ أَجْمَعِينَ .

9. We have inspired the Light of Truth prior to the appearance of darkness. We appeal to each of you, return to the true and tried pathway. Harken to Our Word. Repent from your worldliness. Follow Our precepts. We certainly forgive everyone who will repent, for We are loving and forgiving.

٩) وأنزلنا نورَ الحَقِّ قبلَ ظَلامِ البَاطِلِ فارجعوا الى الحَقِّ القديمِ واسْمَعُوا وتُوبُوا واتَّبِعُوا سُنَّتَنَا فَإِنَّا نغفرُ للتَّائِبِينَ .

10. Furthermore, do not avenge yourselves from your enemies. Instead, seek forgiveness for them. Because of such a loving disposition you yourselves will be forgiven. No forgiveness is granted to those who will not forgive the guilty.

١٠) وَلَا تَنْتَقِمُوا مِنَ المُعْتَدِينَ وَاسْتَغْفِرُوا لَهُمْ يُغْفَرُ لَكُمْ وَلَا يُغْفَرُ لِمَنْ لَا يَسْتَغْفِرُونَ لِلْمُذْنِبِينَ .

11. Our precept is love and forgiveness, not killing and vengefulness. Let those who have gone astray return quickly to Our pathway.

١١) فَسُنَّتُنَا المَحَبَّةُ وَالغُفْرَانُ إِنْ لَا القَتْلُ وَالِابْتِقَامُ فَلْيُهْتَدِ الغَافِلُونَ .

12. The truth is, when you practice deception in dealing with the believers, you are deceiving yourselves. You are absolutely the losers.

١٢) وَيُخَادِعُونَ الَّذِينَ آمَنُوا وَمَا يُخَادِعُونَ إِلَّا أَنْفُسَكُمْ فَأَنْتُمُ الأَخْسَرُونَ .

13. Whenever you are instructed, "Do not cause corruption in the earth," you counter, "We are repairers of the earth." The fact is, you are the corrupters. Somehow, you are unaware of the fallacy of your point of view.

١٣) وَإِنْ قِيلَ لَكُمْ : "لَا تُفْسِدُوا فِي الأَرْضِ" . قُلْتُمْ : "إِنَّمَا نَحْنُ مُصْلِحُونَ" اَلَا إِنَّكُمُ المُفْسِدُونَ وَلَكِنْ لَا تَشْعُرُونَ .

14. Whenever you are instructed, "Follow **The True**

١٤) وَإِنْ قِيلَ : تَعَالَوْا إِلَى سُنَّةِ الحَقِّ وَآمِنُوا

173

Criterion and believe in **The True Furqan**," you haughtily jettison such instructions and renounce them.

بِالفُرْقانِ الحَقِّ اسْتَكْبَرَ وَصَدَدْتُمْ عَنَهُ صُدُوداً .

15. O, people everywhere: We warn you. The Satanic verses are recited in your hearing. They are deception aimed at leading you astray. They are intended to bring you out of the realm of light to an abysmal night. Do not follow the linguistically lofty Satanic verses; instead, consider their author, Satan, your worst of enemies.

١٥) يَأَيُّها النّاسُ إِنّا نُتْلَى عَلَيْكُمْ آيَاتُ الشَّيْطانِ مُضَلِّلاتٍ لِيُخْرِجَكُمْ مِنَ النّورِ إلى الظُّلُماتِ فَلاَ تَتَّبِعوا وَحْيِ الشَّيْطانِ واتَّخِذوهُ عَدَوّاً لَدُوداً .

174

36
FASTING
(Surat Al Siyam)

٣٦) سورةُالصيام

In the Name of the Father, the Word, the Holy Spirit, the One and only True God

بسمِ الآبِ الكلمةِ الروحِ الإلهِ الواحدِ الأوحدِ

1. Whosoever performs a worthwhile deed should not allow even his left hand to know what his right hand has done.

١) وَمَنْ أَحْسَنَ حَسَنَةً فَلَا يَجْعَلَنَّ يَسَارَهُ تَعلمُ ما فَعَلتِ اليمينُ .

2. For We have knowledge of whatever you do secretly and will recompense you openly in the sight of the whole world.

٢) فَإِنَّا نَعلمُ ما تَعْمَلونَ خَفيةً وتُثيبُكمْ عَلانيةً بعينِ العالمينَ .

3. O, you who are hypocrites, yet still count yourselves among Our worshipers: your fasting is not acceptable to Us and will not be rewarded.

٣) يا أيُّها المنافقونَ مِنْ عِبادِنا : إنَّ صيامَكمْ غيرُ مقبولٍ لدينا وغيرُ ممنونٍ .

4. Fasting was not designed just to feel the pangs of hunger periodically.

٤) فما كانَ الصَّومُ تَصَوَّرَ الأجلِ معلومٍ .

175

5. As a matter of fact, you consume more food when fasting than when you are on regular diets. You devour food ferociously just like brute creatures.

٥) تَحْسَبُونَ صَوْماً أَكْثَرَ مِنْكُمْ مَفَاطِرَ وكالأنعامِ تَطْعَمُونَ .

6. You exhaust your bodies and souls as you eat hungrily, as if you have never eaten before and you will never eat again.

٦) تُرْهِقُونَ أَجْسَادَكُمْ ونفوسَكُمْ تَهَماً فكأنَّكُمْ مَا طَعِمْتُمْ مِنْ قبلِ ولنْ تكونوا مِنْ بعدُ طَاعمينَ .

7. Furthermore, you greedily consume the entire year's produce in one month, because you are craving and yearning for nutrition. It is certainly advisable for you not to participate in fasting for there is no recognition for the thirsty and hungry physically.

٧) وتأكلونَ السّنةَ في شَهْرٍ جَشَعاً لضنكُمْ وتَقَتُّرِكُمْ فخيرٌ لكُمْ ألّا تصُومُوا فإنّه لا أجرَ للظِّماء والمُتَضَوِّرينَ .

8. You actually put a frown on your faces and discolor your cheeks so others can observe that you are fasting. Hypocrites, those are the ones who practice this sort of thing.

٨) وتُكَلِّحونَ وُجوهَكُمْ وتُصَعِّرونَ خُدودَكُمْ للنّاسِ لتظهرِوا صَائِمينَ إنّما يَفعلُ ذلكَ القومُ المُنَافِقونَ .

9. True fasting is the cessation of the heart, the tongue,

٩) إنّما الصّيامُ الحَقُّ صِيامُ القلبِ واللسانِ

the hand and the eye from transacting wickedness, vileness and immorality, whether you are famished or full.

والْيَدِ وَالْعَيْنِ عَنِ الْفَحْشَاءِ وَالْمُنْكَرِ وَالْبَغِي سَوَاءَ أَكُنْتُمْ جِيَاعاً أَوْ مُتْخَمِينَ .

37
THE TREASURE
(Surat Al Kanz)

٣٧) سُورةُ الكنز

In the Name of the Father, the Word, the Holy Spirit, the One and only True God

بسـم الآبِ الكلمةِ الروحِ الالهِ الواحدِ الأوحدِ

1. O, you who have gone astray, yet still claim to be counted among Our worshipers: if you acknowledge Us, then relent from doing evil, you will be forgiven. So, follow the right pathway and emulate the believers. No one who follows his own whim will ever enter the Kingdom of Heaven. All the materials that this world has to offer are no more than brightly shining trinkets. They only rebuff you from the straight way to keep you from finding Our pathway.

١) يَأيُّها الذينَ ضَلُّوا مِنْ عِبادِنا : إنْ تُوبوا يُتبْ عليكـم فـاتَّبعوا الهُدى والحقـوا بـالمؤمنينَ فليـس مَـنْ يتَّبـعُ هَـواهُ بداخـل مَلكـوتَ السماواتِ وما مَتاعُ الحياةِ الدنيا سوى زُخْرُفٍ بـرّاقٍ يَصُدّـكـمْ عَـن السَّبيلِ الحقِّ فلا تَهتدونَ .

2. For that reason, do not stash for yourselves a treasure which can be eaten by the cankerworm, or rust, or can be stolen by thieves.

٢) فـلا تكـنزوا في الدنيـا كـنزاً يأكـلهُ السـوسُ ويُتلفهُ الصـدأُ وَيَسرِقهُ

Instead, store up treasures in the better world where there is no cankerworm, neither rust, nor thieves who can steal.

السَّارِقُونَ . بَلِ اكْنِزُوا فِي الأُخْرَى حَيْثُ لَا سُوسٌ وَلَا صَدَأٌ وَلَا يَسْرِقُهُ سَارِقُونَ .

3. Will anyone from among you be willing to be killed, his women taken captives or his properties raided? Then how can you wish this upon your fellowman? We have commanded that you treat others just as you yourselves wish to be treated.

٣) أَيَرْضَى أَحَدُكُمْ أَنْ يُقْتَلَ وَتُسْبَى نِسَاؤُهُ وَتُنْهَبَ أَمْوَالُهُ فَأَيَّ تَرْضَوْهُ لِغَيْرِكُمْ مِنْ عِبَادِنَا . وَقَدْ وَصَّيْنَا بِأَنْ تُعَامِلُوا الآخَرِينَ كَمَا تُحِبُّونَ أَنْ يُعَامِلَكُمُ الآخَرُونَ ! .

4. For such is the heart of the **Criterion**. This **Truth** is what We have commissioned Our messengers and prophets to proclaim throughout the ages to all peoples and in all places.

٤) ذَلِكُمْ هُوَ كُنْهُ الشَّرِيعَةِ وَبِهِ بَعَثْنَا الأَنْبِيَاءَ وَالمُرْسَلِينَ .

5. Your forefathers must have heard of this **Criterion** in **The True Gospel**, but they did not comply.   Noticeably, they proceeded to kill people, take women captive and seize their properties.   Your forefathers even fabricated   the   lies   which

٥) وَسَمِعَ آبَاؤُكُمْ سُنَّتَنَا فِي الإِنْجِيلِ الحَقِّ فَلَمْ يَتَّبِعُوهَا بَلْ رَاحُوا يَقْتُلُونَ النَّاسَ وَيَسْبُونَ النِّسَاءَ وَيَسْلُبُونَ الأَمْوَالَ وَقَدِ افْتَرُوا عَلَيْنَا الكَذِبَ بِأَنَّا أَوْحَيْنَا إِلَيْهِمْ بِأَفْعَالِ

179

proclaimed that We had inspired them to perform the works of depraved criminals.

المُجرمينَ .

6. Behold, anyone who fabricates lies about Us is the worst of imposters and is definitely a cohort of Satan, the accursed one. But We are the mighty and the merciful.

٦) ألَا إنَّ مَنْ يفـتري علينـا الكـذبَ لَهُوَ أكفـرُ الكــافرين وَهـوَ كُلّ شَـيطان رجيمٍ .

38
THE PROPHETS
(Surat Al Anbeya)

٣٨) سُورةُ الأَنبِياءِ

In the Name of the Father, the Word, the Holy Spirit, the One and only True God

بسمِ الآبِ الكلمةِ الروحِ الالهِ الواحدِ الأوحدِ

1. O, you who have blasphemed and gone astray, yet claim to still be among Our worshipers: you fabricate a statement, then recite it. One quickly learns that it is neither poetry nor prose; at times it is not even nuggets of pithy sayings.

١) يَأَيُّها الذينَ كَفَروا مِنْ عِبادِنا الضّالِينَ إِنَّكُمْ لَتُرَدِّدونَ قَوْلاً لَغُواً ما كانَ شِعراً ولا نَثْراً ولا قولاً سَديداً .

2. It is so often no more than gibberish repeated redundantly and incoherently.

٢) إِنْ هُوَ إلاّ لَغْوٌ مُرَدَّدٌ تَرْديداً .

3. Once understood the words terrify Our followers grievously and threaten even the defiant fearfully.

٣) يُرَغِّبُ التّابِعينَ تَرْغيباً وَيُهَدِّدُ المُعْرِضينَ تَهْديداً .

4. The rhyming words found favor even in the souls of Our

٤) حَسُنَ وَقْعاً في نُفوسِ عِبادِنا الضّالِينَ

worshipers who have gone astray, yet claim they belong to Us. Surprisingly, even the ignorant seem to fall for it.

واسْتَمَرَأَهُ الْجَاهِلُونَ .

5.   It is more or less like poison hidden in the heart of tasty dishes of food. Yet this fact is not realized by most of them. Thus, they do not make an effort whatsoever to avoid it.

٥) سُـــــمٌّ فِي دَسَـــــمٍ ولكِــــنَّ أَكْثَرَهُمْ لَا يَشْعُـــرُونَ فَلَا يَبْتَغُونَ عنهُ مَحِيداً .

6.   We have indeed forewarned Our followers concerning the imposters stating, "By their fruits you will know them." Is it really feasible to produce grapes from a thorn bush or figs from a thistle?

٦) وَحَذَّرْنَا عِبَادَنَا الْمُؤْمِنِينَ مِنَ الرُّسُلِ الأَفَّاكِينَ فَمِنْ ثِمَارِهِمْ يُعْرَفُونَ . فَهَلْ يُجْنَى مِنَ الشَّوْكِ الْعِنَبُ أَوْ مِنَ الْحَسَكِ التِّينُ .

7.   The declarations of the imposters cause Our faithful followers sheer terror because of instructions to commit murder. They react with distaste to orders for attacking others and feel some anxiety from the idea of a paradise full of sexual immorality and debauchery.

٧) أَقْوَالٌ يَرْتَعِدُ مِنْهَا عِبَادُنَا الْمُؤْمِنُونَ هَلَعاً مِنَ التَّقْتِيلِ وَنُفُوراً مِنَ الْغَزْوِ وَأَنَفاً مِنْ جَنَّةِ الزِّنَى وَالْفُجُورِ .

8. Whenever Our faithful followers hear of such pronouncements their physical bodies tremble violently out of disgust, seeking refuge in Us from Satan, the cursed one.

٨) فإذا سمعوها اقشعرت أبدانهـم فرقاً
واستعاذوا بنا من الشيطان الرجيم .

9. There is no welcome at the portals of paradise for those who merely repeat prescribed prayers. Paradise is prepared instead for those who have performed Our divine will. Such people are truly triumphant servants of Ours. They attain a lofty place in the Kingdom. No fear is associated within them; neither are they among the regretful.

٩) وما دخل الجنة من كرر الصلاة لغواً
وأما الذين عملوا بمشيتنا فأولئك هـم
عبادنا المفلحون لهـم مقام في الملكوت
ولا خوف عليهـم ولا هـم يندمون .

10. One's personal opinion can never take the place of Truth. Peace, for instance, is nothing like warfare. Neither is the man who welcomes his believing brother with an olive branch like the one who welcomes him with a drawn sword and kills him. For such an individual is counted among the infidels.

١٠) إن الظن لا يغني من الحق شيئاً . وما
السلام كالقتال وليس من يلقى أخاه
المؤمن بغصن زيتون كمن يشرع عليه
سيفاً فيقتله ذلك أنه من الكافرين .

11. You have annulled with your gibberish what **The Torah**

١١) ومسحتـم بلغوكـم قول التوراة

183

and **The True Gospel** declared by camouflaging truth with lies and faith with forgery. You have even fabricated proclamations in Our name which We have never authorized.

والانجيـل الحـقّ فألبسـتـمُ الحـقّ بـاطلاً والايمانَ كفـراً وافتريتـمُ أقوالاً مـا أنزلنا بها من سلطانٍ .

12. The sneaking whisperer, Satan, impersonated Us and whispered into the hearts of his devotees false scriptures which were full of blasphemy and lies. Because he frightened them into surrendering to him, they believed him and thus became supporters of each other in this folly.

١٢) وانتحـل الوسـواسُ الخنّـاسُ اسـمَنا ووَسوَسَ في صُدورِ أوليائه بِمَا ألقى في روعِهـمُ من بَهتٍ وكفرٍ وهـمُ مُصدِّقوه فكـان بعضهــمُ لبعضٍ نصيرا .

13. Additionally, Satan instructed them to perform good deeds and forewarned them concerning debauchery, gross sins and rape. But those instructions were mere words, for he sanctioned all of the vile sins beguilingly. Consequently, his devotees practiced all of the above vices dedicatedly and frequently.

١٣) وأمرهـمُ بـالمعروف مكـراً مـنه ونهاهُمُ عن الفحشاءِ والمُنكرِ والبغيِ قولاً إفكاً وحلّلَهُمُ تحليلاً فكـان فعلاً مفعولاً .

14. Furthermore, Satan enticed the illiterates from among Our Worshipers. They followed him headlong even though they

١٤) وأغوى الجاهلينَ من عبادنا فاتبعوهُ وأبى الجاهلونَ إلا ضلالاً وكفُوراً .

184

would normally reject going astray.

15. Satan cunningly proved his assessment of these illiterates because they willing followed his guiles. Yet, Satan could not beguile the true believers. Neither does he have authority over them. He could neither trick them nor attract them with his promises. Instead, they held on to Our revealed **Truth** and tightly clasped Our lifeline.

١٥) وَقَدْ صَدَّقَ اِبْلِيسُ عَلَيْهِمْ ظَنَّهُ اِذْ اتَّبَعُوهُ وَاِلَّا الْمُؤْمِنُونَ مِنْ عِبَادِنَا فَمَا كَانَ لَهُ عَلَيْهِمْ مِنْ سُلْطَانٍ فَمَا اَغْوَاهُمْ وَلَا بَدَّدَ لَهُمْ شَمْلًا فَهُمْ بِمَا اَنْزَلْنَا مُوقِنُونَ وَبِحَبْلِنَا مُعْتَصِمُونَ .

16. We did not enunciate any prediction to the children of Israel regarding another messenger who would come after Our Living Word. How dare he publish another message after We have revealed the **Word of Truth** powerfully! In the Word, the Messiah, We profoundly inspired the perfect precepts and brought the Good News to all of humanity. None of the divine revelation will ever be annulled or

١٦) وَمَا بَشَّرْنَا بَنِي اِسْرَائِيلَ بِرَسُولٍ يَأْتِي مِنْ بَعْدِ كَلِمَتِنَا وَمَا عَسَاهُ اَنْ يَقُولَ بَعْدَ اَنْ قُلْنَا كَلِمَةَ الْحَقِّ وَاَنْزَلْنَا سُنَّةَ الْكَمَالِ وَبَشَّرْنَا النَّاسَ كَافَّةً بِدِينِ الْحَقِّ وَكَنْ يَجِدُوا لَهُ نَسْخًا وَلَا تَبْدِيلًا اِلَى يَوْمِ يُبْعَثُونَ .

abrogated till the Day of Resurrection.

17. Let Us logically suppose that We did announce to the People of The Book such a prediction. Why would they deny the existence of such a prophecy? For this presumption would mean that We have sent a messenger who could not speak their language. How absurd is the idea that We would send the Israelites a messenger who is neither a Jew nor did he know their Hebrew tongue! They already have Moses, their own Hebrew prophets and messengers. We also fulfilled and sealed their prophecies with Our perfectly manifested Word, Jesus the Messiah!

١٧) ولو بشّرناهم لما كذّبوا وما أرسلنا من رسول إلا بلسان قومه . فأنّى بشّر بنى إسرائيل برسول ليس منهم وما لسانه بلسانهم وعندهم موسى والأنبياء والمرسلون وقفينا على آثارهم بكلمتنا بالحقّ المبين .

18. We admonished Our faithful followers regarding the appearance of a false prophet. They could identify such a person by his anti-Christ statements. They could recognize him by the fruit of his works, and expose his

١٨) وحذّرنا عبادنا المؤمنين من رسول أفّاك تبيّنوه من بيّنات كفره وعرفوه من ثمار أفعاله وكشفوا إفكه وسحره المبين فهو

مَرسُول شَيطانٍ رَجيسٍ لِقومٍ كَافِرِينَ .

treachery and evil sorcery. For the fact is, such a so-called prophet is categorically a messenger of Satan, the rejected one, sent to a people who are infidels through and through.

39
THE CONSPIRATORS
(Surat Al Makireen)

٣٩) سُورةُ المَاكِرِين

In the Name of the Father, the Word, the Holy Spirit, the One and only True God

بسم الآبِ الكلمةِ الروحِ الالهِ الواحدِ الأوحدِ

1. Those of Our worshipers who had gone astray, fabricated the news announcing that We were in competition with the deceptive hypocrites. The fabrication states further that they devised some treachery and We did the same and then We emerged as the best of deceivers and were swiftest in deception. Therefore, those people are transformed into the manipulators of deception!

١) وافترى علينا الذينَ ضَلّوا مِنْ عِبادِنا بأنّا تَنافَسْنا مَعَ القومِ المَاكِرِينَ اِذْ مَكَروا مَكرًا ومَكَرْنا مَكرًا فكنّا خيرَ المَاكِرِينَ وأسْرِعَ مَكراً ونا المَكرِ جميعاً .

2. Let Satan shut up for he is behind their talking tongues. Furthermore, let those who conform to his designs be banished too. They own the entire right to deception and double-dealing. They are the craftiest of the

٢) ألا فليَخرَسِ الشّيطانُ لِسانَهُمْ ولْيَخرَسِ التّابِعونَ فلهمُ المَكرُ جميعاً وهمْ أنكرُ المَاكِرِينَ .

188

counterfeiters.

3. We have never sent a messenger from Us who instructs his disciples to kill others, urges them to get involved in polygamy and leads them as invaders against Our peaceful worshipers.

٣) وَمَا أَرْسَلْنَا مِنْ رَسُولٍ بِأَمْرِ حِزْبَهُ بِالْقَتْلِ وَيُحَرِّضُهُمْ عَلَى الزِّنَى وَيَقُودُهُمْ غَازِياً عِبَادَنَا الآمِنِينَ .

4. Such atrocities are not characteristic of the honorable prophets. Rather, such activities are the delusion of the diabolical and damned devil himself.

٤) وَمَا تِلْكَ مِنْ شِيَمِ الْمُرْسَلِينَ إِنْ هِيَ إِلَّا مِنْ وَحْيِ شَيْطَانٍ لَعِينٍ .

5. No genuine messenger has ever made himself a companion to the God who sent him, confronted Him about the message, manufactured lies, then committed criminal activities and stirred rebellion.

٥) وَمَا كَانَ لِرَسُولٍ أَنْ يُشْرِكَ نَفْسَهُ بِمُرْسِلِهِ وَيُعَارِضَ رِسَالَتَهُ وَيَفْتَرِيَ عَلَيْهِ الْكَذِبَ وَيَقْتَرِفَ الآثْمَ وَالْعِصْيَانَ .

6. O, you from among Our true followers who have gone astray and have been involved in deception: you have judged Our faithful followers wrongly. We have announced long ago, "Thou

٦) يَا أَهْلَ الْمَكْرِ مِنْ عِبَادِنَا الضَّالِينَ . لَقَدْ أَدَنْتُمْ عِبَادَنَا الْمُؤْمِنِينَ وَقَدْ وَصَّيْنَا بِأَلَّا كَدِنُوا لِئَلَّا تُدَانُوا وَلَا تُشْتَمُوا مِنَ الْمُعْتَدِينَ .

shalt not judge that you may not be judged." Furthermore We stated: "Do not avenge yourselves."

7. You have instead appropriated properties of others and have pilfered their supplies of food. Yet, We had given instructions to the effect, "Whosoever owns two robes let him give one of them to the less fortunate, and he should not turn a beggar away."

٧) وَسَلَبْتُمْ أَمْوَالَهُمْ وَنَهِبْتُمْ أَقْوَاتِهِمْ
وَقَدْ وَصَّيْنَا مَنْ لَهُ ثَوْبَانِ فَلْيُعْطِ أَحَدَهُمَا وَلَا
يَرُدَّ السَّائِلِينَ .

8. You have exhorted your people to hate, kill and curse. But We had commanded earlier, "Love your enemies, bless them who curse you, do good to them who hate you and forgive those who wrong you."

٨) وَحَرَّضْتُمْ قَوْمَكُمْ عَلَى الْكُرْهِ
وَالْقَتْلِ وَاللَّعْنِ وَوَصَّيْنَا بِأَنْ تُحِبُّوا
أَعْدَاءَكُمْ وَتُبَارِكُوا لَاعِنِيكُمْ
وَتُحْسِنُوا إِلَى مُبْغِضِيكُمْ وَتَغْفِرُوا
وَتَسْتَغْفِرُوا لِلْمُخْطِئِينَ اسْتِغْفَارًا .

9. Consequently, whosoever rebelled by disobeying Us and desired the eventuality of his ways, Hell itself hastened to prepare its eternal flames, where he will not only burn continuous-

٩) فَمَنْ كَفَرَ وَأَرَادَ الْعَاجِلَةَ عَجَّلْتُ لَهُ
جَهَنَّمَ يَصْلَاهَا مَذْمُومًا مَدْحُورًا وَمَنْ أَرَادَ
الْآخِرَةَ وَسَعَى لَهَا سَعْيًا وَهُوَ مُؤْمِنٌ كَالَهَا

ly, but also end up defeated and defamed. In contrast, whosoever desires Heaven, diligently seeks it, and is a faithful believer in Us, he will definitely reach Heaven and his labors will be richly rewarded.

وَكَانَ سَعْيُهُ مَشْكُوراً .

10. There was never a time in history where evil was substituted for good, warfare considered peace, hatred accepted as love, pillage as virtue, except in the law of Satan, the lawless one and his vile followers.

١٠) فَمَا كَانَ الشَّرُّ خَيْراً وَالحَرْبُ سَلاماً والبغضَاءُ مَحَبَّةً والسَّلبُ حَسَنةً إلاَّ فِي شِرْعةِ الشيطانِ وأوْليائِهِ الفَاسِقينَ .

11. Virtue has its messengers. Evil too has its messengers. Each of the messengers produces his own ideologies. It is unlikely that virtue and vileness are equated in the balance. Consequently, there is no comparison between the godly and the ungodly.

١١) إنَّ للخيرِ رُسُلاً وللشرِّ رُسُلاً وكلٌّ يعملُ على شَاكِلتِهِ ولا يَسْتَوي الطيبُ والخَبيثُ ولا المؤمنونَ والكَافرونَ .

12. The eye is the light of the entire body. Whosoever has a healthy eye will naturally have a body full of light. Yet, whosoever has a sick eye will naturally have a body full of darkness. If,

١٢) العَيْنُ نِبْراسُ الجَسَدِ فذُو العينِ النَّيِّرةِ ذُو جَسَدٍ نيِّرٍ وذُو العينِ المُظلِمةِ ذو جَسَدٍ مُظلِمٍ . فإمَّا كَانَ نورُكُمْ ظَلاماً

191

therefore, your light has gone out, how enormous will your darkness be?

فَظَلَامُكُمْ أَنَّى يَكُونُ ؟

13. Thus, one cannot put a blind person on the exact same footing as one who can see. The same is with darkness and light. If you are actually immersed in the gloom of ignorance and infidelity, will you ever find the True Way?

١٣) فَلَا يَسْتَوِي الْأَعْمَى وَالْبَصِيرُ وَلَا الظُّلُمَاتُ وَالنُّورُ وَأَكُمْ فِي ظُلُمَاتِ الْجَهْلِ وَالْكُفْرِ فَأَنَّى تَهْتَدُونَ ؟

14. Woe unto them who accept deception by rejecting Our precepts, who also wrong others by waging war against the innocents. They are such mean evildoers who cannot leave any evil undone and their wicked deeds are loathsome.

١٤) طُبّا لِلَّذِينَ كَفَرُوا بِمَا عَصَوْا أَمْرِنَا وَكَانُوا يَعْتَدُونَ فَمَا تَنَاهَوْا عَنْ مُنْكَرٍ اقْتَرَفُوهُ لَبِئْسَ مَا كَانُوا يَفْعَلُونَ .

15. Demons descend upon every liar and deceiver. They make him hear impersonators and lies and let him trust such demonic voices, as if they are from Us. We have never conveyed any blasphemous information. Such things are the by-products of

١٥) تَنَزَّلُ الشَّيَاطِينُ عَلَى كُلِّ أَفَّاكٍ أَثِيمٍ يُلْقُونَ السَّمْعَ وَيَأْفِكُونَ وَيُخَادِعُونَ أَوْلِيَاءَهُمْ وَيُوحُونَ إِلَيْهِمُ الْكُفْرَ بِاسْمِنَا وَمَا أَوْحَيْنَا كُفْرًا إِنْ هُوَ إِلَّا إِفْكٌ

the heathen.

المُفتَرِينَ .

16. The unbelievers decided to come after a people who were barefooted, naked and hungry. These false believers urged them to pillage the peaceful citizens and not do good deeds.

١٦) وأتبَعَ الذينَ كَفَروا شِرْعَةَ قَومٍ حُفَاة عُراةٍ جِياعٍ يَأمرونَ بغزوِ الآمنينَ وينهَونَ عن أفعالِ المُحسنينَ .

17. Subsequently, these unbelievers brought vileness upon the earth, such as murdering, raiding and committing sexual immorality. They demonstrated brute aspirations within their own souls rather than human decency, both in this world and the world to come. At the Judgment Day they will pay dearly for their evil deeds.

١٧) فَعاثوا في الأرضِ فَساداً وقَتَلوا وسَلبوا ومَرَّوا وأُتحَموا غرائِزَ البَهائِمِ في نُفوسِهِمْ في الدّنيا وفي الآخرة سَيُجزَونَ سَعيراً ويُحْمَونَ .

18. As for those who fear Us, who humbly and sincerely believe in Our Word, who run swiftly to perform righteous deeds, they will always reach their objectives successfully. For they are on the right path and a people of integrity.

١٨) إنَّ الذينَ هُمْ مِنْ خشْيتِنا مُشْفقونَ وبكلِمتِنا مُؤمنونَ وكمشيئتِنا خاضِعونَ أولئكَ يُسارعونَ في الخيراتِ وهُمْ لها سابقونَ فهُمْ على صِراطٍ مُستقيمٍ وعلى

خُلُقٍ عَظِيمٍ .

١٩) أَمَّا الَّذِينَ ضَلَّ سَعْيُهُمْ فِي الْحَيَاةِ الدُّنْيَا وَهُمْ يَحْسِبُونَ أَنَّهُمْ يُحْسِنُونَ صُنْعًا فَهُمُ الأَخْسَرُونَ .

19. As for those who have chosen the wrong way in this earthly life, though they think they have done well, they are in fact absolute failures.

٢٠) يَحْلِفُونَ إِنْ أَرَدْنَا إِلَّا إِحْسَانًا وَتَوْفِيقًا وَيَحْلِفُونَ عَلَى الْكَذِبِ فَلَا تُصَدِّقُوهُمْ وَلَا تُطِيعُوا كُلَّ حَلَّافٍ مَهِينٍ .

20. They even vow, "All that we desire is only goodness and prosperity." Truth is, they make such vows with forked tongues. Consequently, do not believe them, neither listen to any of their exaggerated vows and instruction ever.

40
THE ILLITERATES
(Surat Al Ummieen)

٤٠) سُورَةُ الأُمّيِّينَ

In the Name of the Father, the Word, the Holy Spirit, the One and only True God

بسمِ الآبِ الكلمةِ الروحِ الالهِ الواحدِ الأوحدِ

1. We have never sent a messenger without equipping him with a miraculous sign. For this is the method of authenticating His prophethood.

١) وَمَا أَرْسَلنا مِنْ رَسُولٍ إلا وآتيناهُ آيةً وكان مِنْ عِبادِنا الصَّادقينَ .

2. Subsequently, the claim that an illiterate person could be teaching illiterate people is much like the blind leading the blind. It is implausible, for they will certainly fall into a deep pit, sooner or later, with the leader and those whom he led perishing.

٢) وَمَثَلُ الأُميِّ يُعلِّمُ أُمّيينَ كَمَثَلِ أَعمى يقودُ عُمياً يَهوونَ جَميعاً في جُبٍّ فيهلكُ القائدُ والمقودونَ .

3. We send messengers with true precepts, showing them the true path and instructing them, that they themselves in turn can

٣) وَبَعثُ الرُسُلَ بِسُنَّةِ الحقِّ وَهَديهمُ وَعَلِّمَهُمْ ليَهدوا عِبادَنا فَأَنّى يَهدي الضالُّ

guide Our people. How can it ever make sense that an individual who himself has gone astray can instruct those who are just like he is, ones who have lost their way too?   Logically, We must ask, "Can an illiterate teach illiterates to read and write?"

الضَّالِّينَ؟ وأنّى يَعَلِّمُ الأُمِّيَّ الأُمِّيِّينَ؟ .

4. Satan did assault the uninformed, which is an easy goal for him to accomplish. Satan beguiled them, brainwashed them and maligned their hearts. What emerged became a race of people who are deaf, dumb and blind. The only thing they understand is what the devil devises. They are subservient to his vices.

٤) وَأَوْقَعَ الشَّيطانُ بِالأُمِّيِّينَ وذلكَ عليهِ هَيِّنٌ فَأَضَلَّهُمْ وَأَفْسَدَ عُقُولَهُمْ وَأَفْسَدَ تهُمْ فَهُمْ صُمٌّ بُكْمٌ عُمْيٌ لا يَفْقَهونَ إلاّ ما يُوحِي الشَّيطانُ وَهُمْ لِوَحْيِهِ طائِعونَ .

5. They recite this gibberish which is nothing but plagiarized wisdom, pitiful enunciation and mystifying instructions.   This reminds one of the dead bones into which people blow their breath to bring them to life. Who in the universe but Us, the True Living God, can bring dead bones to life?

٥) وَيَتْلونَهُ لَغواً فِجّاً فَالأحْكامُ رَثَّةُ الألْفاظِ غَثَّةُ الأنباءِ مِثْلُهُ كَمِثْلِ عِظامٍ نَخِرَةٍ يَنْفُخونَ فيها لِيُحْيوا رَميمَها وَمَنْ غَيْرُنا يُحي العِظامَ وهيَ رَميمٌ .

6. We have sent down this **True Furqan** as standard precepts to mankind everywhere. It is also conveyed so the blasphemers from among Our followers can recognize how cruel they were in their dealings with Our righteous followers in previous centuries. Furthermore, it discloses how they themselves were the infidels who rejected Our Word vehemently.

٦) إِنَّا أَنزَلْنَا هَذَا الفَرْقَانَ الحَقَّ هُدًى لِلنَّاسِ كَافَّةً وَلِنُرِيَنَّ أَهْلَ الكَفْرِ مِنْ عِبَادِنَا كَمْ كَانُوا أُفْظَاظاً عَلَى عِبَادِنَا الصَّالِحِينَ وَكَمْ كَانُوا لِكَلِمَتِنَا جَاحِدِينَ.

7. To expose the design of Satan, people should look at how he beguiled his followers to rebel against Us and to manufacture falsehood about Us. They obeyed him completely and accomplished his evil purpose willingly.

٧) وَبَيِّنَةٌ تَفْضَحُ الشَّيْطَانَ إِذْ أَوْحَى لِأَوْلِيَائِهِ بِأَنْ يَكْفُرُوا بِنَا وَيَقُولُوا عَلَيْنَا شَطَطاً فَأَطَاعُوهُ وَأَتَوْا أَمْراً إِدًّا.

8. Unfathomable as it is, they disputed the Truth but supported falsehood! Thus, they became despairing colossal desperados and gangsters.

٨) وَنَاهَضُوا الحَقَّ وَنَاصَرُوا البَاطِلَ فَكَانُوا جَبَارَةً عُنُداً.

9. They even fabricated lies declaring that We have hoodwinked Our worshipers formidably, devoured them

٩) وَافْتَرُوا عَلَى لِسَانِنَا كَذِباً بِأَنَّا مَكَرْنَا بِعِبَادِنَا مَكْراً وَبَطَشْنَا بِهِمْ

fiercely, taken revenge on them forcefully, put them down flamboyantly, victimized them frequently, put them to utter shame fatefully, decimated them fanatically, made a joke out of them festively, destroyed them fully, tormented them frantically, cursed them factually and planned for them a terrible punishment finally.

بَطشاً وَانتَقمنا مِنْـهُـمُ انتقاماً وتَكَبَّرنا عَلَيـهِـمْ تَكَبَّراً وقَهَرنا فَوْتَـهـمْ قَـهراً وأذلَلنــاهـمْ إذلالاً وأهْلَكنــاهُـمْ إهلاكـاً واسْـتَهزأنا بـهـمِ استِـهْزاءً ودَمَّرْنـاهـمْ تَدميراً وعذّبنـاهـمْ تَعذيباً ولَعنّاهُـمْ لَعناً وَكِدْنا لهـمْ كَيـداً عَظيماً .

١٠)   10. Far be it from Us ever to punish Our worshipers without first giving them an opportunity to repent. The charlatans have fabricated such proclamations as Our Own instructions. Such is but the designs of Satan, the rejected one, in whose inner being poisons of blasphemy boil continuously. Therefore, he deceptively and ingeniously enunciated such declarations through the mouths of his devotees. In turn, they spewed them out into the ears of their adherents. Wherefore the adherents turned away from the True Path angrily.

١٠) حَاشَا لَنا أنْ نُنزلَ بعبادِنا ما افترى علينا بـهِ المُفـترونَ إنْ هـوَ إلاّ كَيـدُ شَـيطان رَجيـم جَاشَتْ فـي صَـدرِهِ سُـمومُ الـكفـر فلفظها فـي أفواهِ رسُله فَتَقَيؤُها فـي آذانِ أتباعِهـم فَصَـدّوا عـن السَّـبيل صُدوداً .

11. Satan has attained enormous wickedness and his messengers have followed suit. But his blasphemous devotees are doomed to a certain horrific destruction at the termination point.

١١) الا سَاءَ الشيطانُ وسَاءَ رُسُلُهُ وَخَابَ أُتبَاعُهُ الكَافِرونَ .

12. For he himself is the one who dispatched to the illiterates a messenger from among them reciting his verses—Satanic verses indeed. Although they staunchly followed him, the fact is they only follow a man's opinion. Opinions of men can never replace the True revelation in any form or fashion.

١٢) فهوَالذي بَعَثَ في الاميينَ رَسُولاً مِنْ أنفُسِهِمْ يَتلو عَليهِمْ آياتِهِ فاتبعوهُ إِنْ يَتَّبِعونَ إلا الظنَّ وإنَّ الظنَّ لا يُغني مِنَ الحَقِّ شَيئاً .

41
THE SLANDERERS
(Surat Al Muftareen)

٤١) سُورَةُ المُفتَرِينَ

In the Name of the Father, the Word, the Holy Spirit, the One and only True God

بسـم الآبِ الكلمةِ الروحِ الالهِ الواحدِ الأوحدِ

1. Worshipers: you have enunciated, "Add no partners to God." Yet, you have joined a partner to Us. He has become an associate to Us in omnipotence, thus, turning yourselves into the worst of polytheists.

١) يأيها المُفترونَ مِنْ عِبادِنا الضّالِينَ: لقـدْ قلتـمْ: "لا تُشـركوا بـاللهِ أحـداً" وأشركتـمْ بنا مَنْ شاركنا الحَوْلَ والقوةَ فكنتـمْ شَرَّ المُشركينَ.

2. You added, "Close not your fist too tightly, neither open it too generously." Yet, you did not close your fists too tightly when it came to killing, fornication and depravity! Neither did you open it generously with love, justice and peace!

٢) وقلتـمْ: "لا تجعلْ يـدكَ مَغلولةً ولا تَبسطها كُـلَّ البسْطِ". فمـا غَلَلتـمْ أيديكـمْ عَنِ القتلِ والزنى والفجورِ، وما بسطتُموها بالمحبةِ والعدلِ والسلامِ.

3. You further emphasized, "Do not commit immorality for it is an abomination and an evil pathway." Then, you proclaimed that committing fornication and

٣) وقلتـمْ: "لا تقربوا الزنى إنّهُ كانَ فاحشةً وساءَ سَبيلاً". ثُـمَّ دعوتُم إلى اقترافِ الزنى والفاحشـةِ فَسُتّمْ سَبيلاً.

immorality, through polygamy, is
sanctioned. This resulted in your
following an evil way.

4. Furthermore, you stated,
"Do not destroy the soul that God
has forbidden to destroy, except
when it is just to do so."
Thereafter, you abrogated your
declaration and encouraged
killing, which is the most savage
of brutalities. We have outlawed
murder among you very emphatically. But you have sanctioned
it for yourselves as a legal
prerogative. Murder has never
been lawful or right for anybody.

٤)   وقلتـمُ : "لاٰ تَقْتُلوا النفسَ التي حَرَّمَها
اللهُ إلاّ بالحقّ" . ثُمَّ نَسَختـمُ قولَكـمُ
وحَرَّضتـمُ على القتـلِ وهـوَ أكـبرُ
الكـبائرِ وقد حرّمناهُ عليكـمُ تحريماً
فحلّلتموه لأنفسكـمُ تحليلاً بالحقّ . وما
كانَ القتلُ حَقّاً حلالاً .

5. "Argue not with the
People of The Book in matters
above your comprehension," is
another of your declarations.
Because you did not seek
answers from the People of The
Book and those who are
established in knowledge and
religion, you very definitely lost
your way.

٥)   وقلتـمُ : "لاٰ تُجادلوا أهلَ الكتابِ
بما ليسَ لكـمُ بهِ علمٌ" وما سألتـمُ أهلَ
الكتابِ والراسخينَ في العلـمِ والدينِ
فضَلَلتـمُ دليلاً .

6. "Deprive not the orphan of
his inheritance unless you have a

٦)   وقلتـمُ : "لاٰ تَقربـوا مالَ اليتيـمِ إلاّ

better plan for him for using it," is another of your sayings. Yet, you abrogated the statement with another, "Enjoy your spoils they are lawful and thrilling." The sustenance of orphans has never been considered delicious food by anyone. Neither was raiding nor plundering ever lawful gain or a method to earn a living.

7.   Therefore, whosoever devours the morsel of the orphan soon after they caused him to become an orphan, will not place into their bellies nutrients, but hellfire.   Their deed is actually despicable.

بـالتي هـي أحسـن" . ثـمّ تَسَـخْتـمْ قوَلكـمْ بقوَلكـمـ: "كُلـوامَّـا غَنمَتـمْ حَلالاً طَيباً" . وما كانَ قـوْتُ اليتـامى أكـلاً طيباً ولا كـانَ الغـزوُ مِرِزْقاً حَلالاً .

٧)   إنَّ الذين يأكلونَ لُقمةَ اليتيـمِ من بعدِ أنْ يُتَّموهُ أولَكَ ما يأكلونَ في بُطونهـمْ إلا النارَ وكانَ فعلُهـمْ وَبَيلاً .

42
PRAYER
(Surat Al Salat)

سُورَةُ الصّلاةِ (٤٢

In the Name of the Father, the Word, the Holy Spirit, the One and only True God

بسم الآبِ الكلمةِ الروحِ الالهِ الواحدِ الأوحدِ

1. A charitable deed without prayer is superior to any evil deed with prayer. Therefore discard gossip and hypocrisy for We can do without the prayers of hypocrites.

١) وَلَحَسَنَةٌ بلاصَلاةٍ خيرٌ مِنْ سَيّئَةٍ مَعَ الصلاةِ فانْبُذوا اللغوَ والنفاقَ فإنّا في غِنىً عَنْ صَلاةِ المُنافقينَ .

2. There is no comparison between the believers who perform righteous works by faith and the ones who perform none.

٢) وَلا يَسْتَوي المؤمنونَ الذينَ يَعملونَ بإيمانٍ والذينَ لا يعملونَ .

3. The ones who perform their ritualistic prayers at street corners, churches and mosques with an ulterior motive, which is to be observed by passersby, are the perfect hypocrites for they do not genuinely pray.

٣) إنّ الذينَ يُقيمونَ الصّلاةَ في زوايا الشوارعِ والمَساجدِ رياءً كي يَشْهَدَهُمُ الناسَ ذلكُمْ هُمُ المُنافقونَ وهُمْ في

203

الْحَقِيقَةَ لَا يُصَلُّونَ .

4. Therefore, whosoever de-termines to pray, let him enter his residence, find a secluded space, shut the door then proceed to pray while in his hiding place. We will reward such a person abundantly and openly.

٤) فَمَنْ نَوَى أَنْ يُصَلِّي فَلْيَدْخُلْ دَارَهُ وَيُغْلِقْ بَابَهُ وَيُصَلِّ خُفِيَةً نَجْزِهِ بِهِ عَلَانِيَةً بِعَيْنِ الْعَالَمِينَ .

5. Your repetition of the ritualistic prayers is much like that of the heathen. You errone-ously believe that by repeating your prayers you will be guarante-ed a hearing.

٥) تُكَرِّرُونَ الْكَلَامَ لَغْواً كَعَبَدَةِ الْأَوْثَانِ تَظُنُّونَ أَنَّكُمْ بِالتَّكْرَارِ تُسْتَجَابُونَ .

6. Are you not aware that We know your prayer requests before you vocalize them?

٦) إِنَّا نَعْلَمُ سُؤَلَكُمْ قَبْلَمَا تَسْأَلُونَ .

7. You presume that your repetitions of rituals will introduce you to the Garden. The Gates of Paradise will never open to let hypocrites inside. Only those who practice obedience to Our will shall enter therein.

٧) وَتُرَدِّدُونَ الدُّعَاءَ طَمَعاً بِدُخُولِ الْجَنَّةِ فَلَنْ تُفْتَحَ أَبْوَابُ الْجَنَّةِ لِلْمُنَافِقِينَ . أَمَّا الَّذِينَ يَعْمَلُونَ بِمَشِيئَتِنَا فَهُمُ الَّذِينَ يَدْخُلُونَ .

8. You judge people falsely. Never forget that the day will come when you will be judged in accordance with the judgments that you meted out to others.

٨) تُدِينُونَ النَّاسَ بِالبَاطِلِ وَسَوْفَ تُدانونَ بِالحَقِّ بِما كُنْتُمْ تُدِينُونَ .

9. None of you can serve two masters. Money is your master and money is what you really worship.

٩) وَلَا يَقْدِرُ أَحَدُكُمْ أَنْ يَعْبُدَ رَبَّيْنِ فَالمالُ رَبُّكُمْ وَإِيَّاهُ تَعْبُدُونَ .

10. All you worship besides Us are no more than idols and names you and your ancestors have concocted. They were the whisperings of Satan in your very hearts for which We have never given authority.

١٠) وَمَا تَعْبُدُونَ مِنْ دُونِنا إِلَّا أَشْياءَ وَأَسْماءَ سَمَّيْتُمُوها أَنْتُمْ وَآباؤُكُمْ وَسْوَسَ بِها الشَّيطانُ فِي صُدُورِكُمْ وَما أَنْزَلْنا بِها مِنْ سُلْطانٍ .

205

43
THE KINGS
(Surat Al Mulook)

٤٣) سُورةُ الملُوك

In the Name of the Father, the Word, the Holy Spirit, the One and only True God

بسم الآب الكلمة الروح الاله الواحد الأوحد

1. You declared, "There is no coercion in religion." Yet you forced upon Our faithful followers rebellion. Whosoever surrendered to you was saved from being killed by your enforcers. However, whosoever held onto the religion of Truth was killed summarily as criminals are killed.

١) وقلتُم: "لا إكراهَ في الدين". ورحتُم تُكرهونَ عبادَنا المؤمنينَ على الكفرِ فمن استسلمَ سلمَ ومن استمسكَ بدينِ الحقِّ قتلَ قتلَهُ المجرمينَ.

2. If We desire it, every soul on earth can be forced to trust Us unconditionally. Are you gods to make people into believers involuntarily?

٢) ولو شئنا لآمنَ مَن في الأرضِ كلُّهم جميعاً. أفأنتم تُكرهونَ الناسَ حتى يكونوا مؤمنينَ؟

3. You conjecture that we proclaimed, "Kill for the cause of

٣) وزعمتُم بأنا قلنا: "قاتلوا في سبيل

206

God and be aware that God is ever-listening and wise."

الله واعلموا أنّ اللّه سَميعٌ عليمٌ".

4. Whosoever orders death to others indiscriminately is not an all-knowing and allwise god. Indeed, such is Satan, the rebellious one.

٤) ألا إنّ مَنْ يأمرُ بالقتل فليسَ بإله سَميع عليم إنْ هوَ إلا شيطانٌ مَرِينٌ.

5. He actually urged his own followers to reject Our decrees. He promised them paradises of fornication and debauchery. Subsequently, they considered Our decrees unbelievable commands. Worldliness bamboozled them; thus, they lost the straight path.

٥) حَرّضَ أتباعهُ على الكفر بِسُنّتِنا ووَعدهُمْ بجنّاتِ الزّنى والفجورِ فاتخذوا آياتِنا هُزوًا وغرّتهُمُ الحياةُ الدنيا فضلّوا سَواءَ السّبيل.

6. The illustration of the ruthless raiders is much like thieves who assaulted a magnificent palace. They murdered the dwellers, seized their wealth and all the treasured riches.

٦) إنّ مَثَل الطغاةِ المعتدينَ كمثل لصُوص سَطوا على قصرٍ مُشيّد فقتلوا أهلهُ وسَلبوا أموالهُمْ وما يَدّخرونَ.

7. They claimed the women as their own and announced, "We have now become lords of palaces."

٧) واستَحيَوا نساءَهُمْ وقالوا: "لقد أصبحنا أربابَ قصورٍ فنحنُ اليومَ مُلوك"

207

مُتْرَفُونَ" .

8.   Nevertheless, the usurpers did not practice the precepts of the palace owners, but they behaved just as marauding raiders.   The result was that their lives became disorganized, the palace turned over into a den of thieves and became barren of royal thrones. Finally, it surfaced as a shelter for criminals only.

٨)   ومَا اتَّبَعَ اللصوصُ سُنَّةَ أهلِ القصورِ بلْ شِرْعَةَ الغُزَاةِ المُعتَدِينَ فأصبحتْ حَيَاتُهمُ فوضى وأصبحَ القصرُ كَهْفاً خَاوياً على عُروشِهِ وأمْسى مَأوىً للمُجرِمينَ .

44
THE EVIL ONE
(Surat Al Taghout)

٤٤) سُورَةُالطّاغوتِ

In the Name of the Father, the Word, the Holy Spirit, the One and only True God

بِسمِ الآبِ الكلمةِ الروحِ الالهِ الواحدِ الأوحدِ

1. This is directed to anyone who has rebelled, yet still claim to be counted among Our followers. There is a rumor that a descendent has arisen from your midst who proclaims that he is equal to Us. In fact, he joined his name to Ours, his will with Our will, adding that to trust him is actually to trust Us too. He deluded people that he is Our elect and companion. There has never been a partner to Us nor any equal to Us in the entire universe.

١) يَأيُها الذينَ كَفروا مِنْ عِبادِنا : لَقَدْ قَامَ مِنكُمْ مَنْ أقَامَ نَفسَهُ كَفوآ لَنا وَطَفِقَ يُوهِمُ الناسَ بأنَهُ مُختارُنا وشَرِيكُنا . الا اِنَهُ لا شَرِيكَ لَنا ولمْ يَكُنْ لَنا كُفوا أحدٌ فِي العَالمينَ .

2. We provided guidance for man and led him out of darkness into the light. Yet, Satan tricked him back into darkness. We brought man from unbelief into

٢) وَهَدينا الإنسانَ وأخرجناهُ مِنَ الظلماتِ إلى النُورِ فأعادَهُ إلى الظلماتِ .

209

faith.   But Satan brought him back into unbelief. We cleansed man from every unclean thing. But Satan polluted him by adultery and immorality.

ونقلناهُ من الكفر الى الإيمان فردّه إلى الكفر، وطهّرناه من كل رجس فنجّسه بالزنى والفجورِ.

3.   Mankind was commanded not to kill. But Satan allowed killing to mankind, by claiming We Ourselves have sanctioned it. We planted in man's heart love, mercy and peace. Satan snatched these virtues from man's heart, overwhelming him with hate and animosity. We wished for man to be a benevolent angel. But Satan turned him into a cursed demon. Then he demoted man into the lowest depravity.

٣) وحرّمنا عليه القتل فأحلّه له باسمنا. وغرسنا بقلبه المحبّة والرحمة والسلامَ فنزعها من قلبه وأفعمه بالكره والخصامِ وأردنا له أن يكون مَلَكاً رحيماً فجعَل منه شيطاناً رجيماً وأنزَل له أسفل سافلينَ.

4.   Satan conspired against Our believing followers purposing to turn them back from their faith. So, he commissioned someone who renounced Our decrees. Thus, he caused those whose hearts were already sick to be misguided; then they rebelled.

٤) وكادَ الشيطانُ لعبادنا المؤمنينَ ليردّهُمْ عن إيمانهمْ فأرسلَ من يُناهضُ سُنّتنا فأضلَّ الذينَ في قلوبهمْ مَرضٌ فكفروا وأمّا عبادُنا المُخلصونَ فلمْ يجدْ إلى قلوبهمْ سبيلاً وظلّوا على إيمانهـمــ

ثَابِتِينَ .

5. We have carved Our precepts into the hearts of the faithful believers. We answer their heartfelt prayers. But the calls of the blasphemers We never hear.

٥) وَطَبَعْنَا سُنَّتَنَا عَلَى قُلُوبِ الْمُؤْمِنِينَ فَنَسْمَعُ دُعَاءَ قُلُوبِهِمْ وَلَا نُصْغِي إِلَى لَغْوِ الْكَافِرِينَ .

6. The followers of the imposter descended into a deep pit. They exchanged peace for warfare, benevolence for raiding, purity for fornication and faith for faithlessness. Subsequently, their trade vanished; their profit was none other than a terrible torment.

٦) وَهَبَطَ الَّذِينَ اتَّبَعُوا الطَّاغُوتَ إِلَى دَرَكٍ سَحِيقٍ فَاشْتَرَوُا الْحَرْبَ بِالسَّلَامِ وَالسَّلْبَ بِالْإِحْسَانِ وَالزِّنَى بِالْعِفَّةِ وَالْكُفْرَ بِالْإِيمَانِ فَخَسِرَتْ تِجَارَتُهُمْ وَكَسِبُوا عَذَابًا وَبِيلًا .

7. They committed debauchery, vileness and rape as they pursued the paradise of adultery. They make false promises and offer insincere rewards from Satan. Flee away from the paradise of the blasphemers. Woe unto them to whom such a paradise appears very desirable.

٧) وَاقْتَرَفُوا الْفَحْشَاءَ وَالْمُنْكَرَ وَالْبَغْيَ سَعْيًا وَرَاءَ جَنَّةِ الزِّنَى يُوعَدُونَهَا وَعْدًا غَرُورًا وَثَوَابًا إِفْكًا مِنَ الشَّيْطَانِ، أَلَا بُعْدًا لِجَنَّةِ الْكَافِرِينَ وَتَعْسًا لِمَنْ بِهَا يُوعَدُونَ .

8. They have also misquoted Us by stating that We have declared, "We have purchased the believer's souls and paradise is theirs. So they should fight for Our enterprise. And such a promise is actually recorded in the Gospel." Let it be known that the fabricators are liars. You see, We do not purchase the souls of criminals. It is Satan, the cursed one, who does this sort of merchandizing.

٨) واقتَروا على لسَانا الكَذبَ: "بأنا اشْتَرِينا من المؤمنينَ أنفسَهم بأنَّ لهم الجنّة يُقاتلونَ في سَبيلنا وعداً علينا حقاً في الإنجيل . "الا إنَّ المفترينَ كاذبونَ . فإنا لا نشتري نفوس المجرمينَ إنما اشتراها الشيطانُ اللعينُ .

9. The imposters have made Us partners with a gang who robs and kills Our creatures. They even arranged that one-fifth of the spoils of war should be given to Us to make them feel justified in their selfish and criminal pursuits.

٩) وأشركونا في عُصبة تقتُل وتَسلُب عبادَنا وفرضوا لنا في خُمُس ما يغنم الغُزاةُ المجرمونَ .

10. The hypocrites exonerated the criminals by saying, "For you have not destroyed them. It is God who did." Do you not realize that We do not destroy Our Own family members in order to take spoils as the marauders and murderers do?

١٠) وبرّأهم المنافقونَ فقالوا : "وما قتلموهم ولكنّ اللهَ قتلهم" الا إنا لا نقتل عبادَنا لنغنمَ مع القتلة والمعتدينَ .

11. They have judged themselves rightly when they announced, "Shall I reveal to you upon whom demons descend? Demons descend upon every wicked deceiver."

١١) وَحَكَمُوا بِالقِسْطِ عَلَى أَنفُسِهِمْ إِذْ كَلوا : "هَـلْ أُنَبِّكُــمْ عَلَى مَـنْ تُنَزِّلُ الشَّياطِينُ؟ تُنَزِّلُ عَـلَى كُــلِّ أَفَّـاكِ أَثِيمٍ."

12. As for those who veil in secrecy what We have conveyed of guidance and prudence in **The True Furqan**, after We had revealed it in **The True Gospel**, denouncers will denounce them. Then, they will roast in the fires of Hell. We are ever Holy and Just.

١٢) والذينَ يَكتُمُونَ مَا أَنزَلنَا مِنَ البَيِّنَاتِ والهُدى فِي الفرقانِ الحَقِّ مِنْ بعدِ مَا بَيَّنَاهُ فِي الإنجِيلِ الحَقِّ أُولئكَ يَلعَنُهُمُ اللاعِـنُونَ وَيَصْلَونَ نَارَ الجَحِيمِ.

213

45
ABROGATION
(Surat Al Naskh)

٤٥) سُورةُالنسخ

In the Name of the Father, the Word, the Holy Spirit, the One and only True God

بسم الآبِ الكلمةِ الروح الاله الواحد الأوحدِ

1. The hypocrite can be likened unto a raider who conquered a village, spoiled it and humiliated its nobility into servitude. He claimed that he is the King's messenger to them providing them with a forged letter to that effect. Therefore, the unenlightened trusted him.

١) إنَّ مَثَلَ المُنافقينَ كَمثلِ غازٍ دَخَلَ قَرْيةً فأفسَدَها وجعَلَ أعِزَّةَ أهلِها أذِلَّةً وزعمَ أنَّه رَسولُ المللكِ إليهمْ وبيَّنَهُ كتابٌ افتراهُ فصَدَّقَهُ الجاهلونَ .

2. Killing, he killed the opposition. But he let live whosoever took his side making them his staunchly faithful followers.

٢) وقتلَ مَن ناهَضَهُ وعَفا عَمَّن أتبَعَهُ وأتَّخذهُمْ أولياءَ كافرينَ .

3. One day a man arrived from a distant city who exposed the treachery of the hypocrite and declared to the entire village the true nature of this person.

٣) وجاءَ رجلٌ من أقصى المدينةِ يَسعى وفَضَحَ خِدْعةَ المفترينَ وأعلَنَ القريةَ بالخَبَرِ

اليقين .

٤) فَحَصْحَصَ الحقُّ وانبلجَ النورُ فاهتدى
الضّالونَ وارتدَّ المُضلّلونَ وتابوا فعَاشوا في
مَحبّةٍ وسلامٍ آمنينَ .

4. Truth was revealed. Light became bright. So, those who were lost were found. The ones who were led astray returned to the right way. Thereafter, they all lived securely with love and peace holding sway.

٥) يأيُّها الذينَ كفروا منْ عِبادنا : هَلْ
وصَّيناكُمْ بِعبادِنا المؤمنينَ أنْ فريقاً
تقتلونَ وتأسرونَ فريقاً . وأوْرثناكُمْ
أرْضَهُمْ ودِيَارهمْ وأموالهمْ وأرضاً لمْ
تطئوها ؟ أهذا جَزاءُ إيمانهمْ بنا ؟ وهلْ
جَزاءُ الإحسانِ إلاّ الإحسانُ ؟

5. O, you who have renounced the faith from among Our people: did We ever command you concerning Our believing servants that you kill some of them and imprison others? And that We gave you their homes, properties, riches and a land which you did not even trod? Is this the reward for their trust in Us? Is not the reward of good deeds also a goodly reward?

٦) أفمنْ كانَ مؤمناً كمنْ كانَ
كافراً ؟ لا يستوونَ ، وسَيرى الذينَ
افتروا علينا الكذبَ أيَّ مُنقلبٍ ينقلبونَ .

6. Can a true believer be compared to one who is an infidel? There is no comparison whatsoever. Consequently, those who have propagated falsehood concerning Us will discover what a terrible punishment awaits them.

7.   You are merely a bunch of illiterates who have no knowledge of **The True Gospel** and debate over Our signs without any authority from any source. Despised are the statements that you make in such ignorance. We, furthermore, stamp "Despised" as Our sign of displeasure on the heart of every arrogant dictator.

8.   You fabricated falsely that We declared, "Such of Our revelations as We abrogate or cause to be forgotten, We bring one better or the like thereof." We have neither made a mistake nor are We absent-minded.

9.   You also stated, "God abrogates what Satan brought forth, then God corrects His own verses."

10. In this manner you have burdened Us down with the weight of your sins and forget-fulness. We never make mistakes thus causing Us to abrogate or annul. Neither do We forget nor must We be reminded. We do not act wickedly and then must rectify

٧) وإنكـــمُ لأمّيّونَ لا تعلمونَ الانجيلَ الحَقَّ وتُجادلونَ في آياتنا بغيرِ سُلطان أتاكــمُ . كَبُرَ مَقْتاً عندَنا أنْ تقولوا ما لا تعلمونَ . كَذلكَ نَطبعُ على قلبِ كُلِّ مُتكبِّرٍ جبّارٍ .

٨) وافتريتمُ على لِسانِنا الكـــذبَ وقلتمُ بأنّا : "ما ننسَخُ مِنْ آيةٍ أو نُنسِهَا نأتِ بخيرٍ منها أو مثلِها" . فما أخطأنا ولا كُنّا غافلينَ .

٩) وقلتمُ : "فينسخُ اللهُ ما يُلقي الشيطانُ ثمَّ يُحكِمُ اللهُ آياتِه"

١٠) وألقيتمُ علينا وِزرَ أخطائكمُ وسيانكمُ . ألا إنّنا لا نُخطئُ فننسَخَ . ولا نَنسى فنتذكَّرَ ولا نُسيءُ فنُحسِنَ . وإذا أردنا أمراً فإنّما قولُـهُ كُـنْ

216

by doing better. The fact is, if We desire anything We simply say, "Let it be done," and it is done in superlative fashion.

فيكون في أحسن تكوين .

11. You have also despised and disdained Our revealed scriptures. Consequently, this motto fitted you well; "Demons are the supporters of the unbelievers who accused Our scripture with falsehood, yet they themselves were oblivious of their lot."

(١١) وكفرتم وكذبتم بآياتنا فحق عليكم القول : " بأنّ الشياطين أولياء الذين كفروا وكذّبوا بآياتنا وكانوا عنها غافلين"

12. Furthermore, if it is rumored, "These sayings are his own invention," he recoils from the criticism and announces, "Bring ten such invented chapters if you have the creative ability."

(١٢) وإذا قيل : " هو قول افتراه" . قلتم : " فأتوا بعشر سور مثله مفتريات إن كنتم صادقين" .

13. No one brings forth such invented chapters except an imposter who recites what demons concocted.

(١٣) ولا يأتي السور المفتريات إلا مفترٍ وممّا توحي الشياطين .

14. We have conveyed it, a **True Furqan**. No deception will ever enter into it. Even Satan himself will not get near this

(١٤) وأنزلناه فرقاناً حقّاً لا يأتيه الباطل من بين يديه ولا من خلفه ولا يقربه الشيطان

217

True **Furqan** because it is an extremely heavy burden for the hearts of the infidels to bear. Let everyone remember, that We are the Most Gracious, The Omniscient God.

فكان على قلوب الكافرين عبئاً ثقيلاً .

46
THE SHEPHERDS
(Surat Al Ru'aah)

٤٦) سُورةُالرِّعاةِ

In the Name of the Father, the Word, the Holy Spirit, the One and only True God

بِسْمِ الآبِ الكلمةِ الروحِ الإلهِ الواحِدِ الأوحدِ

1. An illustration of a good messenger is a shepherd who led his sheep to an excellent watering stream and green pastures.

١) وَمَثَلُ الرسولِ الصَّالِحِ كَمَثَلِ راعٍ أوْرِدَ رَعَيْتَهُ وِرْداً طَهُوراً وَرَعَى حَلالاً .

2. Subsequently, We accepted those sheep into Our fold with great delight. They are indeed Our righteous worshipers. Neither danger nor sorrow will affect them.

٢) فَتَقَبَّلْنَاهُمْ بِقَبُولٍ حَسَنٍ أُولئكَ هُمْ عِبَادُنَا الصَّالِحونَ لا خوفَ عليهِمْ ولا هُمْ يَحْزَنونَ .

3. But an illustration of a wicked shepherd is a thief who climbed over the sheepfold. He killed and snatched, then led astray those who knew the right way, sending them to the pit, where the unrepentant sinners

٣) وَمَثَلُ الرَّاعي الطَّالِحِ كَمَثَلِ لِصٍّ تَسَوَّرَ حَضِيرَةَ الخِرافِ فقَتَلَ وَسَرَقَ وأضَلَّ المُهتَدينَ وأوْرِدَهُمْ مَوْرِدَ الهالِكينَ .

219

forever will stay.

4. They denounced the precept of **Truth**. That decision caused them to become lost people and the very ones upon whom wrath is poured out continually.

٤) فكفروا بسُنةِ الحَقّ فهُمُ المَغضوبُ عليهِمُ وهـمُ الضّالّونَ .

5. The fact is, the good Shepherd sacrifices His very life for His flock. But the wicked shepherd scatters his flock to fulfill his own selfish desire. Therefore, each shepherd demonstrates his character by what he does with the sheep and will receive his fair reward without impartiality.

٥) إنّما الرّاعي الصّالح يبذلُ نفسَهُ في سبيلِ رعيّتِهِ . والرّاعي الطّالح يُبدّدُ رعيّتهُ في سبيلِ رغبتِهِ فكلّ يعملُ على شاكلته ويَنالُ جَزاءً وفاقاً ولا يُظلمونَ .

6. No one will adhere to the creed of the infidel, the unenlightened, the murderer or the depraved except the infidels, the ignorant, the murderers and the depraved. Accordingly, their religion is suitable and accommodative to their characters. For they will definitely reap exactly what they sow.

٦) ولا يعتنق سُنّةَ الكفرِ والجهلِ والقتلِ والفجورِ إلّا الكفرةُ والجهلةُ والقتلةُ والفاجرونَ . فدينُهـمُ على شـاكلتِهـمُ وإنْ يَحصُدونَ إلّا ما يزرعونَ .

47
THE TESTIMONY
(Surat Al Shahada)

٤٧) سورةُالشّهادة

In the Name of the Father, the Word, the Holy Spirit, the One and only True God

بسمِ الآبِ الكلمةِ الروحِ الالهِ الواحدِ الأوحدِ

1. O, you who are hypocrites, yet still claim to be counted among Our worshipers: how can you testify about what your eyes have not witnessed and repeat what you do not comprehend? You have actually testified falsely, declared dishonestly and have spoken fraudulently.

١) يَأَيُّها المُنافقونَ مِنْ عِبادِنا الضّالِينَ: أنَّى تَشهدونَ بِما لَمْ تَشهدوا وتُرَدِّدُونَ مَا لَا تَفْقهونَ . لَقَدْ شَهِدْتُرْ إِفكاً وَقُلْــمْ بَهْتاً ونُكراً .

2. You have related to the people that information of which you are ignorant. You have unloaded your backward knowledge upon the ones who were well-grounded in scholarship and the religion of truth, weighing them down with a heavy burden.

٢) وَبَلّغتُمُ الناسَ مَا ليسَ لكــم بِه عِلمٌ . وأنفذتُمْ جَاهليتَكُمْ على الرّاسِخينَ في العلـمِ والدينِ القويـمِ فأثقلتُمْ كواهلَهمْ وِزْراً .

3. Truth became incarnate in flesh, Jesus of Nazareth, but you

٣) وشُبِّهَ لكــمُ الحـقُّ فَمَا فَقِهتمْ

221

never could comprehend the incarnation one iota! Neither did you understand the meaning of Fatherhood or Sonship. Even redemption was an unfathomable truth for your clouded understanding. Thus, spiritual matters somehow escaped your comprehension.

٤) وعَلَّمَ الْأُمّيِّينَ أُمّيٌّ كَافِرٌ فَزَادَهُـمْ جَهْلاً وَكُفْراً.

4. An illiterate infidel instructed the illiterates, who in turn increased their ignorance and infidelity.

٥) وَأَخْرَجَهُـمْ مِنَ النُّـورِ إِلَى الظُّلُمَـاتِ وَأَضَلَّهُـمْ قَسْراً.

5. Astonishingly, he led them by hook and crook out of light into darkness and led them astray.

٦) فَالنُّورُ يُبَدِّدُ الظَّلامَ وَالظَّلامُ لاَ يُطْفِئُ النُّورَ، بَـلْ يَزِيـدُ الْمُؤْمِنِينَ إِيمَانـاً وَيُسْـراً وَالْكَافِرِينَ كُفْراً وَعُسْـراً.

6. Light dispels darkness and darkness cannot snuff out the light. Instead, it intensifies the faith of the believers with more resolve. But the unbelievers end up with more dread and damnation.

٧) فَمَنْ سَارَ فِي النُّورِ لاَ يَعْثُرُ وَمَنْ سَارَ

7. Consequently, whosoever walks in the light shall not

stumble. But whosoever walks in the dark shall accumulate more wickedness and faithlessness.

فِي الظَّلامِ يَزْدَادُ ضَلالاً وَكُفْراً .

48
THE GUIDANCE
(Surat Al Huda)

٤٨) سُورَةُ الْهُدى

In the Name of the Father, the Word, the Holy Spirit, the One and only True God

بسم الآبِ الكلمةِ الروحِ الالهِ الواحدِ الأوحدِ

1. We aspired for Our worshipers a wholesome body, an enlightened mind and a pure heart. The purpose was to be guided to Our path, to live by Our criterion and to enter Our paradise of abundant grace and eternal peace.

١) وأردنا لعبادِنا جَسَداً سَليماً وَعقلاً مُنيراً وقلباً طَهيراً ليهتدوا إلى سَبيلنا وَيعملوا بُسنَّتنا ويَنالوا جنّاتِ النعيمِ .

2. We have also healed the blind and the leper. But when the imposters arrived they blinded the eyes of those who could see and defiled those who were cleansed.

٢) وَشَفَينا الأكمَهَ والأبرصَ فجئتُمْ تُعشُونَ عُيونَ المبصِرِينَ وتُنجِسُونَ الطاهرينَ .

3. Furthermore, We brought to life those who were dead. But the deceivers commenced to kill those who were living righteous lives.

٣) وأحيَينا المَوتى فَرُحتُمْ تُقتَلونَ الأحياءَ الصَّالحينَ .

4. Additionally, We guided the lost back to the path. But the imposters came along leading them astray.

٤) وَهَدَيْنَا الضَّالِينَ فَجِئْتُمْ تُضِلُّونَ المُهْتَدِينَ .

5. You have even accused Us of lying by announcing that We inspired a new decree unto you, which permits infidelity, killing and oppression.

٥) وافْتَرَيْتُمْ عَلَيْنَا الكَذِبَ إِذْ زَعَمْتُمْ بِأَنَّا أَوْحَيْنَا إِلَيْكُمْ بِشِرْعَةِ الكُفْرِ والقَتْلِ والضَّلالِ .

6. Let it be known that We do not command the killing of Our created beings, even if they are pagans or apostates.

٦) أَلَا إِنَّا لَا نُوحِي بِقَتْلِ عِبَادِنَا وَلَوْ كَانُوا كَافِرِينَ .

7. Such "decree of bad faith" is the inspiration of the wicked and rebellious Satan.

٧) لَكِنَّهَا شِرْعَةُ الكُفْرِ مِنْ وحي شَيْطَانٍ عَنِيدٍ .

8. Had you brought forth what Our righteous messengers have presented you of divine truth and right guidance, you too would have been among Our chosen few.

٨) وَلَوْ جِئْتُمْ بِمِثْلِ مَا جَاءَ بِهِ رُسُلُنَا الصَّالِحُونَ مِنْ حَقٍّ وهُدًى وقُلْتُمْ كَمَا قَالُوا لَكُنْتُمْ مِنْ عِبَادِنَا الصَّادِقِينَ .

9. Instead, you have corrupted the path of Our worshipers. You have also hindered their efforts to reach Us, causing them

٩) لَكِنَّكُمْ أَفْسَدْتُمْ سَبِيلَ عِبَادِنَا وأَحْبَطْتُمْ مَسْعَاهُمْ فَهَبَطُوا إِلَى دَرْكِ

to descend into a deep level of despair.

سَحِيقٍ .

10. Satan made your evil deeds look attractive to you and announced, "No one will conquer you now from among humans. I am a neighbor to you, so do not fear any aggressors or their aggression."

١٠) وَزَيَّنَ لَكُــمُ الشَّــيْطانُ سُــوءَ أَعْمَالِكُمْ وَقَالَ: "لا غَالِبَ لَكُـمُ اليَومَ مِنَ النَّاسِ وِإِنِّي جَارٌ لَكُـمْ فَلا تَخْشَوا بَأْسَ المُعتَدِينَ" .

11. Thus, you trusted the lies and mistrusted the truth. You ended up following the path of the misguided.

١١) فَصَدَّقْتُـمْ بِـالضَلالِ وكَذَّبتُـمْ بِالهُدى وَاتَّبَعتُـمْ سَبِيلَ الكَافِرِينَ .

49
THE GOSPEL
(Surat Al Injil)

سورةُ الإنجيل (٤٩

In the Name of the Father, the Word, the Holy Spirit, the One and only True God

بسمِ الآبِ الكلمةِ الروحِ الإله الواحدِ الأوحدِ

1. O, you who have gone astray, yet still claim to be counted among Our followers: you declare, "Let the people of **The True Gospel** judge what God inspired in it. Those who will not accept what God inspired are the ungodly for certain."

١) يَأيُّها الذينَ ضَلُّوا مِنْ عبادنا: تقولونَ: "وليحكمُ أهلُ الإنجيلِ بما أنزلَ اللهُ فيه ومَنْ لَمْ يحكمُ بما أنزلَ اللهُ فأولئك هـمُ الفَاسقُونَ" .

2. You did not revere what We inspired, rather you accused **The True Gospel** of being lies and perverted Our doctrines. Your conviction about the ungodly became most fitting for yourselves.

٢) فما حكمتـمُ بما أنزلنـا بـل كذّبتـمُ بالإنجيلِ الحقِّ وحرّقتـمُ قولَنا فحقَّ عليكـمُ قولكـمُ بأنّكـمُ الفَاسقُونَ .

3. Is it ever practical for the hand of dishonesty to fight the spike of honesty and win? If you champion the cause of corruption the kingdom of corruption will

٣) وأنّى يَلطمُ كفُّ الباطلِ مخزَرَ الحقِّ . فإنْ تُنصروا الظلمَ فدولةُ الظلمِ ساعةٌ

227

last only for an hour. In contrast, the Kingdom of Truth will last forever and forever.

ودَوْلَـةُ الْحَــقِّ خَــالِدَةٌ لَـوْ كُنْتَـــمْ تَذكُرونَ .

4. You proclaim, "In case you are in doubt of the validity of what We have conveyed, seek the counsel of those who read **The True Gospel**, which was revealed ahead of you." Why then do you persist in your ungodliness and stubbornness by not seeking the counsel of the People of The Book? You actually doubt what We inspired in **The True Gospel** because you do not really trust what you claim to have in yours.

٤) تَقُولُونَ: "إنْ كُنْتَ فِي شَكٍّ مِّمَّا أنزَلَ اللهُ فَسائِلِ الذينَ يَقرَأونَ الانجيلَ الحَـقِّ مِنْ قَبْلِكَ" فَأنَّى تُغالونَ في الكفرِ والضَلال وَلا تَسْألونَ أهْلَ الذِكرِ؟ فإنَّكُـمْ في شَكٍّ مِّمَّا أنزَلْنا في الإنجيلِ الحَقِّ وأنَّكُـمْ لا تَعلَمونَ .

5. Therefore, you did not pursue the conduct of love, compassion and peace. Neither did you pursue the help of those who read **The True Gospel**. Nor did you obtain its divine guidance to emulate it. Thus, you lost your way and turned out to be among the ill-informed until doomsday.

٥) وَما ابْتَغيتُمْ سَـبِيلَ المَحَبَّةِ والرحمة والسَلامِ وما سَألتُمُ الذينَ يَقرَأونَ الانجيل وَما اهتَدَيتُــمْ بِــهُداهِمْ فَضَلَلتُـمْ وَكُنتُمْ مِنْ الجاهِلينَ .

6. O, you who have believed from among Our worshipers: have

٦) يَأيُها الذينَ آمنوا مِنْ عِبادِنا: ألَمْ تَكرَوا إلى

you not taken notice of those who rejected **The True Gospel**, how they purchased falsehood with guidance! They abandoned the perfect principles of conduct and defiled Our scriptures in various sections of The Book degrading True Religion. Had they answered, "We have both heard and obeyed," it would have been to their advantage. Instead, they persisted in their apostasy and no longer trust Us.

الذين كفروا بالإنجيل الحق كيف

اشتروا الضلالة بالهدى وضلّوا سواءَ السبيل

وحرّفوا الكلم عن مَواضعه طغنا في

الدين الحقّ وكوأنهم قالوا سَمعنا وأطعنا

لكانَ خيرًا لهم ولكنهم أمعنوا في

الكفر فهم لا يؤمنونَ .

50
THE POLYTHEISTS
(Surat Al Mushrikeen)

٥٠) سُورَةُ المُشرِكِينَ

In the Name of the Father, the Word, the Holy Spirit, the One and only True God

بِسمِ الآبِ الكلمةِ الرُّوحِ الالهِ الواحدِ الأوحدِ

1.   O, you who have become polytheists, yet still claim to be counted among Our worshipers: you have forced Our believing servants to give up their faith. You then infused the monotheists with polytheism and accused them with apostasy because they have trusted Our manifestation in the Triune God. You did not realize fully that they worshiped Us as the one and only Heavenly Father, accepted Us, The Word, as the most beneficent messenger and believed in Our Spirit as the most Merciful Holy One. Actually, they have neither become polytheists nor added an associate to Us by believing in this manner.

١) يَأَيُّها الذينَ أشرَكوا من عِبادِنا الضّالينَ: لقدْ كَفَّرَّ عِبادَنا المُؤمنينَ وربيتَمُ بالشِّركِ المُوحِّدينَ. ذلكَ أنهـمْ آمنوا بثالوثِ مَظهرِنا فَعبدونا أباً وحيداً وقبلِوا كلمَتَنا رَسُولاً رحمَاناً وآمنوا بروحِنا قُدوسَاً رحيماً. فما كَفروا وما أشرَكوا بِنا شيئاً في العالمينَ.

230

2.   Let us clarify this doctrine. Any human being who joins himself to Us as an associate and assumes to be Our partner in power and might has indeed become a polytheist.   No true prophet has ever made himself a partner with the God who sent him.   Therefore, whosoever adds an associate to Our Person becomes an apostate who has gone astray. No human being can ever attain divinity.   But We Ourselves can be incarnated into a human being as We did in Jesus, the Messiah.

٢) لقد كفر من أشرك بنفسه بنا وشاركنا الحول والقوة فما كان لرسول أن يشرك بنفسه برسله ومن يشرك بنا فقد كفر وضل ضلالاً بعيداً .

3.   Therefore, the one who associates the obedience of Our servants to Us with the obedience to himself has indeed become a polytheist.   He declared, "Whosoever obeys the messenger has actually obeyed God." Without a doubt this is the height of polytheism.

٣) فقد أشرك بنا من شاركنا إطاعة عبادنا إذ قال : "من يطع الرسول فقد أطاع الله" . وهذا هو الشرك العظيم .

4.   Furthermore, the one who associates Our answer to the prayers of Our worshipers as his

٤) وأشرك بنا من شاركنا استجابة عبادنا إذ تلا : "استجيبوا لله والرسول"

polytheist. He announced, "Respond to God and His messenger."

ولا يستجيب للمشرك إلا المشركون .

5. Again, the one who associates Our rule among Our people with his rule has become a polytheist. He proclaimed, "Whenever you quarrel over something bring the problem to God and his messenger." How can a person be just in his ruling when he has previously been tyrannical in dealing with Our believing children?

٥) وأشرك بنا من شاركنا الحكم بين عبادنا إذ قال : "إذا تنازعتم في شيء فردّوه إلى الله والرسول" فأتى يحكم بالقسط من كان ظلاماً لعبادنا المؤمنين .

6. Moreover, this messenger even abrogated what he had just proclaimed, "O, God, you are the one who hands out judgment among your people concerning the matter in which they quarrel."

٦) ثم نسخ قوله بقوله : "اللهم أنت تحكم بين عبادك فيما كانوا فيه يختلفون" .

7. Also, the one who associates the promise of trust in Us as an indication of trust in himself has become a polytheist. He announced, "Put your trust in God and his messenger." No one trusts a polytheist except the apostates.

٧) وأشرك بنا من شاركنا الايمان بنا وقال : "آمنوا بالله ورسوله" ولا يؤمن بالمشرك إلا القوم الكافرون .

8. Furthermore, the one who makes Us an associate of his in his captivities and spoils of war has become a polytheist. He recited, "The spoils of war belong to God and his messenger." Suffice it to say that we have no need for the spoils of war won by the oppressors and the lawless.

٨) وأشرك بنا مَنْ أشركنا في غنائمه وأنفاله إذْ تَلا: "الأنفال لله والرسول" وإنّا لفي غنىً عـن أنفـال المعتدين وأسـلاب المجرمين .

9. Also, the one who claims that he and We are responsible partners whenever his companions betray him has become a polytheist. He said, "Do not betray either God or his messenger." Even if his own adherents betray him, Our righteous worshipers do not betray Us because there are no traitors among them.

٩) وأشرك بنا من أشركنا في خيانة أتباعه له إذ قال: "لا تخونوا الله والرسول" . ولئنْ خَانـه أتبـاعُـه فـلا يَخُونُـا عبادُنـا الصالحون فما بينهم من خائنين .

10. Again, the one who makes Us a partner when his companions rebel against him has become a polytheist. If his companions rebelled against him Our obedient followers certainly do not follow suit.

١٠) وأشرك بنا من أشركنا في عصيان أتباعه له بقوله: "ومَنْ يَعْص الله والرسول" فـإنْ عَصِيـه أتبـاعُـه فمَـا عَصِينـا عبادُنـا المطيعون .

11. Furthermore, the one who makes Us a partner in his warfare and killing has become a polytheist. He claimed, "The punishment of those who fight God and his messenger is execution." We certainly did not create Our worshipers to fight against Us so We would have an excuse to execute them. Such behavior is the height of apostasy and polytheism.

١١) وأشرك بنا من أشرك كنا في حروبه
وقتاله وقال: "إنّما جزاء الذين يحاربون الله
ورسوله أن يُقتلوا" وما خلقنا عبادنا
ليُحاربونا فنقتلهم وما ذلك إلا الضلال
والشرك الكبير.

12. Additionally, the one who claims to share in Our power of redemption has become a polytheist. He affirmed, "Indeed your redeemer is God and his messenger." There has never been a redeemer for Our people who originated from among the polytheists.

١٢) وأشرك بنا من شارك كنا ولايتنا
لعبادنا بقوله: "إنّما وليكم الله ورسوله
"وما كان لعبادنا المؤمنين ولي من
المشركين.

13. And the one who makes himself a partner with Us in justifying Our people has indeed become a polytheist. "Justification comes from God and his messenger," he proclaimed. There has never been a human

١٣) وأشرك بنا من شارك كنا تبرئة عبادنا
إذ تلا: "براءة من الله ورسوله" وما
كان لبشر أن يُبرئ بشرا من قدر
محتوم.

being who is capable to justify or exonerate another human being from a predestined doom.

14. Besides that, the one who makes himself an associate in Our covenants with mankind has become a polytheist. He emphasized, "How can it be that polytheists have a covenant relationship with God and his messenger?" Let Us explain that there is no partner with Us in Our Covenants and never was such. No one makes a covenant with a polytheist except other polytheists.

١٤) وأشرك بنا من شار كنا عُهودنا إذ قال: "كيف يكون للمشركين عهدٌ عند الله وعند رسوله" الا إنه لا شريك لنا في عهودنا ولا يعاهد المشرك إلا المشركون.

15. In addition, the one who joins himself to Us as a partner in the forbidding or the sanctioning of anything has become a polytheist. He recited, "They will not forbid what God and his messenger have forbidden." The authority in the world of sanctioning or forbidding is Ours only and in this supreme prerogative We have no partner.

١٥) وأشرك بنا من شار كنا التحريمَ والتحليلَ إذ كلا: "ولا يحرّمونَ ما حرّمَ الله ورسوله" الا إنّ التحليلَ والتحريمَ من أمرنا ولا شريك لنا في العالمينَ.

16. Furthermore, the one who

١٦) وأشرك بنا من شارَكنا في إغناء

235

counts himself as an associate of Ours in enriching Our followers is a polytheist. His words are, "God and his messenger has enriched them." Is it conceivable that a penniless man can bestow riches upon a penniless people?

عبادنا بقوله: "أغناهُمُ اللهُ ورسُولُهُ" وأنّى يُغني المُعدِمُ المُعدِمِينَ ؟ .

17. Additionally, the one who makes himself a partner with Us by claiming that his followers blasphemed against Us and him is himself a polytheist. He pronounced, "They have blasphemed against God and his messenger." Such pronouncements originate from the apostates and the work of polytheists.

١٧) وأشركَ بنا من أشركَنا كفرِ أتباعِه إذ قال: "كفروا بالله ورسوله" وإنّهُ قولُ الكفَرةِ وفعـلُ المشركينَ .

18. Moreover, the one who makes Us his partner whenever he accuses others of calling him dishonest has become a polytheist. He said, "Those people have accused God and his messenger of dishonesty." In fact, his accusers have told the truth about him, whereas the ones who believed him were dishonest themselves.

١٨) وأشـركَ بنـا مـن أشـركَنا في تكذيبِ الناسِ لهُ فقال: "الذينَ كذّبوا اللهَ ورسوله" لقد صَدقَ الذينَ كذّبوهُ وكذبَ المصدّقون .

19. Again, the one who joins himself to us as a partner in watching over Our worshipers has become a polytheist. He recited, "Go ahead with your good deeds for God and his messenger shall watch over your deeds." How can one see anything when he himself has gone astray? He has neither a heart to understand nor eyes to see what goes on over this vast creation.

٩١) وأشـرك بنـا من شـارك نا مُراقَبَة
عِبادنـا إذ تـلا: "إعملـوا وسَيَـرى الله
عَملك ورَسُولهُ" وأنى يَرى من ضلَّ
وماله من قلب وعيون.

20. Also, the one who makes himself an associate of Ours by the promise of deception on Our part has become a polytheist. It is recorded, "God and his messenger have promised us nothing except a false promise." No one makes a fake promise but Satan, the supreme apostate.

٢٠) وأشرك بنا من أشرك نا في وعد
الغرور بقوله: "ما وعَدَنا الله ورسُوله إلا
غُـرورا" ولا يَعـدُ وعـد الغُـرور إلا
الشيطانُ اللعينُ.

21. The one who joins Us as the One who repays the upright has become a polytheist. He recited, "Whosoever among your women who submits herself to God and his messenger and practices righteousness, We shall reward her twofold." Anyone who lifts himself high and

٢١) وأشرك بنا من شـارك نا أجرَ القانتين
وتلا: "ومن يَقنت منك نَّ لله ورسُوله
وتعمل صَالحاً نؤتها أجرَها مرتين" لقـد
كفـر وذلَّ من استكبَر واستَعلى من

becomes arrogant has blasphemed and will be humiliated. No human submits himself to another human except the slaves, the backsliders and the polytheists.

الدركِ إلى عَلِيِّينَ فلاَ يَمُتُ بَشَرُ لِبَشرٍ إلاَّ الكفرةُ والمشركونَ .

22. The one who joins Us as a participant in experiencing affliction has become a polytheist. He announced, "As for those who afflict God and his messenger. . ." No one can ever afflict Us. But affliction is the punishment of those who hurt Our believing followers.

٢٢) وأشركَ بنا مَنْ أشركنا في الأذى
وكلا : "إنَّ الذينَ يُؤذونَ اللهَ ورسولهُ" ولاَ
يؤذِيَّنَا أحدٌ إنما الأذى جزاءُ الذينِ يؤذونَ
عِبادَنا المؤمنينَ .

23. The one who makes himself a partner to Us in telling the Truth has become a polytheist. He stated, "God has spoken truthfully and so did his messenger." Is it possible that one who comes from among the deceitful would always tell the truth?

٢٣) وأشركَ بنا مَنْ شارَكنا الصّدقَ إذ
تلا : "لقد صَدقَ اللهُ ورسولهُ" وأنّى يَصْدُقُ
من كانَ من الكاذبينَ .

24. The one who makes himself an associate of Ours in endorsement has become a polytheist. He stated, "Those who

٢٤) وأشركَ بنا مَنْ أشركنا في المبايعة
وقالَ : "والذينَ يُبايعونَكَ إنما يُبايعونَ اللهَ" ومَا

238

endorse you are in fact endorsing God himself." We have never been in need of the endorsement of blasphemers. No one supports a deceiver except those who are deceived themselves.

كُنَّا بِحَاجَةٍ لِمُبَايعةِ الكَافِرينَ وَلا يُبَايعُ الماكِرَ إلّا القَومُ الماكِرونَ .

25. The one who makes Us an associate of his in challenging others has become a polytheist. He proclaimed, "And those who challenge God and his messenger. . ." No one in the universe can challenge Us for We are the Mightiest in the universe.

(٢٥) وأشرَكَ بِنا مَنْ أشرَكَنا فِي المُحادّةِ إذ قَالَ : "والذينَ يُحادّونَ اللهَ ورسُولَهُ " ولا يُحَادِدُنا أحَدٌ مِنَ العالمينَ .

26. The one who claims partnership with Us in might has become a polytheist. He recited boldly, "Might belongs to God and to his apostle." Can there be any worse type of polytheism and blasphemy than this declaration?"

(٢٦) وأشرَكَ بِنا مَنْ شَارَكَنا العِزَّةَ وتَحَرّاً فَتلا : "ولِلهِ العِزّةُ ولرسُولِهِ " فَهلْ بعدَ ذلكَ مِنْ شِركِ وكُفرانٍ .

27. O, you who have become polytheists and apostates from Our people: you have accused Our faithful and trusted worshipers of lying by claiming that they are polytheists.

(٢٧) يَأهلَ الشِركِ والبُهتانِ مِنْ عِبادِنا الضّالينَ : لَقد افتريتَمُ على عِبادِنا المؤمنينَ الصّادقينَ الكِذبَ فزعمتمُ بأنّهم مُشرِكونَ .

28. Are you not aware that Our trusting worshipers are the greatest of monotheists! And that whosoever associates himself to Us in might and glory is the worst of polytheists!

٢٨) ألا إنَّ عِبادَنا المؤمِنينَ هـــم خيرُ الموحّدينَ وإنَّ مَنْ شـارَكنا الحُولَ والعِزّةَ فهوَ شَرُّ المُشرِكينَ .

29. Whosoever joins anyone to Us is like unto some creature who has fallen from the sky. Either the vultures will snatch him away or the wild wind will blow him into a bottomless pit where he will never ever see the light of day.

٢٩) ومَنْ يُشرِكْ بنا فكأنّما خَرَّ مِنَ السماءِ فَتَخْطَفُهُ الطيرُ أو تهوي بهِ الريحُ فـي قرارٍ سَحيقٍ .

30. Therefore, We admonish everyone, do not join anyone to Our Person in might, honor or glory. For if you do you will incur a severe curse upon yourself and will be vanquished forever in the infernal Abyss.

٣٠) فلا تَجعلوا معنا شَرِكاً يحوُلنا وقوَّتَنا وعِزَّتَنا فتَقْعُدوا مَذمومينَ مَخذولينَ .

51
THE JUDGMENT
(Surat Al Hukm)

بِسْمِ الآبِ الكلمةِ الروحِ الإلهِ الواحد
الأوحد

In the Name of the Father, the Word, the Holy Spirit, the One and only True God

١) يَأَيُّهَا المُنَافِقُونَ مِنْ عِبَادِنَا الضَّالِينَ: تَقُولُونَ
: "آمَنَّا بِاللهِ وَمَا أُوتِي عِيسَى والنبيونَ لَا
نُفَرِّقُ بَيْنَ أَحَدٍ مِنْهُمْ، وتلكَ الرِّسْلُ فَضَّلْنَا
بَعْضَهُمْ على بعضٍ".

1.   O, you who are fabricators of lies from among Our misled worshipers: you announce, "We believe in God and what was given to Jesus and the prophets. We make no differentiation among them. Yet from among those messengers We have preferred some over others."

٢) وإنَّ أَهْلَ الكتابِ يَتْلُونَ آيَاتِنَا آنَاءَ الليلِ
وهُمْ يَسْجُدُونَ ويؤمنونَ بِنَا ويَأْمُرونَ
بالمعروفِ وينهونَ عَنِ المنكرِ ويُسَارِعونَ
فِي الخيراتِ وأُولئكَ مِنَ الصَّالحينَ.

2.   And the People of The Book, recite Our scriptures even during the nighttime. They bow down and trust Us. They command the practice of goodwill and forbid the works of immorality. They hasten to the performance of good deeds. Such people are among the righteous ones.

3. You remark, "O, People of The Book, you have nothing to stand on until you practice the instructions of the Gospel and whatever your Lord has sent down to you if you truly believe."

٣) وتقولونَ: "يا أهلَ الكتابِ لستُمْ على شيءٍ حتى تُقيموا الانجيلَ ومَا أُنزِلَ عليكُمْ مِنْ ربّكُمْ إنْ كنتُمْ تُؤمنونَ".

4. Then you turned on your heels and denied what you had declared and annulled your statements by proclaiming, "O, People of The Book, why have you blasphemed the signs of God when you witness about Him? If the People of The Book trusted and feared us, we would have redeemed them from their vile deeds." You have lied. You have not spoken truthfully. You are not fair-minded.

٤) ثمَّ نكصتُمْ على أعقابكُمْ وأنكرتُمْ ما ادّعيتُمْ ونسَختُمْ قولَكُمْ بقولِكُمْ: "يا أهلَ الكتابِ لمَ تكفرونَ بآياتِ اللهِ وأنتُمْ تشهدونَ وكوْ أنَّ أهلَ الكتابِ آمنوا واتقوا لكفَرنا عنهمْ سَيّئاتِهمْ". لقد أفكتُمْ ومَا نطقتُمْ بالحقِّ ومَا كنتُمْ مُقسطينَ.

5. O, people who misrepresent the truth, yet still count yourselves among Our worshipers: judge the People of The Book equitably, whether they have blasphemed or should be numbered among the faithful. Then judge yourselves whether you are trustworthy or should be

٥) يَا أهلَ البُهتانِ مِنْ عِبادِنا الضّالّينَ: أحكموا بالقِسطِ على أهلِ الكتابِ أكفروا أمْ كانوا مِنَ المؤمنينَ؟ وعَلى أنفسِكُمْ أصدقتُمْ أمْ كنتُمْ مِنَ

numbered among the deceivers.

6. If you find them to have blasphemed, you must be numbered among the deceivers. But if they are numbered among the believers, then you have spoken truthfully. While the fabricators lied.

7. Why do you assign authority to another document, instead of **The True Gospel**, and the **True Furqan** when they embody our precepts. For if you depart from them you are hypocrites through and through.

8. We have conveyed **The True Furqan** in which there is guidance and light. Use it in your governing and be witnesses to its veracity. Fear not other people, but fear Us. Do not regard Our Scripture as cheap in value.

9. Whosoever will not govern by what We have sent down, will definitely turn out to be blasphemers.

الْكَاذِبِينَ ؟

٦) فَإِنْ كَفَرُوا فَأَنْتُمْ مِنَ الْكَاذِبِينَ
وَإِنْ كَانُوا مِنَ الْمُؤْمِنِينَ فَقَدْ صَدَقْتُمْ وَأَفَكَ
الْمُفْتَرُونَ .

٧) وَأَنَّى تُحَكِّمُونَ غَيْرَ الْإِنْجِيلِ الْحَقِّ
وَالْفُرْقَانِ الْحَقِّ مِنْ قَبْلُ وَمِنْ بَعْدُ وَفِيهِمَا
حُكْمُنَا ؟ فَإِنْ تَوَلَّيْتُمْ فَأَنْتُمُ الْمُبْطِلُونَ .

٨) وَقَدْ أَنْزَلْنَا الْفُرْقَانَ الْحَقَّ فِيهِ هُدًى وَنُورٌ
فَاحْكُمُوا بِهِ وَكُونُوا عَلَيْهِ شُهَدَاءَ وَلَا
تَخْشَوُا النَّاسَ بَلِ اخْشَوْنَا وَلَا تَشْتَرُوا بِآيَاتِنَا
ثَمَنًا قَلِيلًا .

٩) وَمَنْ لَا يَحْكُمْ بِمَا أَنْزَلْنَا فَأُولَٰئِكَ
هُمُ الْكَافِرُونَ .

10. Do you wish to pursue the doctrines of the age of ignorance, a soul for a soul, an eye for an eye, a tooth for a tooth? That was the tradition of the ancients. Do you not realize that the creed of men of old is null and void?

١٠) أفحكـمَ الجَاهليّةِ يَبتغونَ بأنّ النفسَ بالنفسِ والعينَ بالعينِ والسنَّ بالسنّ إنْ هوَ إلاّ سُنّةُ الأوّلينَ وقدْ خلتْ شرْعةُ الغَابرينَ .

11. We proclaim to all mankind, you should not take vengeance. Rather return good for evil in such circumstances, for it can turn into a redemptive act for you. That is if you trust and obey what we say.

١١) فلا تنتقِموا وتَصَدَّقوا بهِ فهو كفّارة لكـمْ إنْ كنتـمْ تُؤمنونَ .

12. Divine Truth is the scale of fairness on the Day of Resurrection. Whosoever's scales tip over will be among those who are victorious. Whosoever's scales go upward will be among those who are vanquished because they firmly denounced Our scriptures as corrupted revelation.

١٢) الحقُّ ميزانُ القِسْطِ يومَ القيامةِ فمنْ ثقلتْ مَوازينُهُ فأولئكَ هـمُ المُفلحونَ ومنْ خفّتْ مَوازينُهُ فـأُولئكَ الذينَ خَسِـروا أنفسَهـمْ بما كانوا بآياتِنا يُكذّبونَ .

13. O, you who have firmly believed from among Our worshipers: make yourselves more dignified witnesses for Us.

١٣) يأيّها الذينَ آمنوا منْ عِبادِنا : كونوا قوّامينَ شُهداءَ لنا واحْكـموا بالقِسْطِ ولا

Do not let your own whim push you to practice injustice, but rule justly. When you are fair-minded you are much closer to Our divine standard. As you live from day to day you must take into account the reckoning Day of Judgment.

يحملنكـم الهوى على أنْ لا تعدلوا اعدلوا هوأقـرب للتقـوى واتقـوا يـوم الحسـاب العسـيرِ.

14. One day there arose a seducer from among the deceived who subjugated them. He also misappropriated their rights, humiliated them and delivered them to The Fire. He left them without an escape hatch from doom. Moreover, he recited, "A believing man or a believing woman has no recourse from whatever God and his Messenger intended for their eternal destiny. Whosoever disobeys God and his messenger turns into a reprobate soul who has lost his way."

١٤) وَقَامَ ضَالٌ مِنْ أهل الضـلال فاسْتعبد رقَابهـمْ وقَهَرَ فوقهـمْ وغَمَط حَقَّهـمْ وأذَلهـمْ وأوردهـمْ النـار ومـا أبقى لهـمْ خِيرةً مِنْ أمرهـمْ وكلا: "مَا كَانَ لِمؤمن ولا مؤمنةٍ إذا قضى الله ورسُولهُ أمـراً أنْ يكونَ لهـمُ الخِيرةُ مِنْ أمرهـمْ ومنْ يعص الله ورسُولهُ فقد ضل ضلالاً مُبيناً".

245

52
THE THREAT
(Surat Al Wa'eed)

٥٢) سُورةُ الوَعيد

In the Name of the Father, the Word, the Holy Spirit, the One and only True God

بسـم الآبِ الكلمةِ الروحِ الالهِ الواحِدِ الأوحدِ

1.   O, you who have lost your way, yet still claim to be counted among Our worshipers: you have threatened Our trusting servants by impersonating Us. You stated, "O, you who have been given The Book, trust in what We have sent as a supporter of what you have had.   If you will not, We will shame some faces and turn them backwards and denounce them just as We denounced the keepers of the Sabbath with a curse."

١)   يَأيُّها الذينَ ضَلّوا مِنْ عِبادِنا : لَقَدْ تَوَعَّدْتُمْ عِبادَنا المؤمنينَ بلسانِنا افتراءً فقلتمُ : "يأيّها الذينَ أوتوا الكتابَ آمنوا بما نزّلنا مُصدقاً لما معكمْ مِنْ قبلِ أنْ نَطمِسَ وجوهاً فنردَّها على أدبارِها ونلعنهمْ كما لَعنّا أصحابَ السّبتِ لعناً"

2.   We have sent down the unchangeable standards in the immutable commandments and **The True Gospel** which are true declarations by Our own eternal decree.   We have even approved them by **The True Furqan** in an

٢)   وقدْ أنزلنا سُنّةَ الحقِّ في الإنجيلِ الحقِّ قولاً حقاً بلسانِنا وصدّقناها بالفرقانِ الحقِّ تصديقاً مُبيناً وما نزّلنا سِواها مُعارِضاً أو

246

outspoken fashion.   Thus, We
have inspired nothing else like
them,   neither contrary to them,
nor abrogating or replacing them.

ناسخاً أو بديلاً .

3.   Had there been another
inspiration We would have caused
it to be a proof of the already
revealed   ones,   (**The   Torah,
Zabur** and **The True Gospel.**)
Therefore, you will never ever
discover any abrogation to Our
decree nor any changing of it
thereof.

٣)   وكونزّلنا لكان مُصدقاً ولنْ تجدوا
لِسُنّتنا نَسْخاً ولا تبديلاً .

4.   Why is it that you conspire
to exchange Our upright path for
a crooked one and our bright
highway for a darkened one?

٤)   فأنّى تبتغون لصراطنا المستقيم عِوَجاً
ولِهُدانا المنير تضليلاً ؟ .

5.   Have you observed your
partners whom you call upon
besides Us?   Display to Us what
they have created on the earth or
who is their partner in the heavens
or if We have sent them a book.
Arrogance is all that the apostates
are capable of displaying.

٥)   أرأيتـمْ شُـركاءَكـمُ الذيـن
تدَّعونَ منْ دونـا أرونا مـاذا خلقـوا مـنْ
الأرض أمْ لهـمْ شِـركُ ـفي السَّماوات أمْ
آتيناهـمْ كِتاباً ، بلْ إنْ يَعدُ المُفتـرونَ إلا
غـروراً .

6. They have promulgated an evil deception. Are you aware that evil deception fits best those who manufacture it? They certainly deserve it. Whether they are warned or not warned they vehemently persist in their apostasy for they have lost their way, ending in total disarray.

٦) ومَكَرَ الذين كَفَروا مَكْراً سَيِّئاً ولا يَحِيقُ المكرُ السيِّءُ إلا بأهله وسَواءٌ عليهمْ أَنذرِهم أمْ لَمْ تُنذرهم فهم لا يؤمنون فقد ضَلّوا سَبيلاً .

7. Therefore, do not make terrifying threats. Unquestionably, your tongue will be held responsible for such threats on that extraordinary Day.

٧) فلا تُوعّدوا وَعيداً عَسيراً إنَّ اللسانَ كانَ مَسؤولاً .

53
THE ATROCITIES
(Surat Al Kabaer)

٥٣) سُورةُالكَبائرِ

In the Name of the Father, the Word, the Holy Spirit, the One and only True God

بسمِ الآبِ الكلمةِ الروحِ الالهِ الواحدِ الأوحدِ

1.   O, you have become ungodly, yet still claim to be counted among Our worshipers: you have transformed Our paradises into brothels for fornicators, shelters for murderers, unholy sleeping quarters for prostitutes and vile dwelling places for drunkards and transgressors.

١) يَأَيُّهَا الذينَ كَفَروا من عبادِنا الضَّالِينَ: لقدْ جَعلتـمُ من جَنَّاتِـنا مَواخِـرَ للزُّنـاةِ ومَغاوِرَ للقَتلةِ ومَخادِعَ رِجْسٍ للزَّانِياتِ وتُزلَ دعارةٍ للسُّكارى والمُجرِمينَ .

2.   Moreover, you have dug up the animal instinct in your souls. You have also planted the roots of bitterness in your hearts. Then you sealed your minds up with hostility and animosity.

٢) ونبشْتُـمُ غَرائـزَ البـهائمِ في نفوسِكـمُ وزَرَعْتُـمُ بُذورِ الحِقدِ في قلوبِكـمُ وطبعتـمُ على عُقولِكـمُ بالمكرِ والعدوانِ .

3.   Your demeanor is blasphemy, paganism, adultery,

٣) فسيماؤكـمُ كُفرٌ وشِرْكٌ وزِنىَ

249

marauding, murder, pillage, taking captives, ignorance and rebellion.

وَغَـزْوٌ وَقَتَـلٌ وَسَـلَبٌ وَسَـبْيٌ وَجَـهـلٌ وَعِصيـانٌ .

4. These characteristics are recognized by Our true followers who can identify you by them. Your conduct and demeanor are a giveaway as to what type of people you really are.

٤) صِفاتٌ يُبَيِّنكُـمْ مِنها عِبادُنا المؤمنونَ فَمِنْ سِيماهُـمْ تُعرَفونَ .

5. As for those who put no faith in what We revealed in **The True Gospel**, denounce what We conveyed in **The True Furqan** and kill the believers from among Our true worshipers, their labors will come to naught both in this world and the world to come. At the end, they will absolutely have no supporters to exonerate whatsoever.

٥) إنَّ الذينَ كَفَروا بِما قُلنا فِي الإنجيل الحَقِّ وكَذَّبوا بِما أَنزلْنا مِنْ الفُرقانِ الحَقِّ وقَتَلوا المؤمِنينَ مَن عِبادِنا فَقـدْ حَبِطَـتْ أعمالُهُـمْ فِي الدنيا والآخِرةِ وما لهُـمْ مِنْ ناصِرينَ .

6. You claimed that Abraham was an adherent to your sect, who believed in Us and surrendered to Us. So you accepted Abraham as your role-model, along with the other

٦) وَزَعَمْتُـمْ بأنَّ إبراهيـمَ كانَ على مِلتِكُـمْ مؤمناً مُسْلِماً لأمرِنا وَثَقْتِـمْ بهِ فكُنتُـمْ أولَ المُسلِمينَ .

faithful patriarchs of old.

7.   Surprisingly enough, you actually did not trust as Abraham trusted.   You did not surrender to the One to whom he surrendered. You, in fact, trusted the Evil One and to the Prince of Darkness you are totally committed.

٧) وَمَا آمَنتُمْ كَمَا آمَنَ وَمَا سَلَّمْتُمْ بِمَا سَلَّمَ بَلْ آمَنتُمْ بِالطَّاغُوتِ فَأَنتُمْ لِأَمْرِهِ مُسَلِّمُونَ .

8.   To Us, it is preferable to have one trustworthy believer who practices Our doctrine than one thousand untrustworthy believers who ignore it.

٨) وَكَمُؤْمِنٌ صَادِقٌ يَعْمَلُ سُنَّتَنَا خَيْرٌ مِنْ أَلْفِ مُؤْمِنٍ مُنَافِقٍ لَا يَعْمَلُونَ .

9.   You also maintained that you trusted in the Book as well as the People of The Book, who have been guided rightly, and the Christians because they trusted in Us and worshiped Us. In spite of such declarations, you assaulted and eliminated them by the sword.   Moreover, you took their wives as captives for your pleasure.   You made their children orphans. You took their belongings as spoils of war. You also robbed the provisions of the poverty-stricken and the orphans.

٩) وَزَعَمْتُمْ بِأَنَّكُمْ آمَنتُمْ بِالْكِتَابِ وَبِأَهْلِ الْكِتَابِ الَّذِينَ هَادُوا وَالنَّصَارَى ذَلِكَ أَنَّهُمْ آمَنُوا بِنَا وَعَبَدُونَا . لَكِنَّكُمْ قَتَلْتُمُوهُمْ تَقْتِيلًا وَسَبَيْتُمْ نِسَاءَهُمْ وَيَتَّمْتُمْ أَطْفَالَهُمْ وَغَنِمْتُمْ أَمْوَالَهُمْ وَوَهَبْتُمْ أَقْوَاتَ الْيَتَامَى وَالْمَسَاكِينِ .

10. The most outrageous atrocity of all is your fabrication of the deception which you ascribe to Us, that We are the Ones who put you up to commit these atrocities. Despite that, it will be your own tongues, hands and feet that will testify against you concerning what you have committed once you arrive at the Judgment Seat.

١٠) وَلأَكْبَرُ الكَبَائِرِ افْتِرَاؤُكُمْ عَلَيْنَا الكَذِبَ بِأَنَّا أَوْحَيْنَا إِلَيْكُمْ بِارْتِكَابِ الكَبَائِرِ . وَسَتَشْهَدُ عَلَيْكُمْ أَلْسِنَتُكُمْ وَأَيْدِيكُمْ وَأَرْجُلُكُمْ بِمَا كُنْتُمْ تَقْتَرِنَ .

11. The ones who hide Our miracles and perfect guidance after We had revealed them to the people in **The True Gospel** and reminded you of them in **The True Furqan** which followed it, are definitely the worst of apostates.

١١) إِنَّ الَّذِينَ يَكْتُمُونَ البَيِّنَاتِ وَالهُدَى مِنْ بَعْدِ مَا بَيَّنَّاهَا لِلنَّاسِ فِي الإنْجِيلِ الحَقِّ وَذَكَّرْنَاكُمْ بِهَا بِالفُرْقَانِ الحَقِّ مِنْ بَعْدِهِ أُولَئِكَ هُمْ شَرُّ الكَافِرِينَ .

12. The illustration of those who had become ungodly is like the one who cries out, screaming and jabbering, unaware of what he is saying because he is deaf. So it is with these people. They are deaf, dumb and blind, oblivious of what is going on.

١٢) وَمَثَلُ الَّذِينَ كَفَرُوا كَمَثَلِ الَّذِي يَنْعَقُ بِمَا لا يَسْمَعُ إِلا دُعَاءً وَنِدَاءً صُمٌّ بُكْمٌ عُمْيٌ فَهُمْ لا يَعْقِلُونَ .

13. We proclaimed in **The True Gospel** what the believers accepted without any disputation. The only expression of any disputation erupted from the apostates once We brought the Scriptures to them. It must be pointed out that whosoever follows anything else besides **The True Gospel** and **The True Furqan**, as a book of guidance, will never be accepted from Him. Furthermore, he will never be rightly guided but will end up among the conscience-stricken.

١٣) وقُلْنَا في الإنجيلِ الحقِّ ما لم يختلفْ فيه المؤمنونَ وما اختلفَ فيهِ إلا أهلُ الكفرانِ مِنْ بعدِ ما جئناهُمْ بالبيناتِ ومَنْ يَبْغِ غيرَ الإنجيلِ الحقِّ والفرقانِ الحقِّ كتاباً هادياً فلَنْ يُقبلَ منهُ ولَنْ يَهتَدِيَ وهوَ في الآخرةِ مِنَ النادمينَ .

14. This earthly life has been glamorized to the apostates who still claim they are among Our worshipers. The apostates scoff at those who believe in Us and practice godly deeds in pursuing the Abundant Kingdom above. This earthly life will never be a profitable substitute for the glories of eternal life. Once they arrive there, each individual will receive his just reward and no one will be treated unjustly.

١٤) زُيِّنَ للذينَ كفروا مِنْ عبادِنا الحياةُ الدُّنيا ويَسخرونَ مِنَ الذينَ آمنوا وعَمِلوا الصالحاتِ في سبيلِ الآخرةِ . ولا تُغني الدنيا عن الآخرةِ وكلٌّ ينالُ جزاءً وِفاقاً ولا يُظلمونَ .

15.As for the apostates who turned away from Our pathway, then died, persisting in their blasphemy, they will never be forgiven. In the end they will absolutely be among the defeated, disappointed and damned.

١٥) إِنَّ الَّذِينَ كَفَرُوا وَصَدُّوا عَنْ سَبِيلِنَا ثُمَّ مَاتُوا وَهُمْ كُفَّارٌ فَلَنْ يُغْفَرَ لَهُمْ وَهُمْ فِي الْآخِرَةِ مِنَ الْخَاسِرِينَ .

54
THE SACRIFICE
(Surat Al Adha)

In the Name of the Father, the Word, the Holy Spirit, the One and only True God

٥٤) سُورَةُ الأضحى

بسم الآبِ الكلمةِ الروحِ الاله
الواحدِ الأوحدِ

1.   O, you who are unenlightened from among Our deceived people: your utterances were not in confirmation of Our articulation in **The True Gospel**. As a result, Our trustworthy followers accused you of deception. They have certainly spoken the Truth but you have told lies.

١) يَأهلَ الجهلِ مِنْ عِبادِنا الضّالِينَ : ما كانَ لغوكـمْ مُصدّقاً لقولِنا في الإنجيلِ الحقِّ فكذّبكـمْ عبادُنا المؤمنـونَ وقـد صَدَقـوا وكنتـمْ مِـنَ الكاذبينَ .

2.   You also proclaimed, "Our book is from God." It is absolutely not inspired by Us. No man is given The Book, the commandments and the prophethood who makes himself a partner to Us. He affirmed, "Whosoever obeys me has indeed obeyed God." Such a statement is a monstrous blasphemy.

٢) وقلتـمْ : "هوَ مِنْ عندِ اللهِ " وما كانَ مِنْ عِنْدِنا . وما كـانَ لبَشَـرٍ أنْ نؤتيـهُ الكتابَ والحُكـمَ والنبوّةَ وهوَ يُشْرِكُ نفسَهُ بِنا قائلاً : "مَنْ يُطعْني فقد أطاعَ اللهَ " وهذا هوَ الشركُ المُبينُ .

3. We can forgive any sin one commits except the sin of shirk, that is refusing to believe in oneness, but adding partners to Our divine person. Who is more wicked than the one who adds partners to Us and fabricates lies about Us. Fundamentally, such liars will never win.

٣) وِإِنَّا لَا نَغْفِرُ أَنْ يُشْرَكَ بِنَا وَنَغْفِرُ مَا دُونَ ذَلِكَ . وَمَنْ أَظْلَمُ مِمَّنْ أَشْرَكَ بِنَا وَافْتَرَى عَلَيْنَا الْكَذِبَ إِنَّهُ لَا يُفْلِحُ الْمُفْتَرُونَ .

4. We have not made a particular religion superior to another religion. No other religion is recognized except the True Religion. It invites people to a more sublime and nobler pathway. How then can We ever inspire a religion for whom We did not send a messenger and in which none of the true believers could trust?

٤) وَمَا أَظْهَرْنَا دِيناً عَلَى دِينٍ فَلَا دِينَ إِلَّا دِينُ الْحَقِّ الَّذِي يَدْعُو إِلَيْهِ هِيَ أَسْمَى وَأَقْوَمُ سَبِيلاً . فَأَنَّى نُظْهِرُ دِيناً مَا أَرْسَلْنَا بِهِ مِنْ رَسُولٍ وَمَا دَانَ بِهِ أَحَدٌ مِنَ الْمُؤْمِنِينَ .

5. Suffice it to say that the True Religion is the religion of love, brotherhood, compassion and peace. We have entrusted it to Our worshipers through **The True Gospel** as a persuasive proclamation. We have supported it with **The True Furqan** as an extraordinary revelation. Whoso-

٥) إِنَّمَا الدِّينُ الْحَقُّ هُوَ دِينُ الْمَحَبَّةِ وَالْأُخُوَّةِ وَالرَّحْمَةِ وَالسَّلَامِ بَلَّغْنَاهُ لِعِبَادِنَا بِالْإِنْجِيلِ الْحَقِّ قَوْلاً جَهْراً وَأَيَّدْنَاهُ بِالْفُرْقَانِ الْحَقِّ وَحْياً مُبِيناً . وَمَنْ يَبْتَغِ غَيْرَ دِينِ الْحَقِّ دِيناً فَلَنْ يُقْبَلَ مِنْهُ .

ever puts his trust in any other religion except the True Religion, it will not be recognized. At the end of the trail he will find himself among the regretful.

وهوَ في الآخرةِ مِنَ النَّادِمِينَ .

6. We have conveyed **The True Furqan** to remind you of the True Religion and to approve the veracity of **The True Gospel**. The purpose is to demonstrate its superiority over all religions no matter whether the hypocrites agree or disagree.

٦) وأنزلنا الفُرقانَ الحقَّ مُذكِّراً بالدين الحقِّ ومُصَدِّقاً للإنجيل الحقِّ لِنُظهِرهُ على الدينِ كلَّهِ وكَوْكَرهَ الكافرونَ .

7. O, you who belong to the family of the antagonists from among Our misled worshipers: you spill the blood of animal sacrifices to seek forgiveness and mercy from Us for what your hands have committed of murder, immorality, wickedness and oppression.

٧) يَا أهلَ العُدوانِ مِن عبادِنا الضَّالِّينَ : تَسفِكونَ دِماءَ البهائمِ أضحياتٍ تَبتغونَ مَغفرةً ورحمةً مِنْ لَدُنَّا عمَّا اقترفتْ أيديكُمْ من قتلٍ وزِنىً وإثمٍ وعُدوانٍ .

8. Are you not aware that an acceptable sacrifice to Us is a clean heart, a heart which bubbles over with compassion, love and

٨) إنَّما أضحيةُ الحقِّ والإيمانِ قلبٌ طهيرٌ يَنفجِرُ رَحمةً ومحبَّةً وسَلاماً لعبادِنا ورِفقا

257

peace toward Our people. On the other hand be merciful to the animals because neither their flesh nor their blood will avail with Us. What will avail is the righteousness of the upright.

9. Had those who lost their way been left alone, they would have discovered the right way and believed in **The True Gospel**. For it surrounds them, close at hand, in the hearts of the trustworthy believers and on the tips of their tongues. What transpired was that Satan rushed them with his ungodliness and blocked the true pathway from them; so they ended up being pagans and rebels.

10. O, people everywhere: do not promote wickedness and animosity. Do not even take vengeance upon your enemies because a kind deed cannot be on the same level as an unkind one. Therefore, reinforce deeds which are more wholesome and treat the one with whom you have hostility like an intimate friend.

بالبهائم فلن يَنالنا لحومُها ولا دماؤها ولكن يَنالنا تقوى المتقين .

٩ وَلَوْ تُرِكَ الذينَ ضَلّوا مِنْ عبادِنا لاهتدوا وآمنوا بالإنجيل الحقّ فهو من حولهم وبين أيديهم وفي قلوب المؤمنين وعلى ألسنتهم ولكنّ الشيطانَ عَاجلهمْ بالكفر فصدّوا عن السبيل فكانوا مِنْ غُلاة الكفرِ والعصيانِ .

١٠ يَأيها الناسُ لا تعاونوا على الإثم والعُدوان ولا تنتقموا مِنَ المُعتدينَ فلا تستوي الحسنةُ والسيّئةُ ادفعوا بالتي هي أحسنُ فإذا الذي بينكمْ وبينـه عَداوةٌ كأنّـه وليٌّ حميمٌ .

55
FAIRY TALES
(Surat Al Asateer)

٥٥) سُورَةُ الأَسَاطِيرِ

In the Name of the Father, the Word, the Holy Spirit, the One and only True God

بسمِ الآبِ الكلمةِ الروحِ الإله الواحد الأوحدِ

1.   O, you who corrupt the scriptures, yet dwell among Our followers: you have certainly rebelled against **The True Gospel**. You have also perverted scriptures from their original intention, even exchanged verses in place of other verses. Nevertheless, We assuredly recognize Our scriptures; We are the Guardian of the same.

١) يَأَهلَ التحريفِ من عبادنا الضّالينَ: لقد كَفَرْزِبالإنجيلِ الحَــقِّ وحَرَّفتــمُ الكَلِــمَ عنْ مَواضِعِه وبدّلتــمْ آيـات مَكانَ آياتٍ وإنّا أعلــمُ بآياتِنا وإنّا لَها لحافظونَ .

2.   There arose among you someone who plagiarized the fairy tales of the ancients. He had them written down when they were recited in his hearing in the morning and the evening. They were but fairy tales spun by pagans who helped him memorize them.

٢) وقامَ منكــمْ مَن انتحَـلَ أساطيرَ الأوّلينَ اكتتبها وأمليتْ عليه بُكـرةً وأصيلاً وهي إفكٌ افتراهُ وأعانهُ عليه قومٌ آخرونَ .

3. Although you command that righteousness and godliness should be practiced, hypocritically you forgo doing them yourselves. Each time verses from **The True Gospel** are recited in your hearing, you accede to some unwillingly but reject most of them voluntarily. Then you change some wise statements cunningly. The punishment for anyone who undertakes such deeds is degradation in this world and a horrific end in the world to come.

4. Furthermore, you overthrow properties and dwellings where Our name is mentioned reverently. You also destroy sacred sanctuaries belonging to Our believing worshipers who gave you refuge, welcomed and even educated you when you were destitute. Why have you defrauded and oppressed them? Is not the true reward of benevolence goodwill?

5. You also snuffed out the souls of human-beings, a vile

٣) تَأْمُرُونَ بِالْبِرِّ وَالتَّقْوَى رِيَاءً وَتَنْسَوْنَ أَنْفُسَكُمْ وَإِذْ تُتْلَى عَلَيْكُمْ آيَاتُ الْإِنْجِيلِ الْحَقِّ آمَنْتُمْ بِبَعْضِهَا مُكْرَهِينَ وَكَفَرْتُمْ بِجُلِّهَا رَاضِينَ وَبَدَّلْتُمْ قَوْلًا غَيْرَ الَّذِي قِيلَ وَمَا جَزَاءُ مَنْ يَفْعَلُ ذَلِكَ إِلَّا الْخِزْيُ فِي الدُّنْيَا وَفِي الْآخِرَةِ أَشَدُّ خِزْياً وَثُبُوراً.

٤) وَهَدَمْتُمْ رِيَعاً وَبُيُوتاً يُذْكَرُ فِيهَا اسْمُنَا وَهَدَمْتُمْ كَنَائِسَ عِبَادِنَا الْمُؤْمِنِينَ الَّذِينَ آوَوْكُمْ وَأَحْسَنُوا إِلَيْكُمْ وَعَلَّمُوكُمْ فَغَدَرْتُمْ بِهِمْ ظَالِمِينَ وَهَلْ جَزَاءُ الْإِحْسَانِ إِلَّا الْإِحْسَانُ.

٥) وَقَتَلْتُمُ النَّفْسَ الَّتِي حَرَّمْنَا تَحْرِيماً.

260

deed which We had totally forbidden. Whenever the trusting souls inquire what was the guilt for which they are slain, you reply "By right." Yet, murdering another human being was never justified except by the doctrines of pagans, the precepts of Satan and the lawless assassins.

فإذا المؤمنون سألوا بأيِّ ذنبٍ قُتلوا ؟ قلتـــمُ : "بالحقِّ" وما كان القتـل حَقّاً إلا ـفي شـرعةِ الكفرِ وسُنّةِ الشـيطانِ وأُتباعـه المجرمينَ .

6.   Incredible, is it not! You murder Our faithful servants, vanquish their orphans, and reprove those who seek to rescue them. Yet, whenever Our faithful servants stumble upon your lost orphans they rescue them, give them shelter and show them the way home. True worshipers continuously offer praise for Our grace (for We are the most Generous and the most Gracious.)

٦)   وتقتلـونَ عِبادنا المؤمنـينَ وتقـهَـرونَ يتَـمَـهُـمْ وتـهـرونَ سَـائلهـمْ وقـدْ وَجَـدوا يتَمَكـــمْ فـآووا وضَـآلَّكـمْ فـهَـدوا وعـائلَكـم فـأغنَوا وهـــمْ نعمتَنـــا يُحدّثونَ .

56
PARADISE
(Surat Al Jannah)

٥٦) سُورةُ الجَنّة

In the Name of the Father, the Word, the Holy Spirit, the One and only True God

بسم الآبِ الكلمةِ الروح الاله الواحدِ الأوحدِ

1.   Paradise is figuratively spoken of as a green pasture for the purified of heart and the righteous of souls. Its nourishment is the fragrance of love and peace. Its wellsprings are the aroma of righteousness and holiness.

١) وما كانتِ الجنةُ إلا مرتعاً للأرواح الطاهرةِ المطهّرةِ وقوتُها عَبقُ المحّبةِ والسلامِ ومنهلُها عيرُ الطهرِ والايمانِ .

2.   Our faithful worshipers do not marry in paradise, neither eat nor drink. They are like the angels of Heaven ever singing Our praises.

٢) لا يتزوجونَ فيها ولا يطعمونَ ولا يشربونَ فهمْ كالملائكـةِ بجُندنا يُسبّحونَ .

3.   In contrast, the Satanic paradise is made up of caverns that smolder with

٣) أمّا جنةُ الشيطان فكهوفٌ تعجُّ بالقَتَلة

murderers, unrepentant pagans and the sexually immoral. They wallow in the cesspools of iniquity, blown by the wind of carnal lust. They are continuously drowning in the den of iniquity and the pit of brutality.

والكفرةِ والزِناةِ يتمرّغونَ في حَمأةِ الفجورِ تلفحهُمْ زفراتُ الغرائزِ وتسوطهم شهوةُ البهائمِ فهمْ بالرِّجسِ والمُوبقاتِ غارقونَ وفي شُغلٍ فاكهونَ .

4. Others recline on arranged couches, while indecent women await them in the houses of ill-repute. Homosexuals circulate among them with goblets of forbidden wine. They indulge in these without ever quenching their lust.

٤) متّكئونَ على سُررٍ مصفوفةٍ والمُسافحاتُ مسجوراتٌ في المواخرِ . يطوفُ عليهمْ ولدانُ اللواطِ بأكوابِ الرِّجسِ والخمرِ الحرامِ يلغونَ فيها فلا همْ يُطفئونَ أوارا ولا همْ يرتوونَ .

5. They imbibe from the rivers of wine, milk and honey just as a dumb beast would do. Additionally, they dress in green garments and wear golden bracelets. They envision erotic fantasies and orgies forever and are fed the meat of cattle and birds when hungry. Yet, they are never satisfied or ever content.

٥) يرِدونَ أنهارَ الخمرِ واللبنِ والعسلِ كالسائمةِ ويلبسونَ ثيابا خُضرا ويحلّونَ بأساورَ من ذهبٍ ويحلمونَ بشهواتِ الجسدِ ويطعمونَ لحومَ البهائمِ والطيرِ جياعا لا يشبعونَ ولا يقنعونَ .

6.   Satan allured them with vileness, debauchery, adultery, depravity and bestial lust as the sensual and eternal activities in their eternal paradise. With such descriptions of self-indulgence he inflamed the fantasies of pagans, atheists and the impoverished.

٦) وصوّر لهـم الشـيطان الرجـس والموبقات والزنى والفجور وشهوة البهائـم جنّات ألهب بها خيـال الكـفـرة والقتلة والمحرومين .

7.   The Romans' ancestors constructed such a paradise for themselves while dwelling on this earth. They achieved such vile luxuries without having to die to get there. Centuries before a promise was made to the marauding tribesmen and infidels, who were willing to be martyred to get there, such a paradise of sensuality was already in existence in Rome.

٧) وعاش الأوّلون من كفّار الروم في جنّة خلقوها في الدنيا قبل أن يوعد بها أهل الكفر والعدوان ويستشهدوا في سبيلها بعدّة قرون .

8.   The Romans ate and drank lustily and acquired paradise in jest. It was not their reward for their martyrdom or recompense for murdering Our trusting followers!

٨) فأكلوا وشربوا هنيئاً مريئاً وتأوّلوها استهتاراً لا ثواباً لا يستشهدوا ولا جزاءً لقتلهم عبادنا المؤمنين .

9. Our righteous worshipers are repelled by the idea of entering into a devil's paradise full of carnality. For it will infest their cleansed souls with the filth of fleshly lust, bestial instincts and debauchery of the pagans.

٩) ويأنفُ عبادُنا الصّالحونَ أنْ يدخلوا جنّةَ الشيطان ويُدَنّسوا طُهرَ نفوسِهـمْ بأقذارِ الشـهوةِ وغرائـزِ البـهائـمِ وفجــــورِ الكافرينَ.

10. Anyone who is a slave to the lust of the flesh becomes engrossed in the works of the flesh. He squanders his soul and ends up among the pagans. But the one who is liberated from such slavery gets involved in matters pertaining to the Spirit. Consequently, he will behold Our face, enjoy Our perfect peace and sing Our praises in heavenly places.

١٠) فمنْ كانَ عبدَ الشهوةِ الجسدِ انهمكَ بأمورِ الجسدِ وخسِرَ نفسَهُ وأمسى مَعَ الكـافرينَ. ومنْ تحـرّرَ من العبوديـة اهتـمّ بأمورِ الروحِ فنالَ ملكوتَنا وسبّحَ بحمدِنا وعاشَ في جنّاتِ النعيـمِ المقيـمِ.

11. As for the doctrines of the apostates and their precepts, such doctrines are like the chanting of an unenlightened singer to the ignoramuses. They trudge along following the sound of the camel-herder's music out of sheer habit.

١١) وما أحاديثُ أهلِ الكفرانِ وسُنَنُهـمْ إلّا حِداءُ الأمّيّ للأمّيّينَ كالسّائمةِ على إثرِه يَسيرونَ.

265

12. Such doctrines are completely fruitless. They are but outdated precepts and convictions of those who lost their way—altogether worthless sayings. Yet, the majorities are unaware of this truth.

١٢) ما أجدَّتهُمُ نَفعاً فهي شِرعةُ الغابرينَ وسُنَّةُ الضّالينَ وما أفلحَ مَنِ اتَّبعَها ولكنَّ أكثرهمْ لا يعلمونَ .

13. There are codes of conduct established by each nation to which its citizens must adhere. The natural law, recognized by all men throughout history is, "Whatever a man sows, he shall also reap."

١٣) ولكلِّ قومٍ شِرعةٌ يشترعونَها وفاقاً فكما يزرعونَ يحصُدونَ .

14. Consequently, the code of ethics of the apostates is the code of a people who were barefooted, naked, marauders, polygamists, illiterates, deceivers, aggressors, wayward and oppressors.

١٤) فشِرعةُ أهلِ الكفرِ شِرعةُ قومٍ حُفاةٍ عُراةٍ غُزاةٍ نُكّاةٍ أمّيّينَ مفترينَ مُعتدينَ ضالّينَ ظالمينَ .

15. They seem to never recognize their own sins and wrongdoings. Ignorance, apostasy and confusion totally

١٥) لا يرونَ مثالبَهمُ وهَنَاتِهمُ فقد طَمسَ الجهلُ والكفرُ والضلالُ على قلوبهمُ

266

overwhelmed their hearts and minds. They became deaf, mute and blind and were unwilling to return back to Us.

وعقولهم، صُـمُّ بُكْـمُ عُـمـيٌ لَا

يرجعونَ.

57
THE INSTIGATORS
(Surat Al Mu'arrideen)

سُورةُ المُحَرِّضين (٥٧

In the Name of the Father, the Word, the Holy Spirit, the One and only True God

بسمِ الآبِ الكلمةِ الروحِ الاله الواحدِ الأوحدِ

1. We outlawed killing by Our faithful followers. Furthermore, We commanded them to treat others with mercy, love and peace. You contradicted Our declaration claiming that We announced, "O, prophet urge the believers to fight." Is it logical that We would urge on the practice of committing atrocities, something We had emphatically prohibited? How can We command Our faithful to practice mercy, love and peace then command you to do the opposite?

١) وَهينا عبادَنا عَنِ القَتلِ ووصّيناهمُ بالرحمةِ والمحبّةِ والسّلامِ فجئتمُ تكذبونَ قولَنا وتزعمونَ بأننا قلنا : "يأيها النبيُّ حرِّض المؤمنينَ على القتالِ" فأنّى نُحرِّضُ على اقترافِ كبائرَ حرَّمناها تحريماً ؟ وأنّى تأمرُ عبادَنا المؤمنينَ بالرحمةِ والمحبّةِ والسّلامِ ثمَّ تأمرُكمُ بالقتلِ والغزوِ والفجورِ أفلا تعقلونَ ؟

2. We would certainly avoid taking Our worshipers backward to the absurdity of savagery and the precepts of the apostates. We had seen to it that

٢) وما كنّا لنردّ عبادَنا إلى جاهليّةِ الكفرِ وشِرعةِ القتلِ بعد أنْ آمنوا بسُنّةِ

268

they practiced the rule of love, mercy and peace. They cooperated in performing godly and righteous deeds, renouncing iniquity and enmity.

المَحَبَّةِ والسَّلامِ وتَعـاوَنوا عَلى البِرِّ والتَّقْوى وَنَبَذُوا الإثْـمَ والعُدوانَ .

3.   O, you who belong to the community of the apostates, yet claim to still belong among Our worshipers: you have blocked the gates of paradise by what your hands have done and what your tongues have spoken. You accomplished this when you trusted in lies and denied the Truth, Jesus. Then you accused Him of falsehood, particularly concerning His divine nature.

٣) يَأهْلَ الكُفْرِ إنْ مِنْ عِبادِنا الضّالِّينَ: لَقَدْ أوْصَدْتُرْ بِأيديكُمْ وألسِنتِكُمْ أبوابَ الجَنّةِ في وجوهِكُمْ يومَ آمَنتُمْ بـالكُفرِ وصَدّقتَمـوهُ وكَفـرْتُ بـالحَقّ وكَذّبتِمـوهُ فـأصبحتُمْ في ضـلالٍ أكيدٍ .

4.   We do not desire for you to follow a misguided shepherd who will lead you to a dried-up pasture in the middle of nowhere!

٤) وإنّا لا نُحبُّ لكُمْ أنْ تَتبعوا راعياً ضالّاً يَقُودُكُمْ إلى مَرتعٍ وَخيمٍ .

5.   Accordingly, you must seek the godly pathway. Search for the light of **The True Furqan**. For it is Jesus who is

٥) فَتَلَمَّسـوا سَبيلَ الخَيرِ والتَمِسُـوا نـورَ الفُرقانِ الحَقّ فهوَ رَحمةٌ وسلامٌ لِعبادِنا فلا

mercy and peace for Our followers and do not be misguided.

تكونوا مِنَ الغافلينَ .

6. Do not claim, "We are practicing the traditions of the religion of our fathers and forefathers, which we found them following, and we are taking them as our role models." Rather you should declare, "We have trusted the religion of love, compassion, truth, peace and brotherhood of mankind." Such would be an outstanding triumph of intelligence and nobility.

٦) ولا تقولوا : "إنما نَّبِعُ مَا أُلفِينا عليه آباءَنا وأجُدادَنا فهوَدينُهـم ونحـنُ بـهـمْ مُقتدونَ" بلْ قُولوا : "آمنّا بدين المحبّةِ والرحمة والحقِّ والسّلامِ وأخوّةِ الإنسانِ" . فهذا هُوَ الفوزُ العظيـمُ .

7. Satan has bamboozled you through your parents just as he misled them through their forebearers. Thus, you inherit apostasy from each other unawares. For Satan infected his virus into the souls of his early devotees and now your turn has come!

٧) وأضلّكـمُ الشّـيطانُ بآبائكـمْ كما أضلّهـمْ بآبائهـمْ تَتوارثونَ الكفرَ بعضُكـمْ عن بعضٍ وأنتـمْ لا تعلمونَ فقدْ دَسَّ سَمَّهُ في نفوسِ أوْليائهِ الأوّلِينَ .

8. He beguiled you too as he beguiled your first father

٨) وَفَتَنكـمْ كما فتنَ أباكـمْ آدمَ

270

Adam, the deceived fountainhead. Satan also precipitated Adam's eviction from Our perpetual Paradise. Will you remember Adam's mistake and take heed?

وأخرجَهُـمِـنَ الْجَنَّـةِ أفـلا تذكَـرونَ
وترعـونَ ؟

9.   The parable of a secure servant, who returned to Us after going astray, is like unto a man who owned a hundred sheep. One got lost. He diligently searched for it. When he found it, his joy over finding that solitary sheep exceeded his joy over the other ninety-nine.

٩)   وَمَثلُ عبدٍ آمنَ كابَ إلينا بعدَ ضَلالٍ
كمثلِ رجلٍ لهُ مِئةُ نعجةٍ ضَلَّتْ إحداها
فجَدَّ ـ في طلبِها حتَّى وَجَدها ففـرحَ بها
اكثرَ مِنَ التِّسعِ والتِّسعينَ .

10.   Therefore return to Us in sincere repentance. Come back to the fold of the faithful. Join Our virtuous servants and enter Heaven to dwell with the immortals.

١٠)   فتوبوا إلينا توبةً نصوحاً وارجعوا إلى
حَظيرةِ الإيمانِ وادخلوا ـ في عِبادِنا الصَّالحينَ
وادخلوا جَنَّاتِنا معَ الخَالدينَ .

11.   We declare unto you a new commandment, follow it! "Love one another and love your enemies. Do good to them too. For love is Our standard of conduct and Our correct

١١)   وَصَيَّـةً جديـدةً نوصيكـــمُ بـها
فأتّبعوها : " أحبّوا بعضكـم بعضاً وأحبّوا
أغداءَكـمُ وأحسِنوا إليهـم فالحَبّةُ سُنَّتنا

271

pathway."

وصراطنا المُستقيمُ"

12. As for those who conceal what We disclosed in **The True Furqan** and trade things with it cheaply, they are actually consuming hellfire into their bellies. For they have traded apostasy for true guidance and torment for forgiveness. We will never, ever, justify them. Everlasting torment awaits them at the end.

١٢) والذين يكتمون ما أنزلنا من الفرقان الحقّ ويشترون به ثمناً قليلاً أولئك ما يأكلون في بطونهم الا النار فقد اشتروا الضلالة بالهدى والعذاب بالمغفرة فلا نزكيهم ولهم في الآخرة عذابٌ مقيمٌ .

13. If anyone reads and accepts **The True Furqan**, We shall erect a protective curtain between him and the infidels. We will also introduce tranquility into the hearts of the trusting ones so they will gain greater faith on top of their existing faith. They will neither feel threatened nor will they be anxious in any way.

١٣) ومن يقرأ الفرقان الحقّ نجعل بينه وبين الذين كفروا حجاباً مستوراً وننزل السكينة في قلوب المؤمنين ليزدادوا إيماناً مع إيمانهم فلا خوف عليهم ولا هم يرهبون .

14. Why do you take vengeance upon those who worship Us? Do they not believe in what We proclaimed in the

١٤) وهل تنقمون من عبادنا المؤمنين إلا أن آمنوا بما قلنا من قبل وما أنزلنا من بعد . ألا

earlier covenant and what We revealed in the latter one. You act as if you are nothing but a company of savage oppressors.

إِنَّكُمْ لَقَوْمٌ ظَالِمُونَ .

15.   You rush to commit evil and aggression. You hardly perform any good and righteous deed.   Woe unto you for the vileness you are transacting.

١٥) تُسَارِعُونَ اِلَى الاِثْمِ والعُدوان وتَقعدونَ عَن البِّرِ والتقوى لَبِئْسَ مَا اَنْتُمْ فاعِلُونَ .

16.   We ruled out in **The True Gospel** and **The True Furqan** after it, the discharging of wickedness and the practice of scandalous   deeds.   Yet, you persist in your folly. (Nevertheless, if you will return unto us in honest   repentance   We   will definitely grant you forgive-ness as well as welcome you back into the fold for We are the Loving and the Forgiving Potentate.)

١٦) ونَهينَا فِي الانْجيل الحَقّ والفُرقان الحَقّ مِنْ بعدهِ عَن اقتراف الاِثْمِ وفعل المُوبِقات ومَا نزلْتُمْ بضلالِكُمْ سَادِرينَ .

273

58
FALSE WITNESS
(Surat Al Buhtan)

٥٨) سُورةُ البهتان

In the Name of the Father, the Word, the Holy Spirit, the One and only True God

بسم الآبِ الكلمةِ الروحِ الالهِ الواحد الأوحدِ

1.   O, you who are false witnesses, yet still claim to be counted among Our followers: the closest person to Our precepts is the one who is the farthest from Satan's dictates and deceptions, if you truly understand what We mean.

١) يَا أهلَ البُهتانِ مِنْ عِبادنا الضَّالِينَ: إنَّ أقربكمْ الى سُنَّتِنا أبعدُكمْ عَنْ شِرعةِ الشَّيطانِ ومكرهِ لوْ كُنتمْ تعلمونَ .

2.   You have discarded **The True Gospel** behind your back. You have also concealed the True Precepts so that no one can see the Truth. Additionally, you have announced with your lips what was not found in your inner being. But We discern better than anyone else secrets hidden in the heart.

٢) لقد نبذتُمُ الإنجيلَ الحقَّ وراءَ ظُهوركمْ وكتمتمْ سُنَّةَ الحقِّ وقلتمْ بأفواهكمْ ما ليسَ في قلوبكمْ ونحنُ أعلمُ بما تُخفي الصّدورُ وبما تكتمونَ .

3.   No created being can

٣) ومَا كانَ لمخلوقٍ أنْ يُفلتَ مِنْ قَدَره

فَكُلٌّ لِسُنَّتِنَا يَخْضَعُونَ .

ever escape his destiny, for each one must bow down his knee to Our decree.

4.   Your so-called inspired recitation brought nothing new. There was no prophecy in it, neither knowledge, nor miracle, not even any spirit or light to guide those who have gone astray!

٤) وَمَا جَاءَ لَغَوُكُمْ بِجَدِيدٍ فَلَا نُبُوَّةٌ وَلَا
عِلْمٌ وَلَا مُعْجِزَةٌ وَلَا رُوحٌ وَلَا نُورٌ يَهْدِي
الثَّائِهِينَ .

5.   In fact, your chanting of your recitation can be likened unto a tattered robe. Time has worn it out to such an extent that it is no longer of any benefit to cover exposed limbs!

٥) فَمَثَلُهُ كَمِثْلِ سَمَلٍ بَالٍ دَرَسَهُ الدَّهْرُ
فَمَا أَجْدَى فَتِيلًا لِقَوْمٍ لَا حَقِينَ .

6.   You inherited your book from your forefathers believing that if they considered it of great value, so should you. But it is worthless.

٦) يَتَوَارَثُهُ خَلَفُكُمْ عَنْ سَلَفِكُمْ
يَحْسَبُونَهُ ذَا شَأْنٍ عَظِيمٍ وَمَا هُوَ بِذِي شَأْنٍ
عَظِيمٍ .

7.   Whenever its fabric became threadbare, other misguided men added patches to it on top of previous patches.

٧) كُلَّمَا نَهَرَأَ زَادُوهُ رِقَاعًا فَوْقَ رِقَاعٍ
حَتَّى أَنْدَثَرَ السَّمَلُ الْقَدِيمُ .

They continued to do that until the original material was completely frayed.

8.   Then the patches themselves became ragged. The ignoramuses sought to bring it back to life. Who among the children of dust can ever make the bones rise again? Everyone knows that such labors by man are in vain. Only We can bring the dead to life again!

٨)   وَرَمَّتِ الرِّقاعُ فَسَعَى الجُهلاءُ لإحيانِها وَأنَّى يُحيُونَ العِظامَ وَهِيَ رَميـــمٌ ؟

9.   For a man to raise the dead is a strange conviction. It belongs only to a people who were barefooted, naked and hungry. That recitation was the best that could be produced by the apostates, who turned out to be among the most unlovable, cowardly terrorists and assassins the world has ever seen.

٩)   إنْ هَوَّلاً شِرعةَ قَومٍ حُفاةٍ عُراةٍ جِياعٍ فَكـــانَتْ خَيْرَ شِــرعةٍ أخرجتْ للكـافِرينَ وَكـانوا شَرَّ أمَّةٍ أخرِجتْ للعالَمينَ .

10.   When the barefooted were given horses to mount, the naked clothed to walk in pride and the hungry fed to feel satisfied, they did not discard the precepts of the pagans. Instead,

١٠)   وإذْ حُمِلَ الحُفاةُ وكُسِيَ العُراةُ وأشبِعَ الجِياعُ فَما نَبذوا شِرعةَ الكُفرِ بلْ ظَلُّوا على مِلّةِ الكُفرِ وسُنَّةِ الغابرينَ .

276

they insisted on practicing the way of apostasy and the precepts of the days of ignorance.

11.   Therefore, they were left behind in everything, but especially in the forward march to progress. As underdeveloped people they will not advance at all, but remain little people, backward and uncivilized.

١١) فَتَخَلَّفُوا عَنْ رَكْبِ الْمُفْلِحِينَ فَهُمْ لَا يَتَقَدَّمُونَ .

12.   Such an insignificant civilization will sooner or later disappear from the horizon of history because it has contributed very little to humanity's march to liberty, justice and knowledge.

١٢) تِلْكَ أُمَّةٌ قَدْ خَلَتْ لَهَا مَا كَسَبَتْ وَلَكُمْ مَا كَسَبْتُمْ وَلَا تُسْأَلُونَ عَمَّا كَانُوا يَعْمَلُونَ فَلَا تَنْتَفِعُوا آثَارَ الْكَافِرِينَ .

59
PROSPERITY
(Surat Al Yusr)

بسمِ الآبِ الكلمةِ الروحِ الإله الواحدِ الأوحدِ

In the Name of the Father, the Word, the Holy Spirit, the One and only True God

١) يَا أَهْلَ النِّفَاقِ مِنْ عِبَادِنَا الضَّالِينَ: إِنَّا نُرِيدُ بِكُمُ الْيُسْرَ وَلَا نُرِيدُ بِكُمُ الْعُسْرَ.

1.   O, you who are hypocrites, yet still claim to belong among Our worshipers: We yearn to see you prosper. We do not wish you to be impoverished.

٢) وَنُرِيدُ لَكُمُ الْمَحَبَّةَ لَا الْكُرهَ والإيمانَ لا الكفرَ والصدقَ لا الإفكَ والسلامَ لا الخصامَ.

2.   Moreover, We seek for you love, not hate; faithfulness, not faithlessness; trust, not mistrust; and reconciliation, not irreconciliation.

٣) وَنُرِيدُ لَكُمُ الأمنَ لا الخوفَ والسلمَ لا الحربَ والطُّهرَ لا النَّجَسَ والرّحمةَ لا العُدوانَ.

3.   We furthermore wish for you security, not fear; peace, not war; and compassion, not aggression.

٤) وَنُرِيدُ لَكُمُ العِفَّةَ لا الزّنى والاحترامَ لا الاحتقارَ. والإحسانَ لا

4.   Additionally, We covet for you chastity, not promiscuity; respect, not disrespect; goodwill,

not pillaging; and forgiveness, not
taking revenge.

الغَزوَ والمَغفِرَةَ لا الاِنتِقامَ .

5.   We also long to see you
educated, not uneducated; charming, not backward; humble, not
haughty; just, not unjust; dwelling
in the Light, not dwelling in
darkness.

٥) ونريدُ لكـــمُ العِلـــمَ لا الاُمِّيَّــة
واللطفَ لا الفَظاظةَ والتَّواضعَ لا الكِبرَ
والعدلَ لا الظلـمَ والنورَ لا الظّلامَ .

6.   Moreover, We desire
for you wisdom, not ignorance;
brotherly love, not hostility; and
enlightenment,   not confusion.
Will you try to discern what We
intend for you?

٦) ونريدُ لكـــمُ الحكمةَ لا الجـــهلَ
والاِخاءَ لا العداءَ والهُدى لا الضّلالَ أفلا
تَفِرقونَ ؟

7.   Subsequently, repent,
be enlightened and pursue the
virtuous pathway. It is preferable
to the path which you have
chosen in the past, a path of
ignorance,   sickness,   poverty,
terrorism and insecurity, which
are by-products of complete
infidelity.

٧) فتُوبوا واهتدوا واتَّبعوا سَبيلَ الخيرِ فقد
استَخرِفُ الجهلُ والدّاءَ والفقرَ وتلكـــمُ
آفاتُ الكفرِ المبين .

8.   Satan has certainly beguiled you through your beautiful
and fascinating classical language
and   what you have repeated from
apostasy and counterfeiting.

٨)   لَقَدْ غَرَّكُمْ فِى لُغَوِكُمُّ مَا
كُنْتُمْ تَنْشُرُونَ وَتَأْفِكُونَ .

60
THE POOR
(Surat Al Fuqara)

٦٠) سُورَةُ الفُقَرَاءِ

In the Name of the Father, the Word, the Holy Spirit, the One and only True God

بسم الآبِ الكلمةِ الروح الاله الواحد الأوحدِ

1.   You bury your children alive in the graves of paganism. You have let them feed on the milk of rebellion and ignorance, so that this earthly life deludes them. They lose their way in this world, become confused and end up perishing before their appointed time.

١) وَتئدونَ نفوسَ أولادِكـمُ فـي مُهودِ الكفـرِ ثـرُ ضعوَتـهـمُ الجهلَ والعصيـانَ فتغرّهــمُ الحيـاةُ الدُنيـا وَيضرِبـونَ فـي الأرضِ وَيضلّونَ فيهلكـونَ.

2.   We urge you to redeem them from the clutches of Satan. It can be done through the Word of Truth, Jesus of Nazareth, His love and faith. Then they can behold Our Light and accompany the faithful.

٢) فـاقتدوهـمُ مـنْ رِبْقَـةِ الشـيطان بكلمةِ الحقّ والمحَبَّـةِ وبالايمـانِ فيشـهدوا نورنا وَيلحقوا بالمؤمنينَ.

3.   True riches are attained in having faith, reason and spirit. Riches are not the sum total of

٣) إنما الغنـى بالإيمـانِ والعقـلِ والنفسِ لا بالقناطيرِ المقنطرةِ مـنَ الذهـبِ والفضّـةِ

tons of silver or gold, houses and cattle, spouses and whatever you own.

ولا الطيـان والأنعـام والازواج ومـا تملكـون .

4.   Conversely, real poverty is made up of paganism, ignorance and confusion. Look at your-selves, you really are a company of impoverished, destitute, forgotten and unforgiven souls.

٤)   وإنما الفقر بالكفر والجهل والضلال وما أنتم أولاء في الدنيا والآخرة فقراء معدمون .

5.   For you have elected the sensual and worldly life and missed the narrow way to eternal life. You have also considered everyone as enemies whenever they rejected your apostasy. The result was that everyone despised you thoroughly.

٥)   إستخرتم الحياة الدنيا فضللتم سبيل الآخرة وعـاديتـم مـن رفـض كفركم فنبذكم الناس أجمعين .

6.   You deliberately by-pass logic, wisdom and love. Thus, you become poverty-stricken people spiritually. You do not comprehend the meaning of spiritual matters and become confused.

٦)   تجتنبون العقل والحكمة والمحبة فتفقرون ولا تدركون للروح معنى فتضلون .

7.   Therefore, you must not acquire unlawful properties. You must not murder for We have not sanctioned murder at any time. You must not steal. You must not be involved in immorality. You must not dance to Satanic music. He is the one who commands you to commit abominations, atrocities and sexual immoralities. Satan also urges you to enunciate statements concerning us which are untrue.

٧) فَلَا تَأْكُلُوا مَالًا حَرَامًا وَلَا تَقْتُلُوا النَّفْسَ الَّتِي حَرَّمْنَا قَتْلَهَا تَحْرِيمًا وَلَا تَسْلُبُوا وَلَا تَزْنُوا وَلَا تَتَّبِعُوا خَطَوَاتِ الشَّيْطَانِ فَهُوَ يَأْمُرُكُمْ بِاقْتِرَافِ الْفَحْشَاءِ وَالْمُنْكَرِ وَالْبَغْيِ وَأَنْ تَقُولُوا عَلَيْنَا مَا لَا تَعْلَمُونَ .

8.   Our trusting worshipers walk upon the earth confidently. Whenever the pagans persecute them the righteous ones declare peace upon them, they forgive and take no vengeance on the pagans. For, Our worshipers are of the highest character.

٨) وَيَمْشِي عِبَادُنَا الْمُؤْمِنُونَ فِي الْأَرْضِ هَوْنًا وَإِنْ آذَاهُمُ الْكَافِرُونَ قَالُوا سَلَامًا وَيَغْفِرُونَ وَلَا يَنْتَقِمُونَ فَهُمْ عَلَى خُلُقٍ كَرِيمٍ .

61
INSPIRATION
(Surat Al Wahi)

٦١) سُورَةُ الوحي

In the Name of the Father, the Word, the Holy Spirit, the One and only True God

بسم الآبِ الكلمةِ الروحِ الالهِ الواحدِ الأوحدِ

1. We single out from among Our trusting worshipers whomever We will. Such a chosen person delivers Our divine message as a guide and reminder and does not speak of his own will. It is unquestionably extraordinary inspiration which We convey upon his heart. It is to be a Light for those who have gone astray; perhaps they will find the right way and repent.

١) ونصطفي من عبادنا المؤمنين من نشاءُ ليبلغ سُنَّتَنا هادياً ومُذكراً وما ينطقُ عن الهوى إن هو إلا وحيٌ يُوحى نُنزلهُ بالحقّ على قلبه نوراً للضالين لعلهم يهتدونَ .

2. On the day that We created humankind, We anchored in the depth of their souls a spark of Our Spirit—the conscience. Alas, the curtain of ignorance, infidelity and paganism caused your souls to deny Our existence and confuse your minds. Conse-

٢) ويوم سلنا الإنس مكنّا في قرارة نفسه قبساً من روحنا لكنّ سجوفَ الجهل والكفرِ والضلال أحدثتْ نفوسَكم وأضلَّتْ عقولكم فأنتم في الأرضِ

284

quently, you are lost upon planet earth and are groping in every valley for the right pathway.

كضرون ونے کل وادٍ تہیمون .

3. Accordingly, whenever truth and deception become intermingled and there is confusion in your state of mind, seek discernment through the Spirit of Truth which is embedded in one's living conscience. The Spirit will lead you to the Ultimate Truth because He is the arbiter for the doubtful. You are urged to ask the People of the Reminder if your inspiration is authentic or counterfeit.

٣) فَإِمَّا اخْتَلَطَ عَلَيْكُمُ الْحَقُّ بِالْبَاطِلِ وَكُنْتُمْ فِى شَكٍّ مِنْ أَمْرِكُمْ فَاحْتَكِمُوا إِلَى رُوحِ الْحَقِّ فِى الضَّمِيرِ الْحَىِّ يُرْشِدُكُمْ لِلْقِسْطِ فَهُوَ فَارُوقُ الْحَائِرِينَ . أَوِ اسْأَلُوا أَهْلَ الذِّكْرِ إِنْ كُنْتُمْ لَا تَعْلَمُونَ .

4. You are able to differentiate light from darkness with your naked eyes, but you are unable to differentiate good from evil with your inner eye! Thus, you are wanderers in your own chaotic state.

٤) تُمَيِّزُونَ النُّورَ مِنَ الظَّلَامِ بِبَصَرِكُمْ وَلَا تُمَيِّزُونَ الْخَيْرَ مِنَ الشَّرِّ بِبَصَائِرِكُمْ فَأَنْتُمْ فِى ضَلَالِكُمْ تَعْمَهُونَ .

5. It is common knowledge that peace is good but murder is evil. Chastity is good but promiscuity is evil. Almsgiving is good

٥) فَالسَّلَامُ خَيْرٌ وَالْقَتْلُ شَرٌّ وَالْعِفَّةُ خَيْرٌ وَالزِّنَى شَرٌّ وَالْحَسَنَةُ خَيْرٌ وَالسَّلْبُ شَرٌّ

285

but stealing is evil. Somehow you yourselves are unable to distinguish one from the other!

ولكنكـم لا تُميزونَ

6. You even swear with an oath that you will distinguish good from evil and command the practice of good works and the prohibition of immoralities. However, your commands and prohibitions are only lip service. There is no power in what you command or prohibit because you are hypocrites through and through.

٦) وتُقسمونَ بأنكـم لتُميزونَ الخيرَ منَ الشـرِّ وتأمرونَ بـالمعروفِ وتنهَونَ عَـن المنكـرِ . ومَا تأمرونَ ومَا تنهَونَ إلا قولاً ظاهراً ولا رُوحَ فيمـا تأمرونَ أو تـنهَونَ فأنـتُمُ المُنافقونَ .

7. Whenever you command the practice of good deeds it is only empty words because you practice evil deeds in real life. You also prohibit the activity of evil in theory. But in practice you do the very thing because you are driven.

٧) وكَتأمرونَ بالخيرِ قولاً وتقترفونَ الشَّـرَّ فعلاً . وتنهَونَ عن الشرِّ قولاً وتقترفونَهُ فعلاً وأنـتُمْ لا تشعرونَ .

8. Repeating mere words can never be a substitute for doing the deeds. Such declarations are more or less the pronouncements of the

٨) وإنَّ القولَ لا يُغني عن الفعلِ شَيئاً . وإنْ تلكَ إلا أقوالُ الثائنينَ وأفعالُ المجرمينَ .

lawless and the pursuit of the transgressors.

9. We have conveyed this **True Furqan** in your very language. We articulated it with fascinating phrases. Some of you frown and turn away. Yet, We hope that the majority of you will turn to Our right pathway.

٩) وأنزلنا هذا الفرقان الحقّ بلسانكم وبلغناهُ كلماً مُعجزاً فمنكـم من عَبَسَ وتولى ولكنّ أكثركـم سَيهتدونَ .

10. We address the hearts of mankind with the enlightenment of faith. Hearts are the ears of Our prophets as well as the tongues of Our Apostles.

١٠) ونُخاطبُ القلوبَ بنورِ الإيمان فالقلوبُ آذانُ الأنبياءِ وألسنةُ المُرسلينَ .

11. Oh how the idolaters yearn to discover some prophecies concerning their book in **The True Gospel** or even a mention of the appearance of their so-called prophet.

١١) وَوَدَّ أهلُ الكفرِ إن لو يجدونَ في الإنجيلِ الحقِّ للغوهـــمُ بُشـــرى أو لأنفسهِمُ ذكراً .

12. Deceivers—that is what some of those are who announce that they have found such references. They are

١٢) وكَذبَ الذينَ قَالوا وَجَدْنا فـهـمُ أُمّيونَ لا يعلمونَ الكتابَ الحقَّ إلا أمانيَّ

287

incompetent scholars who are unacquainted with The True Book. They fantasize such prophecies and are truly oblivious of their own chaotic condition of deception.

13. As for those Who trusted in **The True Gospel,** they know the Gospel as thoroughly as they know their own children. Thus, they do not cover up the Truth, neither do they corrupt Our precepts nor do they counterfeit scripture.

14. O, you who are lost and uneducated, yet still consider yourselves among Our followers: if the idolater comes to you stating, "Your doctrines are the doctrines of truth," do not believe him. Why? Because you know full well that idolaters are incorrigible liars.

15. If a depraved person brings to you some so-called fresh news, investigate it carefully. Otherwise, you may

وإن يتبعــون إلا الظــن وإن هـــم إلا يخرصـون .

(١٣) والذين آمنوا بالإنجيل الحق يعرفونـه كما يعرفون أبناءهم فلا يكتمون الحق ولا يحرّفون سنتنا ولا يفترون .

(١٤) يأهل الجهل من عبادنا الضالين : إذا جاءكم المنافقون وقالوا "إن قولكم هو القول الحق" فلا تصدّقوهـم فإنكم تعلمون أنّ المنافقين كاذبون .

(١٥) وإنّ جاءكم فاسق بنبأ فتبيّنوا أن تصيبوا عبادنا المؤمنين بجهالة فتصبحوا على ما

accuse Our believing followers with ignorance. When such a thing takes place You will become extremely regretful for making a false report.

فَعَلْتُمْ نَادِمِينَ .

16. Furthermore, request from the counterfeiter if he has been sent with an authenticating miracle. Then ask him to perform the sign, if he is indeed an honest prophet.

١٦) واسْأَلُوا الْمُرْسَلَ إِنْ كَانَ أُرْسِلَ بِآيَةٍ أَنْ يَأْتِيَ بِهَا إِنْ كَانَ مِنَ الصَّادِقِينَ .

17. No human being is capable of bringing down a sign or a miracle except by Our permission. We do not inspire any prophecy without absolute accuracy.

١٧) وَمَا كَانَ لِبَشَرٍ أَنْ يَأْتِيَ بِآيَةٍ إِلَّا بِإِذْنِنَا وَمَا نُنَزِّلُ الْآيَاتِ إِلَّا بِالْحَقِّ الْمُبِينِ .

18. There is a company among you who twist their tongues by quoting from a corrupt book and wanting you to accept it as a companion to **Our Divine Revelation**. But it is not totally borrowed from The Genuine Book. Additionally, they claim that it has been sent by Us. Yet,

١٨) وَإِنَّ مِنْكُمْ لَفَرِيقًا يَلْوُونَ أَلْسِنَتَهُمْ بِقَوْلٍ بَاطِلٍ لِتَحْسَبُوهُ مِنَ الْكِتَابِ الْحَقِّ وَمَا هُوَ مِنَ الْكِتَابِ الْحَقِّ وَيَقُولُونَ هُوَ مِنْ عِنْدِ اللهِ وَمَا هُوَ مِنْ عِنْدِنَا وَيَقُولُونَ عَلَيْنَا الْكَذِبَ

289

We did not send it. Therefore, they fabricate these things about Us intentionally in order to deceive people artfully. But We are the All-Knowing Judge of man's heart.

وهـم يعلمونَ .

62
THE RIGHTLY-GUIDED
(Surat Al Muhtadeen)

٦٢) سُورةُ المُهتَدِينَ

In the Name of the Father, the Word, the Holy Spirit, the One and only True God

بسمِ الآبِ الكلمةِ الروحِ الإلهِ الواحدِ الأوحدِ

1.   Wide is the gate which leads to destruction and many there are who enter therein. Yet, narrow is the gate that leads to eternity and few there are who are able to locate it.

١) وكبابُ التهلكةِ رَحْبٌ سَبيلُهُ وما أكثرُ الداخلينَ، وما أعسَرِ بابَ الخُلدِ فقلّةٌ إليهِ يهتدونَ .

2.   O, you who have truly believed from among Our creatures: how the idolaters desire to turn you back from your new faith to idolatry, due to the jealousy in their souls. Perhaps if Truth is clarified to them they may trust Us. We will certainly pardon them also. One of the characteristics of righteous believers is their willingness to grant pardon. We recognize that you are truly righteous because you are a people of high moral character.

٢) يأيها الذينَ آمنوا مِنْ عبادِنا : وَدَّ جميعُ أهلِ الكُفرِ إنْ لو يَردّونكمْ مِنْ بعدِ إيمانِكمْ كفارًا حسدًا مِنْ عندِ أنفسهِمْ فإذا تبيّنَ لهمُ الحقُّ وآمنوا فاعفوا عنهمْ حتّى نأتيَ بأمرِنا . فالعفوُ مِنْ سيماءِ المؤمنينَ الصادقينَ وانكمْ لعلى خُلُقٍ عظيـمٍ .

3. The ones who blasphemed, yet still consider themselves among Our people declared, "Christians have nothing to stand on whenever they recite **The True Gospel**." Who is a worse oppressor than a person who oppresses Our loyal followers by forbidding them to celebrate Our name in Our houses of worship, seeks their destruction and ruin, then murders Our trusting worshipers?

4. This type of people have no right to enter, neither to desecrate these buildings. Embarrassment is their lot in this world and in the world to come, horrific torture.

5. O, you who have believed from among Our followers: do not fight those who fight you. Do not take vengeance upon your persecutors and never victimize others. We definitely do not cherish persecutors.

6. Pardon those who oppress and afflict you. Even do

٣) وقال الذين كفروا من عبادنا : "
ليستِ النصارى على شيء وهـــمْ يَتلونَ
الإنجيــل الحــقَّ" ومـنْ أظلـمُ مِنْ مَنَعَ
كَنائسَنا أنْ يُذكرَ فيها اسْمُنا وسَعى
في خرابها وهدْمِها وقتلَ عبادَنا المؤمنينَ ؟

٤) أولئك ما كان لهـمْ أنْ يَدخلوهـا أو
يُدَسُّوها . فلهـمْ خِزِيٌ في الدنيا ولهـمْ
في الآخرةِ عَذابٌ أليـمٌ .

٥) يَأيها الذين آمنوا من عبادنا : لا تُقـاتلوا
الذينَ يُقـاتلونكـمْ ولا تَنتقموا ولا تَعْتدوا
فإنّا لا نُحبُّ المُعتدينَ .

٦) واعفـوا عَنِ الذيـنَ يُعــادونكـمْ

good to them, forgive them, and seek Our forgiveness for them also. With such a disposition no rebellion shall rise among You and religion in its entirety is Ours only. But if those who persecute you stop their evil, repent and trust in **The True Gospel** and Jesus the Messiah, We shall definitely pardon the repentants.

ويُؤْذُونَكُمْ وأَحْسِنُوا إِلَيْهِمْ وَاغْفِرُوا لَهُمْ وَاسْتَغْفِرُوا حَتَّى لَا تَكُونَ فِتْنَةٌ وَيَكُونَ الدِّينُ كُلُّهُ لَنَا . فَإِنِ انْتَهَوْا وَتَابُوا وَآمَنُوا بِالانْجِيلِ الْحَقِّ وَالْفُرْقَانِ الْحَقِّ فَإِنَّا نَعْفُو عَنِ التَّائِينَ .

7. We did not predeter-mine punishment upon you arbitrarily. Punishment was originated as a method of warning to you who have understanding; perchance you will take heed and turn away from your wrong creed.

٧) وَمَا كَتَبْنَا عَلَيْكُمُ الْقِصَاصَ فَلَكُمْ فِي الْقِصَاصِ بَوَائِرٌ يَا أُولِي الأَلْبَابِ لَعَلَّكُمْ تَتَّقُونَ .

8. O, you who have gone astray, yet still consider your-selves party to Our followers: why, O why do you deny Our signs when We are observers of all your insincere manipulations? Furthermore, why do you mislead the ones who have already been rightly guided away from the straight and narrow path? You definitely seek to follow the

٨) يَا أَيُّهَا الَّذِينَ ضَلُّوا مِنْ عِبَادِنَا : لِمَ تَكْفُرُونَ بِآيَاتِنَا وَنَحْنُ شُهَدَاءُ عَلَى مَا تَعْمَلُونَ . وَلِمَ تُضِلُّونَ عَنِ السَّبِيلِ الَّذِينَ اهْتَدَوْا تَبْغُونَهَا لَهُمْ عِوَجاً وَأَنْتُمْ تَشْهَدُونَ وَمَا نَحْنُ بِغَافِلِينَ عَمَّا تَفْعَلُونَ .

293

wrong path and promote such evil paths contently. Are you not aware that We do not overlook whatever you are doing? (For We are the Almighty, the Wise.)

63
THE BEATITUDES
(Surat Al Thouba)

٦٣) سُورةُ طُوبى

In the Name of the Father, the Word, the Holy Spirit, the One and only True God

بسـمِ الآبِ الكَلِمَةِ الروحِ الالهِ الواحدِ الأوحدِ

1. O, people everywhere: We announce to you, blessed are the true believers for theirs is the Kingdom of Heaven.

١) يَأَيُّها النَّاسُ طُوبى للسَّاجدينَ بالحَقِّ فإنَّ لهـمُ جنَّاتِ النعيـمِ .

2. Blessed are the meek for they shall be the inheritors of this earth.

٢) طُوبـى للوُدعـاءِ فإنَّهـــمُ الأرضَ سيرِثونَ .

3. Blessed are the merciful for they shall attain mercy.

٣) طُوبـى للرُحمـاءِ مـن عبادنـا فانـهـم سيُرحمونَ .

4. Blessed are the peacemakers for they shall be Our favorite children.

٤) طُوبـى للدَّاعيـنِ للسَّـلامِ فهـــمُ أبناؤنـا المُقرَّبونَ .

5. O, you who are faithful believers from among Our creatures: We consider you as

٥) يَأَيُّها المؤمنونَ من عبادنا المُقرَّبينَ: أنتَـمُ المِلحُ للعالَمِينَ فإنْ فَسَدَ المِلحُ فبِماذا عَسَاهـمُ

salt for the earth. If salt loses its essence, with what shall people season their food? Salt which has lost its savor shall be discarded for the passersby to trample upon it.

٦)   أَنْتُمُ النُّورُ لِلْعَالَمِينَ لَا تُطْفِئُهُ أَفْوَاهُ الْكَافِرِينَ .

6. You are the light of the world. The intimidating roar of the idolaters can never quench your light.

٧)   فَاشْرِقُوا بِنُورِكُمْ عَلَى النَّاسِ كَافَّةً فَيَشْهَدُوا أَتْقْوَاكُمْ فَيَسْبِّحُونَا وَيلْحَقُوا بِالْمُؤْمِنِينَ .

7. Let your light shine brightly upon people everywhere. Once they have observed your virtuous conduct, they will glorify Us.

٨)   وَلَا يُلْهِكُمُ التَّكَاثُرُ وَتَكْدِيسُ الْأَقْوَاتِ وَتَجْمِيعُ مَا تَشْتَهُونَ .

8. Do not get caught up in the pursuit of worldly prosperity, the piling of sustenance or the accumulation of things you covet.

٩)   فَالْحَيَاةُ أَعَزُّ مِنَ الْغِذَاءِ وَالْجَسَدُ أَغْلَى مِنَ الْكِسَاءِ وَمَا تَمْلَكُونَ .

9. For life is more valuable than provisions. The body is more precious than clothing or what you possess.

10. Observe the birds of the air. They do not sow, neither reap nor gather any food for storage. Do you feed them? No! We are the One who grants them their necessary provisions.

١٠) إنّ الطير لا تـزرع ولا تحصد ولا
تدّخر جَناهـا ونحـن نرزقـها نصيبـاً
مقسـوماً .

11. Think seriously now! Are you not more valuable than the birds of the sky? For you are the crown of Our entire creation?

١١) فلأنتـم أعظـم منها درجةً وأرفعُ
تكريماً .

12. Therefore, pursue the pathway to the Kingdom of Heaven. Then the lesser things in life will be added to you in generous portions.

١٢) واسْعوا في سـبيل ملكـوتِ السـماء
وما دونَه تؤتونه نافلةً ومرسَرقاً كريماً .

13. On the Assigned Day of Judgment, when some faces will be brightened and others darkened, the ones whose faces are darkened will identify the blasphemers. They will taste of the torture that is the payback for what they have done.

١٣) ويومَ تبيضُّ وجوهٌ وتسودُّ وجوهٌ : فأمـا
الذين اسودّت وجوههـم فقد كفـروا مـن
بعد إيمان فذاقوا العذابَ بما كانوا يفعلونَ .

14. As for the ones whose faces are brightened, they will

١٤) وأمـا الذين ابيضّـت وجوههـم ففـي

297

enjoy Our mercy forever. For
We and We alone are the
Supreme Judge of the living and
the dead.

رَحْمَتِنَا هُمْ فِيهَا خَالِدُونَ .

64
THE ALLIES
(Surat Al Awli-ya)

٦٤) سُورَةُ الأَولِياءِ

In the Name of the Father, the Word, the Holy Spirit, the One and only True God

بسمِ الآبِ الكلمةِ الروحِ الاله الواحدِ الأوحدِ

1.   Do not count those who were killed in the Cavalcade for Truth and for Faith to be lifeless. No, not at all. They are in fact alive rejoicing in Our Mansions of Glory. We do not withhold the recompense of the martyrs for truth and genuine faith, who perished by the hands of the savage infidels.

١) ولا تحسبنَّ الذينَ قُتلوا في سَبيلِ الحقِّ والإيمانِ أمواتاً بل أحياءٌ في جناتِنا ينعمونَ . فإنّا لا نُضيعُ أجرَ شهداءِ الحقِّ والإيمانِ بالدينِ القويمِ على أيـدي الكـفرةِ المُجرمينَ .

2.   Some of Our people were informed, "The infidels are preparing to attack you. Therefore take cover." Their apprehension generated more faith in Us. Consequently, they put their trust in Us and triumphed over the enemy through Our grace and good pleasure. So, no evil touched them. Certainly,

٢) والذينَ قال لهمُ الناسُ إنَّ الكفارَ قد جَمَعوا لكمُ فاخشوهمُ فزادَهمُ إيماناً فتوكّلوا علينا فانقلبوا بنعمةٍ مِنّا وفضلٍ لم يمسسهمُ سوءٌ . ألا إنَّ أولياءَنا لا خوفَ عليهمُ ولا همُ يحزنونَ .

299

Our redeemed children have no reason to be fearful neither to be sorrowful because they are Our allies for surety.

3.   By using his cohorts, Satan tries to strike terror in your soul. We admonish you, do not fear them at all. Rather fear the torments of the Abyss.

٣) إِنَّمَا ذَلِكُمُ الشَّيْطَانُ يُخَوِّفُكُمْ بِأَوْلِيَائِهِ فَلاَ تَخَافُوهُمْ بَلْ خَافُوا عَذَابَ الْجَحِيمِ .

4.   Do not let those who rush into apostasy dishearten you. They have not really harmed you in a lasting manner. Recognize that they will have no part in Heaven, but monstrous anguish awaits them and it will last and last and last.

٤) وَلاَ يُحْزِنْكُمُ الَّذِينَ يُسَارِعُونَ فِي الْكُفْرِ إِنَّهُمْ لَنْ يَضُرُّوكُمْ شَيْئًا فَلاَ نَصِيبَ لَهُمْ فِي السَّمَاءِ وَلَهُمْ عَذَابٌ عَظِيمٌ .

5.   We do not withhold the reward for anyone who practices good deeds, who has trusted Us and who has repented from his sinful ways. We will also atone for the misdeeds of those who were forced out of their homes, were injured as a result of serving Us and were

٥) إِنَّا لاَ نُضِيعُ عَمَلَ عَامِلٍ صَالِحٍ آمَنَ وَتَابَ . وَالَّذِينَ أُخْرِجُوا مِنْ دِيَارِهِمْ وَأُوذُوا فِي سَبِيلِنَا وَقُتِلُوا وَمَا قَاتَلُوا لَنُكَفِّرَنَّ عَنْهُمْ سَيِّئَاتِهِمْ وَلَنُدْخِلَنَّهُمْ جَنَّاتِ النَّعِيمِ ثَوَاباً

attacked but did not retaliate by killing the offenders. We shall usher them into the heavenly Mansions of Glory as a reward for their sacrifices. Such will be Our recompense for everyone of Our faithful servants.

لِمَا قَدَّمُوا وَهَكَذَا نَجْزِي الْعَامِلِينَ .

6.   You can observe that those who repented and believed what We delivered in **The True Furqan**, prostrated themselves in humble worship. They do not exchange Our scripture for a pitiful price. They shall definitely be rewarded with generosity and festivity.

٦) وَتَرَوْنَ الَّذِينَ تَابُوا وَآمَنُوا بِمَا أُوْحِينَا فِي الْفُرْقَانِ الْحَقِّ خَاشِعِينَ لَا يَشْتَرُونَ بِآيَاتِنَا ثَمَناً قَلِيلاً أُولَئِكَ لَهُمْ أَجْرُهُمْ وَلَا يُظْلَمُونَ .

7.   The hypocrites preten-ded that they have trusted what We conveyed in **The True Furqan**. Furthermore, they want the evil one to give the verdict in their disputes with each other. Satan seems to work overtime just to lead them astray from Us and take them far, far away.

٧) وَتَرَى عَمَدَ الْمُنَافِقُونَ بِأَنَّهُمْ آمَنُوا بِمَا أُوْحِينَا فِي الْفُرْقَانِ الْحَقِّ يُرِيدُونَ أَنْ يَتَحَاكَمُوا إِلَى الطَّاغُوتِ وَيُرِيدُ الشَّيْطَانُ أَنْ يُضِلَّهُمْ ضَلَالاً بَعِيداً .

8.   When it is enunciated to the blasphemers, "Trust in

٨) وَإِذَا قِيلَ لِلَّذِينَ كَفَرُوا : "آمِنُوا بِمَا

what is disclosed in **The True Furqan,**" one can notice how vehemently the hypocrites dispute it.

9.   Their hearts are utterly sick. Still, do preach to them and admonish them. Relate to them also some words of wisdom.

10.   Those who have disbelieved in Us will surely envy the ones who believed; because of the wisdom and guidance which We placed in **The True Gospel** and **The True Furqan.** Moreover, disbelievers are insanely jealous because We have prepared for the believers Mansions of Glory, where the spirit, not the flesh, finds eternal joy. For the Mansions of Glory are dwellings of purity, love and peace. They will also see what eyes have never seen, hear what ears have never heard and behold what the mind of mankind has never imagined. Because they have walked in the right path We shall let them behold Our countenance. That experience

أَنزَلَ ـ في الفرقانِ الحقّ" . ﴿ رأيتَ المنافقينَ

يصدّونَ عنهُ صُدُوداً .

٩) ـ في قلوبهـمْ مـرضٌ فعِظوهـمْ وقولـوا

لهـمْ قَوْلاً مرشيداً .

١٠) إنَّ الذينَ كفـروا لَيحسـدونَ الذيـنَ

آمنوا على مَا آتيناهـمْ ـ في الإنجيـل الحـقّ

والفرقانِ الحقّ من الحكمة والهدى ومَا

أعددنا لهـمْ من جنّاتٍ يَنعـمُ فيها الأرواحُ

لا الأجسادُ ـ في طُهرٍ ومحبةٍ وسلامٍ يَرونَ

مَا لَمْ تَرهُ عينٌ ولمْ تسمعْهُ أذنٌ ولمْ يخطرْ على

قلبِ بَشرٍ ، ونُريهـمْ وجهَنَا وهذا هوَ الفوزُ

العظيمُ فقد اتّبعوا صراطاً سَديداً .

will be their ultimate triumph.

11. Now regarding the ones who disbelieved and murdered Our servants. Let us declare that if they owned all that is on this terrestrial ball and could offer it for their redemption from the torments of that Great Judgment Morning, it would not be accepted. Of course, they will intensely struggle desperately to get out of hellfire. Nonetheless, they neither can avoid going therein nor find an exit to escape their lot but forever stay within.

١١) إِنَّ الذِينَ كَفَرُوا وقَتَلُوا عِبَادَنَا لِوأَنَّ لَهُـمْ مَا فِي الأَرْضِ جَمِيعاً لِيَفْتَدُوا بِهِ مِنْ عَذَابِ يَوْمِ القِيَامَةِ مَا تُقُبِّلَ مِنْهُمْ يُرِيدُونَ أَنْ يَخْرُجُوا مِنَ النَّارِ وَمَا هُمْ بِخَارِجِينَ أَوْ بِالغَيْنَ عَنْهَا مَحِيداً.

12. We must state unequi-vocally that those who disbe-lieved and turned away from Our Own way, have indeed gone astray, far, far away.

١٢) والذِينَ كَفَرُوا وصَدُّوا عَن سَبِيلِنَا فَقَدْ ضَلُّوا ضَلَالاً بَعِيداً.

65
THE RECITATION
(Surat Iqraa)

٦٥) سُورةُ إِقرأ

In the Name of the Father, the Word, the Holy Spirit, the One and only True God

بسـم الآبِ الكلمةِ الروحِ الالهِ الواحدِ الأوحدِ

1.   Satan determined in his heart, "I will take control of mankind and entice them to commit monstrous sins. Inevitably, practicing such evil things will shut the gates of Heaven and open the gates of Hell for them. Thus, I will enslave them until the Day of Resurrection and that will be my crowning conquest."

١) وقال الشيطانُ في قلبه:
"لأختنِكنّ الانسانَ ولأغويتّه ليقترفَ أكبرَ الكبائرِ فتوصدُ بوجهِه أبوابُ النعيمِ وتُفتحُ أبوابُ الجحيمِ فأستعبدتّه الى يومِ يُبعثونَ وهذا هوَ النصرُ العظيمُ" .

2.   The One and only True God considers that the most monstrous sins are murder, robbery and adultery. All other sins are inferior among the monstrous and degrading sins. (Of course, the worst is unbelief in God—being an infidel, an atheist.)

٢) "فإنّ أكبرَ الكبائرِ عندَ اللهِ هيَ القتلُ والسرقةُ والزنى وما دونَها فنافلةٌ الكبائرِ والفجورِ" .

304

3.   "Therefore, I, Satan, will definitely infuse these sins deep into mankind's soul and bloodstream.   In this manner, they will not even contemplate my being the source of such thoughts and will be terrified of My fury."

٣)   فَلَأُدْخِلَنَّهَا فِي قَلْبِهِ وَنَفْسِهِ مَدْخَلاً بَلِيغاً فَلَا يَظُنُّ بِيَ الظُّنُونَ وَلَا يَخْشَى كَيْدِي وَإِنَّ كَيْدِي لَعَظِيمٌ" .

4.   "Furthermore, I, Satan, will assuredly create in mankind's heart a god whom they will worship and obey, and will call him by excellent names that will be pleasant to hear in one's ear.

٤)   "وَلَأَخْتَلِقَنَّ فِي رَأْسِهِ رَبّاً مَعْبُوداً مُطَاعاً أَدْعُوهُ بِأَسْمَاءٍ حُسْنَى تَسُرُّ السَّامِعِينَ"

5.   "I, Satan, will also implant in these names such deception that the difference between good and evil will not be recognized.   The purpose is to cause mankind to lose the straight way, obey my command with a secure heart everyday, then conclude that mankind has found heaven's passageway.

٥)   "وَلَأَدُسَّنَّ فِيهَا الكُفْرَ فَلَا يُمَيِّزُ الطَّيِّبَ مِنَ الخَبِيثِ وَيَضِلُّ سَوَاءَ السَّبِيلِ وَيُطِيعُ أَمْرِي مُطْمَئِنَّ القَلْبِ قَرِيرَ العَيْنِ، ظَنّاً مِنْهُ أَنَّهُ عَلَى صِرَاطٍ مُسْتَقِيمٍ" .

6.   "Then, a man-god whom I, Satan, will create will

٦)   "فَلِرَبِّهِ مِنْهُ مَظَاهِرُ البَدَنِ وَلَغْوُ اللِّسَانِ .

305

also demonstrate leadership qualities and linguistic eloquence. Additionally, my intention for this man-god includes sensual lust and visions of grandeur.

وليَ منهُ ما يكتـمُ القلبُ ومـا تقـترفُ الجوارحُ والابدانُ" .

7. "I, Satan, will cause this unusual man to seek refuge in his god from me, and accuse me of blasphemy and confusion. These tricks are intended to misguide him as to who I really am and make me look innocent of these activities. His faith in his god, which I, Satan, have created within his heart by deception, will prompt him to undertake these three monstrous sins, murder, robbery and adultery. This man-god will do these things in obedience to the command of the counterfeit god voluntarily. This will become the greatest conspiracy of all, for I am Satan, the best of all conspirators in the universe.

٧) "وسأجعلهُ يستعيذُ مني بربّهِ المختَلق ويرميني بـالكفرِ والضلال، تضليـلاً لـهُ وتبرئةً لنفسي وايماناً منهُ بربّهِ الذي اختلقتهُ في رأسهِ اختلاقـاً بـهْتاً، فيرتكبُ الكبائرَ الثلاثَ بأمرِ ربّهِ المزعومِ طَوْعاً أو كُرهاً، لا بأمري، وهذا هوَ المكرُ الكبيرُ فإنّى لأمكرُ الماكرينَ" .

8. "Additionally, I, Satan, will address his basic instincts

٨) "ولأخاطبنَّ غرائزهُ بلغةٍ أعجزُ بلغوها

with a language so miraculously eloquent that the followers would be utterly captivated. Even the illiterates will understand it because I, Satan, will simplify its meaning.

9. "The lust of the man-god's basic instincts will propel him to carry out the most monstrous sins and wickedness. I, Satan, will accomplish this by urging them to do these things by periodically inspiring erroneous scriptures which are weighty with meaning. These in turn will flow into the souls of mankind like undetected poison, which strikes them unawares."

10. We warn you that Satan has manipulated all of these things as his procedure to reach his intended victim, mankind. So he deliberately drew several illiterates to his plan. He taught them a new counterfeit book without any divine wisdom. He also caused them to elevate blasphemy, promiscuity and rebellion. The terrible end result

was, of course, now guaranteed.

11. Satan came to them proclaiming, "I am your Lord and I have chosen you above all other human beings to bestow my extraordinary inspiration upon you. Therefore, accept whatever I grant you and be grateful."

١١)   وقـال الشـيطانُ لأوليائـه : "إنِّـي أنـا ربكــمُ اصطفيتكــمُ علـى النــاس كافــةً فخــذوا الوحــيَ منــي واعبــدوني" .

12. Once their hearts were encouraged, by remembering their counterfeit lord, they accepted what they were given. Then they recited the fresh, but false, words clearly and convincingly.

١٢)   وإذا اطمأنتْ قلوبهـمُ بذكـرٍ ربّهـم المزعومِ أخذوا ما أتُوهُ وقرؤوهُ قرآ جلّياً .

13. This is the scheme with which demons inspire the fake revelation of old and the counterfeit book to their deceived messengers.

١٣)   هكـذا تُوحي الشياطينُ لرُسُلها وحياً إفكاً وقولاً فَرِياً .

14. As a result Satan dressed up truth with falsehood and falsehood with truth. Thus these people could not distinguish good from evil. Consequently, Satan propelled them to hellfire.

١٤)   وقـد التبسَ عليهـم الحـقُّ بالبـاطل والباطلُ بالحقّ فما تبيّنوا الطيبَ من الخبيثِ فوَردوا النارَ سَوِيّاً .

(Remember that We are the One
who reveals and conceals.)

66
THE INFIDELS
(Surat Al Kafereen)

٦٦) سُورَةُالكَافرِينَ

In the Name of the Father, the Word, the Holy Spirit, the One and only True God

بسم الآبِ الكَلِمةِ الروحِ الالهِ الواحدِ الأوحدِ

١.   O, you who have blasphemed, yet consider yourselves among Our followers: you have stated that Jesus the Messiah, the son of Mary, is a Breath from Our Spirit, as well as Our Word and Our Messenger. And you further believed that We have granted Him miraculous powers, supported Him by the Holy Spirit and have taught Him the Torah, the Gospel and wisdom. You affirmed that by Our permission He healed the dumb-mute, the leper and even raised the dead. Jesus, you said, is also exalted in this world and the world to come and He is also among the closest to God's Throne. He is God.

١) يَأَيُّها الذينَ كفروا مِنْ عِبادِنا الضّالِينَ: لقدْ آمنتمْ بأنَّ عيسى المسيحَ ابنَ مريمَ هو نفخةٌ منْ روحِنا وهو كلمتُنا ورسولُنا وإنّا آتيناهُ البيّناتِ وأيّدناهُ بروحِ القدسِ وعلّمناهُ الكتابَ والحكمةَ والتوراةَ والإنجيلَ وأنّهُ أبرأَ الأكمَهَ والأبرصَ وأحيى الموتى وأنّهُ وجيهٌ في الدنيا والآخرةِ ومنَ المقرّبينَ.

2. After all of these beautiful declarations you backed off in your tracks. You rejected your original statement of faith. You abrogated your earlier proclamations. You split up Our Breath from Our Spirit. You disconnected Our Word from Our Person. You also opposed Our precepts which were revealed in **The True Gospel**. Therefore, we condemn you as vile reprobates and stamp on your foreheads "shirkers and infidels."

٢) ثُمَّ نَكَصْتُمْ عَلى أَعْقَابِكُمْ
وَكَفَرْتُمْ بِإِيمَانِكُمْ وَنَسَخْتُمْ
أَقْوَالَكُمْ وَفَرَّقْتُمْ نَفَخْنَا عَنْ رُوحِنَا
وَسَلَخْتُمْ عَنَّا كَلِمَتَنَا وَعَارَضْتُمْ
سُنَّتَنَا فِي الإِنْجِيلِ الْحَقِّ فَأَنْتُمُ الْكَفَرَةُ
الْفَجَرَةُ الْمُشْرِكُونَ .

3. Your latter declarations in your book did not authenticate **The True Gospel**. Your pronouncements were actually denials of Our revelation, rejection of Our rule, modification of Our precepts and the encouragement of the deceivers.

٣) وَمَا جَاءَ قَوْلُكُمْ مُصَدِّقاً لِلإِنْجِيلِ
الْحَقِّ وَلاَ خَاضِعاً لأَمْرِنَا إِنَّمَا جَاءَ مُكَذِّباً
لِقَوْلِنَا عَاصِياً لأَمْرِنَا مُحَرِّفاً لِسُنَّتِنَا وَنَاصِراً
لِلْمُسْتَكْبِرِينَ .

4. The result is, your disclosure of goodness became evil, your faith became faithlessness, your love became hate and your peace became animosity because Satan set himself up as the worst of enemies against the

٤) فَكَانَ خَيْرُهُ شَرّاً وَإِيمَانُهُ كُفْراً
وَمَحَبَّتُهُ حِقْداً وَسَلاَمُهُ عُدْوَاناً فَقَدْ كَانَ
الشَّيْطَانُ لِلْمُؤْمِنِينَ عَدُوّاً أَلَدُودّاً .

311

true believers.

5.　　But the Word of Truth, (Messiah Jesus), was unveiled, overflowing with goodness, faith, love and peace. He was destined to guide humanity to the straight path (and to become the Ultimate Sacrifice).

٥) وَتَرَكَتْ كَلِمَةُ الْحَقِّ تَفِيضُ خَيْرًا وَمَحَبَّةً وَسَلَامًا أَتَهَدِّي النَّاسَ الى صِرَاطٍ مُسْتَقِيمٍ .

6.　　A counterfeit word erupted spewing vileness, blasphemy, hatred and animosity. As a matter of course it confused humanity. It's intention was to hurl them into the very bottom of the Abyss.

٦) وَخَرَجَتْ كَلِمَةُ الْبَاطِلِ تَنْفُثُ شَرًّا وَكُفْرًا وَحِقْدًا وَعُدْوَانًا فَأَضَلَّتِ النَّاسَ وَأَلْقَتْهُمْ فِي قَرَارِ الْجَحِيمِ .

7.　　Nonetheless, Our loyal believers never changed or corrupted **The True Gospel**. Nor did they oppose it. However, those who blasphemed were the ones who manufactured such ideas of apostasy and expressed such wild opinions about the true believers in the Messiah.

٧) وَمَا حَرَّفَ عِبَادُنَا الْمُؤْمِنُونَ الْإِنْجِيلَ الْحَقَّ وَمَا عَارَضُوهُ وَلَكِنْ شُبِّهَ لِلَّذِينَ كَفَرُوا فَظَنُّوا بِهِمِ الظُّنُونَ .

8.　　Each time We announced to Our worshipers,

٨) وَإِذْ قُلْنَا لِعِبَادِنَا اتَّبِعُوا سُنَّةَ الْحَقِّ فِي

"Follow the True Doctrine in **The True Gospel**," they did not oppose Our command. Neither did they alter **The True Gospel**, nor are they involved in such an effort now.

الإنجيل الحق فما عارضوا قولنا وما حرّفوه
ومَا عَسَاهُمْ يُحرّفُونَ .

9. No one has altered or opposed Our revelations except the reprobate apostates. The apostates even ordered their devotees to murder, steal and commit immorality against everybody. Does anyone care to find out that such is the standard of the lawless, which is inspired by a vile demon?

٩) ومَا حَرّفُهُ ومَا عَارضَهُ إلاّ الكَفرةُ
الضّالُونَ فأمروا أتباعَهُمْ بأنْ يَقتلوا ويَسْرِقوا
ويَزْنوا وهـذهِ شِـرْعةُ المجرمـينَ مَنْ وَحـي
شَيطانٍ زَنِيمٍ .

10. On that great Judgment Morning, We intend to arbitrate the Truth using Our Word as the Righteous Judge and break the back of every heathen, once and for all.

١٠) ونُريدُ أنْ نُحقَّ الحقَّ كلمتِنا ونَقطعَ
دَابِرَ الكَافرينَ .

11. As for those who lost their way, became apostate and led others astray, their destiny is perpetual humiliation, ignorance and confusion every day. The evidence of their state is first

١١) والذيـنَ ضَلّـوا وكَفـروا وأضَلّـوا ،
ضُربتْ عَليهـمِ الذلّةُ والجهلُ والتخلّفُ ذلك
بأنّهـمْ كـانوا كَفـرونَ بآيَاتـا وَيَقتلونَ

their continuous denial of Our miracles, then the murdering of Our servants—whom they are murdering still.

عِبَادَنَا وَمَا نَزَالُوا يَقْتُلُونَ .

12.   The following attractions were made glamorous for them: lust of the flesh, gathering of women and children, owning piles upon piles of gold and silver, acquiring thoroughbred horses, cattle and tillable land. All of these are mere earthly possessions. Earthly possessions will never be a worthy substitute for the heavenly. We have a glorious and a more superior reward for the upright.

١٢)   وَزُيِّنَ لَهُـمْ حُبُّ الشَّهَوَاتِ مِنَ النِّسَاءِ وَالْبَنِينَ وَالْقَنَاطِيرِ الْمُقَنْطَرَةِ مِنَ الذَّهَبِ وَالْفِضَّةِ وَالْخَيْلِ الْمُسَوَّمَةِ وَالْأَنْعَامِ وَالْحَرْثِ ذَلِكَ مَتَاعُ الْحَيَاةِ الدُّنْيَا وَمَا تُغْنِي الدُّنْيَا عَنِ الْآخِرَةِ وَعِنْدَنَا حُسْنُ الْمَآبِ لِلْمُتَّقِينَ .

67
THE SEAL
(Surat Al Khatim)

٦٧) سُورةُالخَاتَم

In the Name of the Father, the Word, the Holy Spirit, the One and only True God

بسـمِ الآبِ الكلمةِ الروحِ الالهِ الواحد الأوحدِ

1. O, you who are uninformed, yet still claim to belong to Our loyal subjects: We yearn to clarify to you what kind of principles the apostates before you lived by. Our purpose is to alert you to stay away from things which We prohibit. We will atone for your sins and welcome you into the glorious Kingdom.

١) يأهلَ الجهلِ من عِبادنا الضالينَ: نودُّ أنْ نُبَيّنَ لكـمْ سُنَنَ الذينَ كفـروا مـن قلـكـمْ فاجْتنبوا كبائرَ ما تُنهَونَ عنهُ نكفّـرْ عنكـمْ سَيّئاتكـمْ وندخلكـمْ مَدخلاً كريماً .

2. Above all, join no companion or anything else to Our Divine Personage. Then express willing obedience to your parents. Do the same in regard to other believers, as well as to all of your brethren in humanity.

٢) فلا تُشرِكوا بنا شيئاً ولا أحـداً ونوصيكـمْ بالوالدينِ إحسـاناً وبـالمؤمنينَ وبإخوانكـمْ منْ بني الإنسانِ جميعاً .

3. Suffice it to say, some of

٣) فقـدْ أجْمَعتـمْ أمركـمْ علـى

315

you have united together as a people group to follow the wrong path of apostasy. Instead of uniting together to perform good and righteous deeds, you united to exercise wickedness and exploitation on the earth. Thus, you decided to follow Satan's commands and in the process became subservient to his orders.

الكفرِ والضلالِ وما تعاونتم على البرِّ والتقوى بل على الإثم والعُدوان واهتديتم بأمرِ الشيطانِ فأنتم لأمرِهِ مُطيعونَ.

4. Consequently, Satan pulled down the curtains of ignorance over your eyes. He taught you wickedness and rebellion. Then he led you astray by lying to you night and day.

٤) فأسدل سُجوفَ الجهلِ على عُقولِكم وعلّمكم الإثمَ والعصيانَ وأضلّكم بالإفكِ والبُهتانِ.

5. Yet, Our own principles are: truth, love, mercy and peace. Therefore, Our principles will never be abrogated or changed.

٥) فسُنّتُنا الحقُّ والمحبّةُ والرحمةُ والسلامُ ولن تجِدوا لسُنّتِنا نَسْخاً ولا تبديلاً.

6. The Satanic law is founded on evil sinfulness, sorrow and suffering. The destiny of those who submit to such a law is continuous death in eternity.

٦) وشريعةُ الشيطانِ أُسُّها الشرُّ والكفرُ والضلالُ ومصيرُها البوارُ وسَيلقى أتباعُها عذاباً وبيلاً.

7.   Satan placed his own seal on the manifesto of apostasy and placed it in your hearts. Thereafter, you mistakenly proclaimed that Satan is the final spokesman of divine revelation. Consequently, you locked the gates of Heaven and opened the gates of Hell before your faces! Subsequently, you erected a visible barricade as well as an invisible veil between us and those who would repent from among you.

٧) وَإِذْ خَتَمَ الشَّيْطَانُ عَلَى قَوْلِ الْكُفْرِ فِي قُلُوبِكُمْ وَمِنْ عِنْدِكُمْ بِأَنَّهُ خَاتَمُ الْقَوْلِ فَقَدْ أَوْصَدْتُمْ أَبْوَابَ السَّمَاءِ فِي وُجُوهِكُمْ وَفَتَحْتُمْ أَبْوَابَ الْجَحِيمِ وَجَعَلْتُمْ بَيْنَنَا وَبَيْنَ التَّائِبِينَ مِنكُمْ سَدًّا مَنْظُورًا وَحِجَابًا مَسْتُورًا .

8.   In case you are skeptical of the trust-worthiness of what We communicated in **The True Furqan** concerning light, love, mercy, truth and peace; then bring a similar chapter and call other witnesses except Us—if you are an honorable people. But if you cannot bring such chapters—for you will never be able to do that—then fear the fire of Hell that is fueled by ungodly and reprobate people.

٨) وَإِنْ كُنْتُمْ فِي رَيْبٍ مِمَّا أَنْزَلْنَا فِي الْفُرْقَانِ الْحَقِّ مِنْ نُورٍ وَمُحَبَّةٍ وَرَحْمَةٍ وَحَقٍّ وَسَلَامٍ فَأْتُوا بِسُورَةٍ مِنْ مِثْلِهِ وَادْعُوا شُهَدَاءَكُمْ مِنْ دُونِنَا إِنْ كُنْتُمْ صَادِقِينَ فَإِنْ لَمْ تَفْعَلُوا وَلَنْ تَفْعَلُوا فَاتَّقُوا النَّارَ الَّتِي وَقُودُهَا النَّاسُ وَالْحِجَارَةُ أُعِدَّتْ لِلْكَافِرِينَ .

9.   O, you who have trusted Us from among Our created subjects:

٩) يَا أَيُّهَا الَّذِينَ آمَنُوا مِنْ عِبَادِنَا : إِذَا رَأَيْتُمْ

317

when you observe great hosts of people joining the True Religion, rejoice. For this is the signal that falsehood has been vanquished while Satan, his demons and the world's apostates have been defeated. On that glorious day none will support the apostates no matter what they say.

النَّاسَ يَدخلونَ في الدِّين أفواجاً فاستبشروا فقد زُهِقَ الباطلُ وهُزِمَ الشيطانُ وجنودهُ وأتباعهُ الكافرونَ فما لهم يومئذٍ من ناصرينَ .

١٠) Satan enticed his devotees by saying to them, "If anyone assaults you, assault him in precisely the very same manner with which he assaulted you." Accordingly, they disobeyed Our command and forgot Our declaration, "Do not avenge yourselves, 'Vengeance is mine, I will repay,' says the Lord."

(١٠   وأغوى الشيطانُ الذينَ اتبعوهُ وقالَ لهم : "مَنِ اعتدى عليكم فاعتدوا عليه بمثل ما اعتدى عليكم" فعَصَوا أمرنا ونسَوا قولنا بأنْ لا تنتقمـوا مِنَ المُعتدينَ .

11. Enmity can be detected by what the apostates say. Yet their hearts cover up even worse things every day. Nevertheless, We have expounded the Scripture to them; perhaps some of them will find the right guidance one day.

(١١   وقد بدتِ البغضاءُ من أفواهِ الكافرينَ وما تُخفي صدورهُـم أكبرُ وقد بيّنـا لهم الآياتِ لعلّهم يهتدونَ .

12. O, you who have trusted Us from among Our servants: you have become a people who love their enemies, despite the fact that they do not love you in return. Whenever they meet you, they announce, "We trust in what you trust." Yet, behind your back, they bite their fingertips in despair. Each time a blessing comes your way they fall apart in disarray. When a calamity befalls you, they shout joyfully. However, if you persevere and trust Us everyday, their vile attitude toward you will have no sway. In fact, their attitude of animosity will hurt only themselves every single day.

يَأَيُّهَا الَّذِينَ آمَنُوا مِنْ عِبَادِنَا: هَا أَنْتُمْ ١٢)
أُولَاءِ تُحِبُّونَ الَّذِينَ يُعَادُونَكُمْ وَهُمْ لَا
يُحِبُّونَكُمْ . وَإِذَا لَقُوكُمْ قَالُوا آمَنَّا بِمَا
آمَنْتُمْ وَإِذَا خَلَوْا عَضُّوا عَلَيْكُمُ الأَنَامِلَ
مِنَ الْغَيْظِ . إِنْ تَمْسَسْكُمْ حَسَنَةٌ
تَسُؤْهُمْ وَإِنْ تُصِبْكُمْ سَيِّئَةٌ يَفْرَحُوا بِهَا
وَإِنْ تَصْبِرُوا وَتَتَّقُوا لَا يَضُرُّكُمْ
كَيْدُهُمْ شَيْئًا وَلَا يَضُرُّونَ إِلَّا أَنْفُسَهُمْ
وَمَا يَشْعُرُونَ .

13. Terror is what We shall strike in the hearts of those who will not relent from rebelling against Our revelation. They demonstrate their rebellion by joining partners to Us and denouncing the words of **The True Furqan** and the Documents of Wisdom.

وَسَنُلْقِي فِي قُلُوبِ الَّذِينَ كَفَرُوا ١٣)
الرُّعْبَ بِمَا أَشْرَكُوا بِنَا أَوْ كَذَّبُوا بِآيَاتِ
الْفُرْقَانِ الْحَقِّ وَالذِّكْرِ الْحَكِيمِ .

14. Mercy and glad tidings are what Our first and foremost intention is in providing this **True Furqan** to everyone, but particularly to all the apostates. Also, it is given to encourage the hearts of Our believing people and to be a balm of healing to those whose hearts are diseased and whose minds doubt the Illustrious Truth.

١٤) وَمَا جَعَلْنَا هَـذَا الفُرْقَانَ الْحَـقَّ إِلَّا
رَحْمَةً وَبُشْرَى لِلْكَافِرِينَ وَلِتَطْمَئِنَّ بِـهِ
قُلُوبُ المُؤْمِنِينَ وَشِفَاءً لِلَّذِينَ فِي قُلُوبِهِمْ
مَرَضٌ وَفِي صُدُورِهِمْ شَكٌّ بِالْحَقِّ
المُبِينِ .

68
THE ASSERTION
(Surat Al Israr)

٦٨) سُورةُ الإصرارِ

In the Name of the Father, the Word, the Holy Spirit, the One and only True God

بسمِ الآبِ الكلمةِ الروحِ الالهِ الواحدِ الأوحدِ

1. O, feuding people who dwell among Our worshipers: you insisted on living a life of infidelity and the practice of promiscuity. While We persisted in guiding people to a life of fidelity and the practice of chastity.

١) يأهلَ العدوانِ من عبادنا الضالينَ: لقد عكفتمْ على الكفرِ والتضليلِ فأمعنا في الهدايةِ والتنويرِ .

2. You instigated a life of murder and debauchery. Yet, We reiterated necessity to live a life of compassion and tranquility.

٢) وحرّضتمْ على القتلِ والفجورِ فكررنا دعوةَ المحبّةِ والسلامِ .

3. The legacy, which you left for your devotees, ended up becoming the laws of paganism and the inadequate knowledge of the age of ignorance.

٣) وأورثتمْ أتباعكمْ شرعةَ الكفرِ وعلمَ الجاهلينَ .

4. Moreover, you clutched

٤) واستمسكتمْ بسُنّةِ الأولينَ وقد

the doctrines of your ancestors, which are completely out-of-date. (You need to recognize that such doctrines from your ancestors are irrelevant for this technological age.)

عفتْ ولا نفعَ من سُنّةِ الغابرينَ .

5. Their grandiose dreams were simply to overindulge themselves in sexual gratification, sensuality and debauchery.

٥) فأحلامُهمْ إتخامُ الغرائزِ بالشهواتِ والفجورِ .

6. Even their paradise was depicted as a den of iniquity for the promiscuous and criminal types.

٦) وجنتُهمْ مواخرُ للزّناةِ والمجرمينَ .

7. For them, the ultimate purpose of life for a man was to show off his physical prowess. A woman lived to propagate, and the children prowled the earth with no restraint.

٧) والرجلُ فحولةٌ والمرأةُ مسؤولةٌ والولدُ سائمةٌ في الأرضِ يسرحونَ .

8. Any nation that followed your religion regressed speedily and its citizens were left behind in the forward march of progress. In

٨) ومَا أتبعَ قومٌ ملّتكمْ إلا وتخلّفوا عن ركبِ المفلحينَ وصاروا موئداً للفكرِ

addition to that they became graves for thoughts, pockets of poverty, vast fields of disease and a burden to bear by the rest of the world's people.

ومَوْئِلاً لِلْفَقْرِ ومَرْتَعاً لِلْأَدْواءِ وحُثَالةً لِلعالَمِينَ .

9. Each individual, who has committed himself to the sect of those who lost their way, has virtually fastened a millstone around his neck and thrown himself into the bottom of the sea.

٩) ومَنِ اعْتَنَقَ مِلَّةَ الضَّلالِ فَقَدْ شَدَّ إلى عُنُقِهِ حَجَرَ رَحىً وألقى بِنَفْسِهِ في قَرارٍ بِحْرٍ سَحِيقٍ .

10. As for Our believing servants, We answer them when they pray to Us and support them whenever they need Us. No power on earth can vanquish them for they lean on Us.

١٠) وإذا دعانا عِبادُنا المؤمنونَ اسْتَجَبْنا لهُمْ ونَصَرْناهُمْ فلا غالِبَ لهُمْ في العالَمِينَ .

11. Yet, when the unbelievers pray, there is no body to answer them. Satan, who can never meet their needs hears them. Sadly enough, they stand alone and will have no supporter.

١١) وإذا دعا الكافِرونَ فما لهُمْ مِنْ مُجِيبٍ إلّا الشَّيطانُ وما لهُمْ مِنْ ناصِرِينَ .

69
REVELATION
(Surat Al Tanzeel)

٦٩) سُورَةُ التَّنزيل

In the Name of the Father, the Word, the Holy Spirit, the One and only True God

بسم الآبِ الكلمةِ الروحِ الإلهِ الواحدِ الأوحدِ

1.   We did not reveal **The True Gospel** as you understand revelation. We actually expressed it in the Perfect Word, with a compassionate tongue. Furthermore, We supported Him with a gracious Spirit for He is the tenderhearted and the Savior of mankind.

١) ومَا نزّلنا الإنجيل الحقّ تنزيلاً كما تأفكون بل قلناهُ قولاً سديداً وبلغناهُ بلاغاً مُبيناً بلسانٍ رحمانٍ وأيدناهُ بروح رحيمٍ هُدى ورحمةً للعالمينَ .

2.   Therefore, We did not reveal a book, neither a chapter nor even a verse of scripture to you. We definitely did not inspire any revelation for you through anyone from your midst. We certainly did not inspire such a person.   But you yourselves imagined it to be a revelation in a book and believed the man who said so. Consequently, you lost the straight and narrow pathway.

٢) ومَا نزّلنا عليكـمْ كتاباً أوْ سُورةً أوْ آيةً ولا أوْحينـا إليكـمْ قوْلاً بلسانِ أحدٍ منكـمْ ومَا ألهمناهُ ولكنْ شُبّهَ لكـمْ فصدَّقتمـوهُ فضللتـمْ سَـواءَ السَّـبيلِ .

324

3.   It is inconceivable that We Ourselves would inspire any scriptures which may abrogate Our revelation, contradict Our decree, mislead Our rightly-led servants, corrupt the verses of **The True Gospel** and overwhelm humanity with the speech of slanderers!

٣) فَأَنَّى نُنْزِّلُ قَوْلاً يَنْسَخُ قَوْلَنَا وَيُعَارِضُ سُنَّتَنَا وَيُضِلُّ عِبَادَنَا الْمُهْتَدِينَ وَيُحَرِّفَ كَلِمَةَ الإِنْجِيلِ الْحَقِّ وَيُعْجِزُ النَّاسَ بِلَغْوِ الْمُفْتَرِينَ.

4.   We have conveyed this **True Furqan** as an inspiration. We have also poured it into the heart of Our chosen man, so he would announce it with articulation in the classical Arabic language.

٤) وَلَقَدْ أَنْزَلْنَا هَذَا الْفُرْقَانَ الْحَقَّ وَحْياً، وَأَلْقَيْنَاهُ نُوراً فِي قَلْبِ صَفِينَا لِيُبَلِّغَهُ قَوْلاً مُعْجِزاً بِلِسَانٍ عَرَبِيٍّ مُبِينٍ.

5.   This **True Furqan** is a confirmation of what mankind already had in **The True Gospel**. It is of similar value, an authentication of the Truth and a destroyer of falsehood. It is also Good News and an admonition to the unbelievers.

٥) مُصَدِّقاً لِمَا بَيْنَ يَدَيْهِ مِنَ الإِنْجِيلِ الْحَقِّ صِنْواً فَارُوقاً مُحِقّاً لِلْحَقِّ وَمُزْهِقاً لِلْبَاطِلِ وَبَشِيراً وَنَذِيراً لِلْكَافِرِينَ.

6.   For that reason, we implore you to accept it willingly

٦) فَتَقَبَّلُوهُ بِقَبُولٍ حَسَنٍ وَآمِنُوا بِهِ فَهُوَ سَبِيلُ

and believe in it completely. For **The True Furqan** is the path to right guidance and the Way to Salvation. The promises to whomever receives its message are:

We shall strengthen his hand,
Refresh his heart,
Release him from his discouragement,
Forgive his guilt
And let him enter Our Paradise. Moreover, We shall show him what an eye has never seen and an ear has never heard of Our glory.

الهدى وطريق الخلاص فمن يأخذ به نأخذ بيده ونشرح له صدره ونفسح عنه كربه ونغفر له ذنبه وندخله جنّاتنا ونريه ما لم تره عين وتسمعه أذن في العالمين.

7.   Let it be recognized by all mankind forevermore, that love is Our supreme characteristic and law. Love is the passport to enter into Our Kingdom and the straight pathway to Us. The mystery of mysteries is hidden in love if you seriously want to know.

(٧) إنّ المحبّة سنّتنا وباب ملكوتنا وصراطنا المستقيم وسرّ الأسرار في المحبّة لو كنتم تعلمون.

8.   You see, We Ourselves are:

(٨) فنحن محبّة ورحمة وسلام فمن أحبّنا

326

Love,
Truth,
Mercy
And Peace.
Whosoever loves Us and loves Our servants sincerely, mercifully and peacefully, We shall make a covenant between him and Us. It will be a covenant of love, mercy and peace. In addition to that We will welcome him into Our mansions in the company of the true believers.

وأحبَّ عِبادَنا بحقٍّ ورحمةٍ وسَلامٍ جَعَلْنَا

بينَا وبينَهُ عـهدَ مَحبـةٍ ورحمـةٍ وسـلامٍ

وأدخلناهُ جناتِنا معَ الصالحينَ .

70
PLAGIARISM
(Surat Al Tahreef)

٧٠) سُورةُ التحريفِ

In the Name of the Father, the Word, the Holy Spirit, the One and only True God

بســمِ الآبِ الكلمةِ الروحِ الالهِ الواحدِ الأوحدِ

1. O, you who are involved in plagiarism and false witness, yet still claim to be among Our followers: you have definitely lost your way.   You have not fathomed the spirit of wisdom in **The True Gospel**. So, you were suspicious of it. Then you claimed that it was plagiarized and denied the Perfect Religion.   Furthermore, you charged Our faithful followers with idolatry. You also did not bother to seek answers from those who understood **The True Gospel** from among the People of The Book. Thus, you went astray from the straight pathway.

١) يا أهلَ التحريفِ والبهتانِ منْ عبادِنا الضّالينَ: لقدْ ضَلَلْتُمْ ومَا أدركتـمُ للإنجيلِ الحقِّ روحاً أوْ حكمةً وكنتـمْ في شَـكٍّ منــهُ فـادّعيتـمْ تحريفَـه وكذّبتـمْ بالدّينِ القيّـمِ وكفّرتُمْ عبادَنا المؤمنينَ ومَا سَأَلتـمُ الذينَ يعلمونَ منْ أهلِ الكتابِ الحقِّ فضَلَلتـمْ سَواءَ السبيلِ .

2.   We commanded people everywhere that they should not

٢) ووصّينا الناسَ كافةً بأنْ لا يَقتُلوا ولا

328

murder, should not steal and should not commit immorality. Moreover, We commanded that they should encourage each other to implement righteous and godly deeds as well as refrain from vileness and persecution of others.

يَسْرِقوا ولا يَزنوا وأنْ يتعاونوا على البِرِّ والتقوى ويَجتنبوا الإثمَ والعُدوانَ .

3. Those who trusted Us, responded favorably to this superior code of ethics. They neither distorted it nor did they plagiarize it.

٣) واستجاب الذين آمنوا بسُنَّة الحقِّ وما بدَّلوها ولا كانوا لآياتنا مُحرِّفينَ .

4. You, however, have twisted the message from its original meaning. You have accused Our divine proclamation with deception. You have opposed Our revelation and you have urged your adherents to commit vileness and atrocities in the earth. You have also legalized what We had disapproved and have forbidden what We have sanctioned. May the hands of plagiarizers be restrained. Despicable are the activities which they have sanctioned or forbidden.

٤) ولكنكم حرَّفتمُ الكلمَ عن مَواضعِه وكذَّبتمُ بقولنا وعاندتمُ سُنَّتنا وحرَّضتمُ الناسَ على ارتكاب الإثمِ والعُدوان وحلَّلتمُ ما حرَّمنا وحرَّمتمُ ما حلَّلنا الأثبتَ أيدي المحرِّفينَ وساءَ ما كانوا يُحلِّلونَ ويحرِّمونَ .

329

5. Disastrous retribution is awaiting those who take credit for changing Our Words and objecting to **Our Divine Revelation**.

٥) فَوَيْلٌ لِلْمُحَرِّفِينَ الَّذِينَ هُمْ لِكَلِمَاتِنَا مُبَدِّلُونَ وَلِسُنَّتِنَا مُعَارِضُونَ .

6. Heaven and earth shall pass away. But not even a letter or a dot from the decalogue which is summarized within **The True Gospel** and **The True Furqan** will ever pass away. We Ourselves guarantee their protection in every way.

٦) تَزُولُ السَّمَاوَاتُ وَالأَرْضُونَ وَلَا يَزُولُ حَرْفٌ أَوْ نُقْطَةٌ مِنَ الشَّرِيعَةِ الْحَقَّةِ فِي الإِنْجِيلِ الْحَقِّ وَالفُرْقَانِ الْحَقِّ وَإِنَّا لَهَا لَحَافِظُونَ .

7. Our authentic Revelation identified for you the difference between the earthly and the heavenly treasures. Yet, you shielded yourselves from that Truth by lying, cheating and distorting it. As a matter of fact, you eliminated the prohibited endeavors by legalizing them. You replaced faith with faithlessness. You even supercharged your sensual desires and over-stuffed your lusts of the flesh. You performed any depraved thing which your minds

٧) وَحَالَتْ سُنَّةُ الْحَقِّ بَيْنَكُمْ وَبَيْنَ مَتَاعِ الدُّنْيَا فَتَذَرَّعْتُمْ بِالإِفْكِ وَالإِفْتِرَاءِ وَالتَّحْرِيفِ فَنَسَخْتُمُ التَّحْرِيمَ بِالتَّحْلِيلِ وَالإِيمَانَ بِالكُفْرِ وَأَمَتُّمْ غَرَائِزَكُمْ وَأَشْبَعْتُمْ شَهَوَاتِكُمْ وَاقْتَرَفْتُمْ مَا سَوَّلَتْ لَكُمْ أَنْفُسُكُمْ مِنَ الإِثْمِ وَمَا زَيَّنَ لَكُمُ الشَّيْطَانُ رُمِنْ

fantasized. Whatever else Satan glamorized for you, from your wicked lifestyle of shame, you also carried out joyfully.

سُوءِ فَعَلَكُـــمُ الْمُهِين .

8. It is obvious that those who are busily seeking after what this passing world offers will end up as heirs of the Abyss. But those who are busily seeking after the hereafter, through fulfilling Our will, shall certainly reach Our Kingdom. After all, is it not their ultimate goal?

٨) الا إنَّ أصحابَ الدنيا في دنياهـمُ سَادِرونَ وبجهنَّمَ وارِثونَ وأصحابَ الآخرةِ في مَرْضاتِنا يتفكَّرونَ وبنيلِ مَلكوتِنا يستبشرونَ .

71
THE DILIGENT
(Surat Al'Amileen)

سُورةُالعَامِلِينَ (٧١

In the Name of the Father, the Word, the Holy Spirit, the One and only True God

بسمِ الآبِ الكلمةِ الروحِ الاله الواحد الأوحد

1. There is no one like the backslidden believers except those who continue to harm others. As for those who are active in Our cause through their very souls and their financial means, We have preferred them over the backslidden believers. We will also recompense them with the greatest reward, enjoying Our Presence forever.

١) ولا يَسْتوي القاعدونَ من المؤمنينَ غيرِ أولي الضَرَرِ والعاملونَ في سَبِيلنا بأموالهِمُ ونُفوسهِمُ وفضّلنا العاملينَ على القاعدينَ أجراً عظيماً .

2. As for those who have repented from infidelity, believed in Us, held on to **The True Gospel** and accepted **The True Furqan**, they are numbered among Our righteous servants. They will also be singing our praises and rejoicing in the gardens of purity, love and peace

٢) إنَّ الذينَ ارتدّوا عن الكفرِ وآمنوا بنا وتمسّكوا بالإنجيل الحقِّ وصَدَقوا بالفرقان الحقِّ أولئك من عِبادنا الصالحينَ يُسبِّحونَ بحمدِنا وينعمونَ بجنّاتِ الطهرِ والحبّةِ والسلامِ

forever.

المُقِيمِ .

٣) يأيها الذين آمنوا من عبادنا : أتريدون أن
تهدوا من أضلهم الشيطان فلن تجدوا إلى
ذلك سبيلاً ولن تغيروا ما بهم حتى يغيروا
ما بأنفسهم من حقد ونحن أعلم بما تخفي
النفوس وما يسرون .

3. O, you who have believed from among Our servants: do you wish to rightly guide those whom Satan has misguided? You will not find an easy way to accomplish your goal. For you will not transform what is within them until they themselves decide to change the bitterness that is within them. We are fully aware of what hearts cover up and what they keep in secret.

٤) فرفقاً بالكافرين من عبادنا الضالين
ولينوا لهم فلو كنتم أفظاظاً غلاظ
القلوب لانفضوا من حولكم فاعفوا
عنهم واستغفروا لهم وإن تنصركم
فلا غالب لكم وإن أعرضوا عن الحق
فقد خذلوا وما لهم من ناصرين .

4. Demonstrate compassion toward the infidels from among Our misled servants. Show them kindness. Because if you display rude manners and uncompassionate hearts, they will surely depart from you. Therefore, pardon them and seek God's forgiveness for them. If We support you no one will be able to conquer you. However, if the infidels turn away from the Truth, they will definitely be vanquished and will never find anyone to support them.

5. O, you who have believed: take not the counterfeit book as Our revelation, rather despise it and abandon it completely.

٥) يَأَيُّهَا الَّذِينَ آمَنُوا لَا تَّدَبَّرُوا قَوْلَ الْبُهْتَانِ وَانْبِذُوهُ وَاتَّخِذُوهُ مَهْجُورًا .

6. If such scriptures were truly inspired by Us, you would certainly discover no plagiarism or any significant difference between it and The True Revelation.

٦) فَلَوْ كَانَ مِنْ عِنْدِنَا لَمَا وَجَدْزُ فِيهِ نَسْخًا أَوِ اخْتِلَافًا كَبِيرًا .

7. The hypocrites are craving to see you blaspheme as they do, so that you will be on the same inferior spiritual level as the pagans. Never, ever will they be on the same footing with you until they are willing to repent and trust Our Creed absolutely.

٧) وَدَّ أَهْلُ النِّفَاقِ لَوْ تَكْفُرُونَ كَمَا كَفَرُوا فَتَكُونُونَ سَوَاءً . كَلَّا لَا يَسَاوُونَ حَتَّى يَتُوبُوا وَيُؤْمِنُوا بِسُنَّتِنَا يَقِينًا .

8. Satan has enticed them by calling them to enunciate beautiful words with their tongues. Yet, he prodded them to commit wickedness with their hands and feet. Mere words can never be an acceptable substitute for beautiful works. Have they not done

٨) فَقَدْ خَدَعَهُمُ الشَّيْطَانُ إِذْ دَعَاهُمْ إِلَى الْقَوْلِ الْحُسْنِ بِأَلْسِنَتِهِمْ وَدَفَعَهُمْ إِلَى اقْتِرَافِ الشَّرِّ بِأَيْدِيهِمْ وَأَرْجُلِهِمْ وَلَا يُغْنِي الْقَوْلُ عَنِ الْفِعْلِ شَيْئًا كَفَاكُمُ الْيَوْمَ كُفْرًا

334

enough of blasphemy and debauchery?

وفجوراً .

9. Satan made fallacious promises to the hypocrites. Everyone, who trusted in such promises, went astray. Their eternal residence became Hell itself, where they will burn night and day.

٩) وَوَعدهـــمُ الشــيطانُ غُــروراً فمـنْ صدّقَ وضَلَّ فمأواهـمْ جهنّـمُ فلايجدونَ عنها مَحيصاً .

10. Of course, anyone who sought to do Our will can never be equated with those who sought to disobey it. The latter will be punished by Our wrath and outrage.

١٠) وليسَ مَنِ أتَّبعَ رَضواناً كمـنْ باءَ بسُخط وغَضَب فلا يستوونَ .

11. Would the unclothed ever dismiss the illusion of having green finery? They do not desire the straight path for their covering, nor do they seek from Us the protective Robe of Righteousness.

١١) وأنّى للعُراةِ أنْ يَنسوا ما وُعدوا بهِ مـنْ ثيـاب خُضـر فهـمْ لا يطيقـونَ للصـراطِ المستقيـمِ لَفحاً ولا يَبغونَ مـن لَدُنّـا لَبوساً ستيراً .

12. Would the thirsty and hungry turn away from the rivers of wine, milk and honey, the meat of birds or whatever their

١٢) وأنّى للجياعِ العِطاشِ أنْ يَصُدروا عـن أنهُرِ الخمرِ واللبنِ والعَسـلِ وعَنْ لَحـمِ الطيرِ

appetites lust after? Alas, they have exchanged Our Mansions of Glory for a pitiful price for which they will forever be very sorry.

وما يشتهون . فقد اشتروا بجناتنا ثمناً قليلاً .

13. Would the sexually abusive husbands leave their numerous wives on earth and abandon their fantasies with girls endowed with gorgeous breasts and captivating eyes, the fulfillment of sensual instincts, in order to dedicate themselves to purity, love and peace?

١٣) وأنى للمسافحين أن يطلقوا النساء والحور العين والولدان ونهم الغرائز ويعرجوا إلى أعتاب الطهر والمحبة والسلام ؟

72
THE MARVELS
(Surat Al'Alaai)

سورةُ الآلاء (٧٢)

In the Name of the Father, the Word, the Holy Spirit, the One and only True God

بسمِ الآبِ الكلمةِ الروحِ الالهِ الواحدِ الأوحدِ

١) يَأهلَ الكفرِ والطغيانِ من عبادِنا الضالينَ: لا تَغلوا في دينكمُ غيرِ الحقِّ ولا تتمادوا في الكفرِ والعصيانِ .

1. O, people of paganism and oppression who still consider yourselves among Our followers: do not boast about your man-made religion. Tell only the truth. Moreover, do not go over the threshold of no return with your apostasy and rebelliousness.

٢) واشهدوا بعينِ الحقِّ واحكموا بنورِ العدلِ واسلكوا صراطَنا المستقيمَ .

2.We demand that you testify of the whole truth before a world court of justice. Judge with the illumination of honesty. Pursue Our straight path.

٣) وانظروا إلى الرحماءِ المؤمنينَ وإلى القتلةِ الكافرينَ لا يستوونَ فبأيِّ الآنا

3.Consider the compassionate believers and the murderous infidels. There is no comparison between the two groups. There-fore, what wonder from among

337

Our marvels do you deny?

تكـــذبونَ ؟ .

4. Consider the people of integrity and those of depravity. There is no comparison between the two groups. Therefore, what wonder from among Our marvels do you deny?

٤) وانظـروا إلى الأبــرارِ الأطهـارِ والى الزنـاةِالفُجَّارِ لا يَسـتوونَ فبـأيّ آلاتـا تكـــذبونَ ؟ .

5. Consider the charitably meek people and the marauding oppressors. There is no comparison between the two groups. Therefore, what wonder from among Our marvels do you deny?

٥) وانظـروا إلى الودعـاءِ المحســنينَ والى الغُــزاةِالمعتدينَ لا يَسـتوونَ فبـأيّ آلاتـا تكـــذبونَ ؟ .

6.Consider the lovingly forgiving people and the vengeful murderers. There is no comparison between the two groups. Therefore, what wonder from among Our marvels do you deny?

٦) وانظـروا إلى ذوي الحَبَّـةِ والغُفـرانِ والى ذوي القَتلِ والانتقـامِ لا يَسـتوونَ فبـأيّ آلاتـا تكـــذبونَ ؟ .

7. Consider those who pardon others as well as control their anger and those who hold a grudge and are vengeful. There is

٧) وانظـروا إلى العـافينَ عَــنِ النـاسِ والكـاظمينَ الغيظَ والى الحـاقدينَ عليهـمُ

no comparison between the two groups.   Therefore, what wonder from among Our marvels do you deny?

والمنتقمــيـن لا يَسْــتَوونَ فبــأيِّ آلاتِـا نُكـــذِّبونَ ؟ .

8.   Consider the benevolent humanitarians and the ruthless transgressors. There is no comparison between the two groups. Therefore,   what wonder from among Our marvels do you deny?

٨)   وانظـــروا إلى اللطفــاء المُحبِّــين وإلى الأفظاظِ الجرمـين لا يَسْتَوونَ فبـأيِّ آلاتِـا تُكـذِّبونَ ؟

9.Consider those who have learned as well as practice good deeds and those who are illiterate and do not practice such. There is no comparison between the two groups. Therefore, what wonder from Our marvels do you deny?

٩)   وانظروا إلى الذينَ يَعلمونَ ويَعمَلونَ وإلى الذينَ لا يَعلمونَ ولا يَعمَلونَ لا يَسْتَوونَ فبـأيِّ آلاتِا تُكـذِّبونَ ؟

10. Subsequently, wisdom has been   distinguished from folly. There is definitely no compelling in ones choice of a religion. Therefore, what is it that you are waiting for, and   what wonder from among Our marvels do you deny?

١٠)   لقدْ تبيَّنَ الرشدُ مِنَ الغيِّ فلا إكـراهَ في الدينِ فمـاذا تنتظـرونَ وبـأيِّ آلاتِـا تُكـــذِّبونَ ؟ .

73
THE ARGUMENT
(Surat Al Mahajat)

بِسْمِ الآبِ الكَلِمَةِ الرُوحِ الإلهِ الواحِدِ الأوحدِ

٧٣) سُورَةُ المُحاجَّةِ

In the Name of the Father, the Word, the Holy Spirit, the One and only True God

1. O, you who have believed from among Our followers: a company of the pagans desires to mislead you. They are unaware that the ones whom they mislead are really themselves.

١) يَأَيُّها الذينَ آمنوا مِنْ عِبادِنا : وَدَّتْ طَائِفَةٌ مِنْ أَهْلِ الكُفْرِ لوْ يُضِلّونَكُمْ وما يُضِلّونَ إلا أنفُسَهُمْ ومَا يَشْعُرونَ .

2. O, rebellious people who are among Our lost servants: if you state that you are witnessing for Us then why do you deny Our signs? Additionally, you dress up Our truth with a robe of falsehood and cover up the obvious facts, knowingly!

٢) يَأَهْلَ العِصيانِ مِنْ عِبادِنا الضَّالِينَ : لِمَ تَكْفُرونَ بِآياتِنا وأنتُمْ تَشْهدونَ وتُلبِسُونَ الحَقَّ بالباطِلِ وتَكْتُمونَ البَيناتِ وأنتُمْ تَعلمونَ .

3. We, therefore, have destroyed falsehood with Our Truth. Behold falsehood is

٣) وقذفنا بالحَقِّ على الباطِلِ فَدَمَغَهُ فَإذا هوَ

dead.

زَاهِقٌ مَدْحُورٌ .

4. You argue with Our trusting servants that Our disciples were actually from your particular sect. In fact, nothing could be any further from the Truth because your sect, chronologically, emerged long after the disciples brought the Religion of Truth. In other words, they are the ones who are right and you are the ones who are wrong.

(٤) وتُحَاجُونَ عِبَادَنَا المُؤمنينَ بأَنَّ الحَوارِيينَ كَانُوا مِنْ مِلَّتِكُمْ وَمَا جَاءَتْ مِلَّتُكُمْ إِلاَّ مِنْ بَعْدِ مَا جَاءُوا بِدِينِ الحَقِّ فَهُمُ المُحِقُّونَ وأَنتُمُ المُبْطِلُونَ .

5. So far you have argued about matters which are known to you and still lost the argument. How then are you capable of arguing about matters which are unknown to you and hope to win? We are the All-Knowing; you are the unenlightened.

(٥) هَا أَنتُمْ حَاجَجْتُمْ فِيمَا لَكُمْ بِهِ عِلمٌ فأَنَّى تُحَاجُّونَ فِيمَا لَيسَ لَكُمْ بِهِ عِلمٌ . ونحنُ نَعلَمُ وأَنتُمْ لا تَعلمونَ .

6. O, people who cheat and speak untruths, yet still number yourselves among Our loyal populace: why don't you agree with Our believing servants on these proclamations:

(٦) يأَهلَ الإفكِ والنِفاقِ مِنْ عِبادِنا الضَّالِينَ : تعَالوا إلى كَلِمَةٍ سَواءٍ بينكُمْ وبينَ عِبادِنا المُؤمِنينَ ألاَّ تتَّبِعوا الشَّيطانَ ولا

341

Do not tread on Satan's highway of lawlessness.

Do not blaspheme Our Word, Messiah Jesus, by rejecting Him.

Do not blaspheme the Creed of Truth by ignoring it.

Do not blaspheme true love by not practicing it.

Do not blaspheme peace by fighting against it.

Do not commit atrocities by rejecting reconciliation.

If you undertake these responsibilities, let it be known to the world.

تَكْفُرُوا بِكَلِمَتِنَا وَسُنَّةَ الْحَقِّ وَالْمَحَبَّةِ
وَالسَّلَامِ وَلَا تَرْتَكِبُوا كَبَائِرَ الْإِثْمِ
فَإِنْ تَوَلَّيْتُمْ فَاعْلَمُوا إِنَّمَا عَلَى عِبَادِنَا الْمُؤْمِنِينَ
الْبَلَاغُ الْمُبِينُ .

7. Therefore, whosoever is rightly-guided is in fact doing good for his own soul. But whosoever is misled is in fact doing evil to his own soul. No soul will ever be held responsible for the guilt of another at the Day of Judgment. We are not interested in tormenting people in Hell, but in saving them from it and welcoming them into Our Presence in Heaven. (That is precisely why We sent the Righteous Messenger, Jesus the Messiah.)

٧) فَمَنِ اهْتَدَى فَإِنَّمَا يَهْتَدِي لِنَفْسِهِ وَمَنْ ضَلَّ
فَإِنَّمَا يَضِلُّ عَلَيْهَا وَلَا تَزِرُ وَازِرَةٌ وِزْرَ
أُخْرَى وَمَا كُنَّا مُعَذِّبِينَ حَتَّى نَبْعَثَ
رَسُولًا صَدُوقًا مِنْ عِبَادِنَا الصَّالِحِينَ .

8. Consequently, We do not send messengers except as evangelists and prophets. We certainly did not send messengers as judges of eternal consequences or to kill sinners now, instead of on the Day of Judgment. Neither did We send such a man to debate the Truth with illogical arguments in order to refute it. Let it be established here and now that in the end oppressors will never win.

(٨) وَمَا نُرْسِلُ الْمُرْسَلِينَ إِلَّا مُبَشِّرِينَ
وَمُنذِرِينَ وَمَا أَرْسَلْنَا مِنْ رَسُولٍ يَدِينُ
عِبَادَنَا قَبْلَ يَوْمِ الدِّينِ وَيَقْتُلُهُمْ تَقْتِيلًا
وَيُجَادِلُهُمْ بِالْبَاطِلِ لِيَدْحَضَ الْحَقَّ إِنَّهُ لَا
يُفْلِحُ الْمُعْتَدُونَ .

74
THE SCALE
(Surat Al Meezan)

٧٤) سُورةُ الميزان

In the Name of the Father, the Word, the Holy Spirit, the One and only True God

بسمِ الآبِ الكلمةِ الروحِ الالهِ الواحدِ الأوحدِ

1. Moses declared to his nation, "You are not to kill the soul of any human because God has intensely forbidden murder," although people did that in the past.

١) وقَالَ مُوسى لقومِهِ: "لا تَقتلوا النفسَ التي حرَّمها اللهُ تحريماً". فقد كـانوا يقتلونَ.

2. Moreover, Jesus proclaimed, "O, people everywhere, whosoever hurts another human being even with an abusive word, deserves the torments of the fiery pit."

٢) وقَالَ عيسى: "يأيها الناسُ مَن آذى أحداً ولو بكلمةٍ خبيثةٍ استحقَّ عذابَ الجحيمِ".

3. Then you exclaimed, "Kill them wherever you find them. When you confront your opponents strike off their necks." With such a creed you regressed

٣) وقُلتـــمُ: "واقتلوهـــمُ حَيثمـــا وجدتُموهـــمُ وإذا لَقيتموهـــمُ فضَــربُ

344

to the lifestyle of the days of ignorance and paganism—the principles of murder and vengeance.

الرقابِ" فرجعتـمُ إلى جَاهليّةِ الكفـرِ

وشرِيعةِ القتلِ والانتقامِ فأنتـمُ الجرِمونَ .

4. Moses declared, "O, my people, do not steal," even though people did that in the past.

٤) وقَالَ مُوسى: "يا قومُ لا تسـرِقوا "

فقدْ كَانُوا يَسرِقونَ .

5. Moreover, Jesus announced, "If anyone owns two robes, let him give one away to him who is needy and do not return a beggar empty-handed."

٥) وقَالَ عيسى: "مِنْ لـهُ ثوبانِ فليُعطِ

أحدَهما ولا ترُدُّوا السائلِينَ" .

6. Then you exclaimed, "Eat from whatever you gained in fighting and in robbing, for it is sanctified unto you." By such activities you went backwards into the uncivilized practice of marauding, stealing and exploitation. You certainly are the oppressors of your fellowman.

٦) وقُلتـمُ: "كُلوا مِمّا غَنِمتـمُ حَلالاً

طيّباً وممّا تسلُبونَ" فرجعتـمُ إلى جَاهليّةِ

الغزوِ والسلبِ والعدوانِ فأنتـمُ المعتدونَ .

7. Moses declared, "O, my people, do not practice sexual

٧) وقَالَ مُوسى: "يا قومُ لا تقرِبوا الزِنى"

immorality," although people practiced sexual immorality in the past.

فَقَدْ كَانُوا مُسَافِحِينَ .

8. However, Jesus warned, "Whosoever adds another woman to his first and only wife, has committed adultery. Additionally, whosoever marries a divorcee, who was guilty of an adulterous relationship, commits adultery too. And whosoever looks upon a woman, with a lustful eye, has committed adultery with her in his sinful heart."

٨) وقَالَ عِيسَى : "مَنْ أَشْرَكَ بِزوجتِه أُخْرى فَقَدْ زَنَى وَمَنْ تَزوّجَ مُطَلَّقَةً فَقَدْ زَنَى . ومَنْ نظرَ لامْرأةٍ بِعينِ الشهوةِ فَقَدْ زَنَى بها فِي قَلبِهِ السقيمِ " .

9. Then you exclaimed, "Marry whosoever looks good in your eyes from among women, two, three or even four. That is in addition to the females whom you own as slaves." By such practice you have reverted to the sensual desires of the uncivilized and the vulgarity of immorality and promiscuity. No cleansing is available to sinners, unless you repent.

٩) وقُلتُمْ : وأنكِحوا مَا طابَ لَكُمْ مِنَ النساءِ مَثْنَى وثُلاثَ ورُباعَ أوْمَا ملكتْ أيمانُكُمْ " . فَرجعتُمْ إلى جاهليّةِ الغَرائزِ وبَجَسِ الزِّنَى والفجورِ فأنتُمْ لا تَطْهُرونَ .

10. Moses declared, "O, my people, love your neighbor as yourselves," although people used to despise them in the past.

١٠) وقال موسى: "يا قوم أحبّوا ذَوِيكم كنفوسكم". فقد كانوا مُبغضين.

11. However, Jesus proclaimed, "Love your enemies. Bless those who curse you. And do good even to them who abuse you."

١١) وقال عيسى: "أحبّوا أعداءكم وبـاركوا لاعنيكم وأحسـنوا للمسيئين."

12. Then you exclaimed, "Make no friends from among the Christians and Jews. There is enmity and hatred between you and them; they are unclean infidels and polytheists who have incurred Our wrath and are really lost." By these attitudes you have reverted back to the uncivilized practices of bitterness, hatred and vengeance. By such deeds you have turned yourselves into a company of untouchables by God, and rejected misfits by man.

١٢) وقلتم: "ولا تتخذوا اليهود والنصارى أولياء فينكم وبينهم عداوة وبغضاء وهم مجس كفار مشركون ومغضوب عليهم وضالّون". فرجعتم إلى جاهليّة الحقد والبغضاء ولا انتقام فأنتم الأرذلون.

13. O, lost people of false accusation: let him who has ears

١٣) يأهل الضلال والبهتان: فليسمع من له

to hear, listen. Let him who has eyes to see, testify of Our righteousness. Let him who has a heart of wisdom judge with equity and impartiality.

14. Since you yourselves are responsible for these senses, be very vigilant of what you hear, see, think and speak.

15. Therefore, if you are truly an honorable people, you would not say, "The Devil made me do it," every time you did something wrong.

أذنان تسمعان . وليشهد من له عينان

تشهدان وليعدل من له قلب سليم

وليحكم بالقسط والميزان .

١٤) فإن السمع والبصر والفؤاد كل أولئك

كنتم عنه مسؤولين .

١٥) فلا تلوموا الشيطان بل لوموا أنفسكم

إن كنتم مقسطين .

75
THE SPARK OF INTELLIGENCE
(Surat Al Qibs)

٧٥) سُورةُ القَبس

In the Name of the Father, the Word, the Holy Spirit, the One and only True God

بِسمِ الآبِ الكلمةِ الروحِ الإلهِ الواحدِ الأوحدِ

1. O, you who are hypocrites, yet still claim to be among Our loyal followers: you have testified that Jesus the Messiah is a breath from Our own Spirit. Why then did you not sniff the fragrance of the Spirit; but elected to smell the putrefied odor of Satan, the contemptible one?

١) يأهلَ النفاقِ مِنْ عِبادِنا الضَالِّينَ: لقـدْ شَهِدتُم بأنَّ عيسى المسيحَ هوَ نفخةٌ مِنْ رُوحِنا. فمَا تَسَّمتُمْ نفحَةَ الروحِ بـلِ استخرَمتُّنَ الشيطانِ الذميمِ.

2. Furthermore, you testified that The Messiah is in fact Our Word. Why then did you not harken to Our Word; but followed the gibberish of the apostates?

٢) وشَهِدتُم بأنَّ المسيحَ هوَ كلِمتُنا فما اسْتمعتم لكلمتِنا وأتبعتــمْ لغـو المارقينَ.

3. You also stated that We granted Jesus miraculous proofs to authenticate His identity. Why did you not seek illumination

٣) وقلتــمْ بأنّا آتينا عيسى البيِناتِ فلــمْ تَّبِينوها وكفرتُم بالدينِ القويمِ.

from these signs; but repudiated the Perfect Faith?

4. Moreover, you asserted that We supported Him with the Holy Spirit as well as taught Him The Book and wisdom. Why then did you not seek enlightenment through The Book, neither apprehend even a spark from the brilliant intelligence We display in it.

٤) وشَهِدتُّرْ بأَنَّا أَيَّدْناه بروح القدس وعلَّمناهُ الكتابَ والحكمةَ فَما اسْتَنرْتُرْ بالكتاب ولا قبستـمْ مِنْ نورِ الحكمة قَبَساً .

5. You also accepted as fact that We were the One who inspired **The True Gospel** as a guidance and a loving kindness to the peoples of the world. Why then did you not beseech Our loving kindness and search for Our guidance? Instead you turned yourselves into Satan's advocates.

٥) وآمنتـمْ بأَنَّا أَنزلنا الانجيلَ الحقَّ رحمةً وهُدىً للعَالمِينَ فما سأَلتـمْ رَحْمَنَا وما التمسْتُـمْ هُدانا وصِرْتُرْ للشيطان أتْبَاعاً .

6. Amazingly enough, when some people get the opportunity to listen to what We have conveyed in **The True Furqan**, one observes that their eyes overflow with tears. As a result of learning such truth they exclaim, "O, Lord our God, We

٦) ومِنَ الناس مَنْ إذا سَمعوا ما أَنزلنا مِن الفُرقان الحقِّ تَرى أَعينهـمْ تفيضُ مِنَ الدمع ممَّا عَرفوا مِن الحقِّ يقولونَ : ربَّنـا آمنَّا بما أَنزلتَ مِنَ الانجيـل الحقِّ والفُرقان الحقِّ

have trusted in **The True Gospel** and **The True Furqan**. We implore You, include us in the company of those whose entire life has been truly committed to You."

فاكتبنا مَعَ الشّاهدينَ"

7. We declare to any one who rejects this trustworthy religion, becomes high and mighty and would rather have what this temporal world offers, that misery is his destiny but the infernal regions shall be his final destination.

(٧) ومَنْ كَفَرِ بِالدينِ القَيِّمِ وطَغَى وآثَرَ الحياةَ الدنيا فَإِنَّ الجحيمَ رَكَهُ المأوى .

8. We furthermore declare to anyone who believes in the True Manifestation, Jesus of Nazareth, and exhibits such faith through integrity of character and good works, that he is saved from Hell. He has truly found Our saving grace—The Ultimate Reality.

(٨) ومَنْ آمَنَ بِسُنَّةِ الحَقِّ وعملَ صَالحاً فقد اهتدى واسْتَمسَكَ بالعروةِ الوثقى .

76
THE EXCELLENT NAMES
(Surat Al Asma' Al Husna)

٧٦) سُورةُ الأسْماءِ

In the Name of the Father, the Word, the Holy Spirit, the One and only True God

بسمِ الآبِ الكلمةِ الروحِ الالهِ الواحدِ الأوحدِ

1. O, people who have become pagans, yet still consider yourselves among Our followers: you have given Us excellent names, some of which were turned into wretched and wicked titles by your actions. Thus, you have done Us a disservice.

١) يأيها الذينَ كفروا من عِبادنا الضّالينَ: لقدْ دَعوتُمونا بأسْماءٍ حُسنى قبّحتمْ حُسْنها وما كنتمُ مُحسنينَ.

2. You called us "The Merciful," but you did not demonstrate a merciful attitude toward others. Instead, you robbed and killed Our peaceful followers without mercy.

٢) فدعوتُمونا (الرّحيمَ) وما عرفتمُ الرّحمةَ فقتلْتمْ وسَلبتمْ وما رَحمتمْ عِبادَنا الآمنينَ.

3. You called Us "The Compassionate," but you disre-

٣) ودَعوتُمونا (اللطيفَ) ونبذتُمُ اللطفَ

garded compassion. Instead, you exploited Our servants, brutalized and assaulted them.

وأَجْهَدْزَ عِبَادَنَا وأَغْلَظْتُمْ عَلَيْهِمْ وكُنتُمْ مِنَ الْمُعْتَدِينَ .

4. You called Us "The Truth," but your hearts wandered away from the truth. Instead, you persecuted people and became infamous due to your mistreatment of others.

٤) ودَعَوْتُمُونَا (الْحَقَّ) وَمَراغَتْ قُلُوبَكُمْ عَنِ الْحَقِّ فَظَلَّتُمُمْ وَمَا كُنتُمْ مِنَ الْمُقْسِطِينَ .

5. You called Us "The Forgiver," but you condemned Our worshipers. You took vengeance upon them. You did not control your tempers and anger in dealing with them. Instead of being forgivers, you displayed the very opposite.

٥) ودَعَوْتُمُونَا (الْعَفُوَّ) وَدَتُّسُمْ عِبَادَنَا وَنَقَمْتُمْ مِنْهُمْ وَمَا كَظَمْتُمُ الْغَيْظَ وَمَا كُنتُمْ مِنَ الْعَافِينَ .

6. You called Us "The Giver of Life," but you put to death the very people to whom We gave life and terrified the peace-loving souls.

٦) ودَعَوْتُمُونَا (الْمُحْيِيَ) وقَتَلْتُمْ مَنْ أَحْيَيْنَا ورَوَّعْتُمْ نُفُوسَ الْآمِنِينَ .

7. You called Us "The Faithful," but you rejected Our

٧) ودَعَوْتُمُونَا (الْمُؤْمِنَ) وكَفَرْتُمْ

Word, the Perfect role model for all humanity and the Light of the World, Jesus of Nazareth.

بكلمتنا وسُنّةِ الحقِّ وبنورِ العالمينَ .

8. You called Us "The Guide," but you went astray, did not seek the right way nor did you show the wanderer the true pathway.

٨) ودَعوتمونا (الهادِيَ) وضَلَلْـــمْ ومَا اهتديتمْ ومَا هَديتمُ الضّالينَ .

9. You called Us "The Just," but you took the untested direction, brutalized Our worshipers and acted unjustly in your treatment of others.

٩) ودَعوتمونا (العَدْلَ) واتّبعتمُ الباطلَ وظَلمتمْ عبادَنا ومَا كنتمْ منَ العادلينَ .

10. You called Us "The Only One," but you added partners to Us. Other women became partners to your wives. You definitely were not among those who worship the One and only true God!

١٠) ودَعوتمونا (الواحدَ) وأشركتمْ بنا وأشركتمْ بأزواجكمْ أخريات ومَا كنتمْ منَ الموحّدينَ .

11. You called Us "The Light," but pressed hard on your eyes with your hands causing your very hearts to go blind. Subsequently, you led people out of light into darkness. Let

١١) ودَعوتمونا (النورَ) وطَمسْتمْ على أعينكــمْ بــأيديكــمْ فَعَميــتْ قلوبكمْ وأخرجتمُ النّاسَ منَ النورِ الى

everyone be cognizant of the fact that pagans are the only people who walk in darkness.

الظُّلمَاتِ وَلا يَسِيرُ فِي الظُّلمَةِ إِلّا الضَّالُونَ .

12. Ignorantly, you branded Us with ugly names which somehow captivated you with their lackluster sounds. In time you yourselves turned into unlovable people.

١٢) ووَصَمْتُمونا جِهلاً مِنكُمْ بِأسْماءَ قُبَحَى اسْتَحْسَنتُمْ قُبحَها فَكنتُمْ مِن المَقبوحِينَ .

13. You branded Us with "The Tyrant." Thus, you treated Our servants tyrannically and caused their faces to ooze with misery. Therefore, you turned into stubborn and arrogant tyrants.

١٣) فَوَصَمْتُمونا (بالجَبَّارِ) وَتَجَبَّرْتَ على عِبادِنا وأرْهقتُمْ وُجوهَهُمْ ذِلَّةَ وكنتُمْ جَبابِرةً عِنْداً ظالِمِينَ .

14. You branded Us with "The Proud." Thus, you became haughty because of infidelity and rebellion. Therefore, you were numbered among the company of the conceited.

١٤) وَوَصَمْتُمونا (بالمُتكبِّرِ) وتكبَّرْتَ بِالكفرِ والعِصيانِ فَكنتُمْ مِنَ المُستكبِرِينَ .

15. You branded Us with "The Enforcer." Thus, you enforced

١٥) وَوَصَمْتُمونا (بالقهَّارِ) وَقَهرْتَ فوقَ

persecution over Our followers and attempted to shut the gates of Heaven in their faces.

عِبادَنا ظُلماً وَأوْجفتـــمْ ـفي وُجوهِــهِمْ أبوابَ النعيــمِ .

16. You branded Us with "The Disgraceful." Thus, you disgraced the noble status of Our worshipers with unjustified shame and oppression. Therefore you will be brought low into a bottomless terminal point.

١٦)   وَوَصمتُمونا (بالخافض) وخفضتـــمْ جَنـاحَ عِبادِنا ذُلاً وَظُلماً فانخفضتُمْ ـفي قراس سَحيقٍ .

17. You branded Us with "The Demeanor." Thus, you demeaned Our servants and embarrassed their honorable leaders. None is left to encourage or rescue them except Us.

١٧)   وَوَصمتُمونا (بالمُذِلّ) وَأذْلَلتُـــمْ عِبادَنا وَجَعَلتُــمْ أعزَّتَهمْ أذِلَّةً ما لهُـمْ مِنْ دُونِا وَليٍّ وَلا نَصيرٍ .

18. You branded Us with "The One Who takes away life." Thus, you took away the lives of Our worshipers by the edge of the sword because they refused to believe in the creed of ungodliness. Therefore, when they continued to believe in the Perfect Religion, they were martyred by you!

١٨)   وَوَصمتُمونـا (بــالمُميت) وأمَتُّـــمْ بالسيفِ عِبادَنا الصالحينَ أوْ يؤمنوا بشـرعة الكفـرِ فاسْتُشْـــهدوا وَبِدينِ الحـــقِّ مؤمنينَ .

19. You branded Us with "The Restrainer." Thus, you restrained Our people from progress by refusing to educate them. Before you appeared on the horizon of history, these very people were among the most advanced.

١٩) وَوَصَمْتُمُونَا (بِالْمُؤَخِّرِ) وأَخَّرْتُمْ بِالْجَهْلِ عِبَادَنَا وكَانُوا مِنَ الْمُقَدَّمِينَ .

20. You branded Us with "The Avenger." Thus, you took vengeance upon Our people. This you promulgated, despite the fact that We had commanded, "Do not avenge yourselves for We do not love the avengers."

٢٠) وَوَصَمْتُمُونَا (بِالْمُنْتَقِم) وانْتَقَمْتُمْ مِنْ عِبَادِنَا وقَدْ وَصَّيْنَا بِأَنْ لَا تَنْتَقِمُوا فَإِنَّا لَا نُحِبُّ الْمُعْتَدِينَ .

21. You branded Us with "the Afflictor." Thus, you afflicted Our people. The afflictors cannot be rightly compared to the benefactors.

٢١) وَوَصَمْتُمُونَا (بِالضَّارِّ) وأَضْرَرْتُمْ بِعِبَادِنَا ولَا يَسْتَوِي الضَّارُّونَ والنَّافِعُونَ .

22. You branded Us with "the Prohibitionist." Thus, you prohibited Our people from getting Our blessings. Therefore, whosoever participates in such behavioral problems is a prohibitionist of Our blessing and a wicked oppressor.

٢٢) وَوَصَمْتُمُونَا (بِالْمَانِعِ) ومَنَعْتُمْ عِبَادَنَا الْخَيْرَ ومَنْ يَفْعَلْ ذَلِكَ فَهُوَ مَنَّاعٌ مُعْتَدٍ أَثِيمٌ .

23. O, people who have lost your way and still dwell among Our servants today: the whole idea of the excellent names is a device of Satan. These excellent names and titles are slanders and lies which Satan concocted for himself. Thus, he baffled you through such fanciful names. We have never had such ridiculous titles given to us before. Sadly enough, you trusted him so completely that you selected him as your savior-redeemer instead of Us! He tricked you so cunningly that you went along with him before you realized what had happened.

٢٣) يأهلَ الضّلالِ مِنْ عِبادِنا : إنْ تلكَ إلا خِدعةٌ دَعا الشيطانُ بها نفسَهُ بأسماءٍ حُسنى إفكاً وافتراءً فأضلّكم باسمِنا وما كانَ لنا سَمِيٌّ فصدّقتمُوهُ واتخذتمُوهُ وليّاً مِنْ دُونِنا فكفرتم وأنتُمْ لا تشعرونَ .

24. Nonetheless, Our believing folk, who are anchored in wisdom and perfect religion, have exposed the treachery of Satan, the despicable one, as well as the double-dealing of his followers. How did We unveil this treason? Very simply—by their fruits they shall be known!

٢٤) أمّا عِبادُنا المؤمنونَ الراسخونَ في العلمِ والدينِ القويمِ فقدْ فَضَحوا إفكَ الشيطانِ الرجيمِ ومكرَ أتباعِهِ الكافرينَ فمِنْ ثمارِ أعمالهِمْ يُعرفونَ .

25. O, people everywhere, be attentive: do not allow Satan and

٢٥) يأيها الناسُ لا يخدعنّكم الشيطانُ

358

his devotees to deceive you through their double-talk and counterfeit documents. The acid test of authenticity is not what one proclaims with his mouth but what he does in everyday life with his hands.

وأتباعُهُ بالإفكِ والبهتانِ فإنّا نَشْهدُ الأفعالَ

ولا نَسمعُ أقوالَ المُفتَرِينَ .

77
THE MARTYR
(Surat Al Shaheed)

VV) سُورةُ الشهيد

In the Name of the Father, the Word, the Holy Spirit, the One and only True God

بسم الآب الكلمة الروح الاله الواحد
الأوحد

1. Let it be proclaimed everywhere and to everyone. The following are the ones who will never be forgiven but shall be banished into hellfire forever and ever:

The ones who reject Our Divine Principles of ethical conduct,

The ones who put to death our chosen servants and

The ones who kill those who admonish others to be even-handed in their treatment of their fellowmen.

١) إنَّ الذينَ يَكفرونَ بآياتنا وَيَقتلونَ
أصفياءَنا وَيَقتلون الذينَ يأمرونَ بالقسطِ مِنَ
الناس فَبَشِّرهـمُ بأنَّ لهـمُ عذاباً شديداً .

2. We have sovereignly selected this special man and permeated his heart with much divine faith. We have also granted him: an observant eye, a

٢) واصطفيناهُ وشـرحنَا صَـدرهُ للإيمـان
وجَعلنا لهُ عيناً تُبصرُ وأذناً تَسمعُ وقلباً يعقلُ
ولساناً ينطقُ بالحقِّ وأوحَينا إليـهِ بالفُرقـان

listening ear, a reasoning mind and a tongue which speaks truth and no guile. We have, furthermore, disclosed to him **The True Furqan** so much so that he was enabled to deliver it with brilliant articulation in moment-ous time of seven days and seven nights.

الحقِّ فخــطّهُ بالحقِّ ـفى سـبعةِ أيامٍ وسـبعِ ليالٍ جليداً .

3. If you shed his blood by your own hands, he will testify against you on the Day of Resurrection.

٣) دَمُرُ رَكي تُسْنفِكونهُ بأيديكُـمُ فيكونُ عَليكُـمُ يومَ القيامةِ شَهيداً .

4. He is but an intelligible sign given to rational people for the purpose of urging them to walk on the highway of prudence.

٤) وآيةٌ بَيِّنـةٌ لقومٍ يعقلونَ فيتبعونَ سَبيلاً رَشيداً .

5. If you commit yourselves to make an attempt on his life, he will not retaliate in the same manner toward you. His goal is to help you to be rightly-guided by leading you out of darkness and into the Light, Jesus the Messiah.

٥) ولئنْ بَسَطتـمُ إليهِ أيديكُـمُ لتقتلوهُ فما هوَ بباسطٍ يدِيهِ إليكُـمُ ليقتُلكُـمُ بل لِيُخرِجَكُـمُ منَ الظلمـاتِ إلى النـورِ لعلّكُـمُ تهتدونَ .

6. Your own minds will pressure you to kill Our chosen one. Such a despicable deed will simply underscore your true identity as godless apostates. It is inconceivable that after destroying a blameless soul, you will still expect Us to demonstrate compassion toward you—even though you have become unrepentant savages.

٦) لقَدْ طَوَّعتْ لكمُ أنفسُكمُ قتَلَ
صفيِّنا شَاهدينَ على أنفسِكمُ
بالكفر، أفتقتلونَ نفساً زركيَّةً وتطمعونَ
برَحمتِنا وأنتمُ المُجرمونَ؟

7. It should be no great surprise to find out at the very end, that in both earthly and heavenly realms you are abysmal losers!

٧) لا جَرمَ أنكمُ في الدنيا والآخرة
أنتمُ الأخسرونَ.

8. Therefore, by such a brutal act, you will end up using the martyr's innocent blood to engrave upon your own foreheads a seal. The seal will attest to three significant facts. First, it will unveil your real character as criminals and infidels. Second, his martyrdom will certify that he is our faithful and chosen one. Third, **The True Furqan** will be recognized as our disclosed Word,

٨) وختمتمُ بدمهِ آيةً تُكوى بها
جباهُكمُ وتشهدُ عليكمُ
بأنكمُ كفرةٌ مجرمونَ وأنهُ الصفيُّ
الأمينُ وأنَّ الفرقانَ الحقَّ هو كلمتُنا وهوَ
الحقُّ اليقينُ ولو كرهَ الكافرونَ.

362

the unadulterated Truth, even if
unbelievers reject its authenticity.
Let it be remembered, it is our
Truth which will finally triumph
on that Great Judgment Day.

Z
EPILOGUE
(Surat Al Khatimah)

ي) الْخَاتِمَةُ

In the Name of the Father, the Word, the Holy Spirit, the One and only True God

بســـمِ الآبِ الكــلمــةِ الـروحِ الالـهِ الواحـدِ الأوحدِ

1.   O, you who have wandered away, yet still number yourselves among Our godly followers: do not block Our Light. Do not excuse yourselves by claiming that you are uneducated, uninformed and illiterate.

١)   يَأَيُّها الذينَ زَاغوا من عبادِنا الصَّالِحينَ: لا تحجبوا نورَنَا عن جهلٍ منكــمْ وأنتــمْ لا تشعرونَ .

2.   Furthermore, do not interpolate Our Truth with your own gibberish, thereby acting as unrepentant heathens.

٢)   ولا تُقحمــوا لغوكــمْ ـفي أقوالنـا مُحرّفينَ الحقَّ كالكـافرينَ .

3.   No one in the entire cosmos has ever been authorized to alter any portion of Our written Scriptures. We implore you to obey it and understand it. Seek restoration from your foolish

٣)   فـلا مُبـدّلَ لكلماتـا . فاسمعوهـا وعوها وارجعوا عنْ غيّكــمْ ولا ترتابوا من صَفِّينا ومّا اصطفيناهُ لكــمْ مِنَ الهُدى

364

backsliding. Do not be skeptical concerning Our Chosen One, neither of what We have sent down for you concerning reasonable guidance and undeniable truth.

والحقِّ المبين .

4. Yes, there are, even among the true believers, some individuals who are quite hypocritical inwardly. Such an individual speaks about matters which really confound him. By his boisterous speech he somehow thinks such rhetoric supports the cause of truth. He also imagines that because of such activity he is brought much closer to Us. Plainly speaking, a person of this type reveals that he has not been honorable regarding the Whole Truth.

٤) ومِنَ المؤمنينَ مَن يُنافقُ في قلبِهِ ويقولُ ما ليس لَهُ بِهِ علمٌ ويحسبُ أنهُ يُناصرُ الحقَّ ومِنَ المقرَّبينَ وهو ليس على الحقِّ بأمينٍ .

5. We have revived Our Covenant in **The True Gospel.** Moreover, We have sought to remind you of that revelation through **The True Furqan.** We ascertain that there will never be any further renewal of Our New Covenant through Messiah Jesus,

٥) وجدَّدنا العـهدَ في الانجيـل الحـقّ وذكَّرناكـمُ بِهِ بالفرقانِ الحقّ فلا تجديدَ لعهـــدِنا الجـــديدِ الى يــومِ تُبعثونَ .

until the Day of Resurrection.

6.   If any one adds to Our Covenant a single letter, his torture in hellfire will be intensified.   If anyone takes away a single letter, his opportunity to enter Our Heavenly Kingdom will be forever denied.

٦)   فمَنْ زادَ بعهدِنا حرفاً زادَ عَذابهُ في نارِ الجحيمِ . ومَنْ حذفَ حرفاً فأُحْذفَ حظُّهُ من جناتِ النعيمِ .

7.   We urge you to utilize wisdom and love in propagating Our Scriptures.   Whenever there is a definite opportunity to share **The   True   Furqan** and its wonderful   message,   do   it wholeheartedly.
For We are The Most Loving, Compassionate   and   Forgiving Potentate in this entire universe.

٧)   واستعينوا علـى تبليـغ كلمتِنـا بالحكمةِ والمحبةِ وحينَ تَحينُ ساعةُ اليقينِ للفرقانِ الحقِّ والبلاغِ المبينِ .

AMEN

آمــين